Gender
4th Edition

SHORT INTRODUCTIONS SERIES

Gender
In World Perspective
4th Edition

Raewyn Connell

polity

First edition first published in 2002 by Polity Press
Second edition first published in 2009 by Polity Press
Third edition first published in 2015 by Polity Press
This fourth edition first published in 2021 by Polity Press

Reprinted 2022 (twice)

Polity Press
65 Bridge Street
Cambridge CB2 1UR, UK

Polity Press
101 Station Landing
Suite 300
Medford, MA 02155, USA

ISBN-13: 978-1-5095-3899-7
ISBN-13: 978-1-5095-3900-0(pb)

A catalogue record for this book is available from the British Library.

Library of Congress Cataloging-in-Publication Data
Names: Connell, Raewyn, 1944- author.
Title: Gender : in world perspective / Raewyn Connell.
Description: 4th edition. | Medford : Polity Press, 2020. | Series: Short
    introductions ; 4 | Revised edition of the author's Gender, 2015. |
    Includes bibliographical references and index. | Summary: "The
    indispensable guide to gender studies by one of the world's foremost
    experts"-- Provided by publisher.
Identifiers: LCCN 2020023820 (print) | LCCN 2020023821 (ebook) | ISBN
    9781509538997 (hardback) | ISBN 9781509539000 (paperback) | ISBN
    9781509539017 (epub)
Subjects: LCSH: Sex role--Research. | Gender identity--Research. |
    Sexology--Research.
Classification: LCC HQ1075 .C658 2020 (print) | LCC HQ1075 (ebook) | DDC
    305.4072--dc23
LC record available at https://lccn.loc.gov/2020023820
LC ebook record available at https://lccn.loc.gov/2020023821

Typeset in 10 on 12pt Sabon
by Fakenham Prepress Solutions, Fakenham, Norfolk NR21 8NL
Printed and bound in Great Britain by TJ Books Limited

For further information on Polity, visit our website:
politybooks.com

In memory of
Pam Benton
1942–1997

She, who had Here so much essentiall joy
As no chance could distract, much lesse destroy;
... she to Heaven is gone,
Who made this world in some proportion
A heaven, and here, became unto us all,
Joy, (as our joyes admit) essentiall.

Contents

Preface

Gender is a key dimension of personal life, culture, institutions and economic life. In the worldwide arenas of gender relations we face large issues about justice, power, environment and even survival.

A great deal of prejudice, myth, and outright falsehood about gender issues circulate. It is therefore important to develop accurate knowledge and deeper understanding. Research and theory in the human sciences provide vital tools for this task. My aim in this book is to use these tools to present an accessible, research-based, globally-informed, and intellectually coherent account of gender.

For readers who are new to these questions, the book introduces gender research through specific examples, describes the main findings on key topics, and outlines the history of debates and ideas. For readers who already have some background in the field, the book proposes an integrated approach linking issues about embodiment, difference and social learning to issues about states, violence and the global economy. The book draws on a spectrum of the human sciences from psychology and sociology to political economy, cultural studies, education and history.

Modern research on gender was launched by the women's movement for gender equality. There is a simple reason for this: most gender orders, around the world, privilege men and disadvantage women. Yet the details are not simple. There are many forms of advantage and disadvantage; there are privileged women and oppressed men; and even the definition of who is a man and who is a woman can be contested.

Though politicians still tend to think gender issues are just about women, it is recognized by researchers and activists that they also concern men. There is now extensive research about masculinities, fatherhood, men's violence, boys' education, men's health and men's involvement in achieving gender equality. I have woven this knowledge into the picture of gender through the book.

Most gender research comes from the rich countries of the global North – which is not unusual in any research field, given global inequalities. The view from the global North matters, and does influence thinking everywhere else. Yet most humans live in other parts of the world, with different histories and social experiences. Therefore the book gives sustained attention to gender research and theory from countries outside North America and Western Europe, places as diverse as Finland, Chile, Australia, South Africa, Indonesia, and Japan. It has never been more important to share knowledge. Previous editions of this book have been translated into nine languages, and I hope the new version will be as useful.

Practical questions about gender range from ending domestic violence, economic injustice and environmental destruction to improving peace-making, education, health and relations between generations. Really, they concern all the conditions for living well. There has never been a greater need for knowledge to inform action. Yet gender research and teaching are themselves under political attack (see chapter 8), and this too needs careful thought and response.

This fourth edition tries to bring all chapters up to date. It includes new case studies, and revises the treatment of politics, environmental issues and embodiment. I have tried to make the presentation as clear and concise as possible, following my own principles in the booklet *Writing for Research* (free to download at *www.raewynconnell.net*).

An attempt to synthesize knowledge across a broad field rests on the labour of many people: social movement activists, researchers, theorists, the operations workers in universities, the participants in research studies, and more. Many intellectual debts are acknowledged in the text. Particular thanks to my colleague Rebecca Pearse, co-author of the third edition; her work has influenced this edition too, and her illuminating discussion of Tsing's work is still included in chapter 2. I am grateful for help and ideas from Christabel Draffin, John Fisher, Kirsten Gomard, Carol Hagemann-White, Robert Morrell, Ulla Müller, Toni Schofield, Katherine Selkirk, Patricia Selkirk, Taga Futoshi, Teresa Valdés, Lin Walker, and my co-editors on the inspiring book *Gender Reckonings*, Patricia Martin, James Messerschmidt and Michael Messner. I am immeasurably grateful to Kylie Benton-Connell, who has made all this possible.

The book is dedicated to the memory of Pam Benton; I hope her spirit of enquiry and action is reflected in the text. The epigraph is from John Donne's poem 'The Second Anniversary'.

Raewyn Connell
Sydney, May 2020

1

The question of gender

Noticing gender

In 2020 the world was swept by a previously unknown but deadly virus, soon named COVID-19. As individual cities and then whole countries went into lockdown, economies slowed and hospitals were flooded, governments around the world intoned 'we are all in this together'.

In one sense we certainly were: no group was immune to this infection. In other ways the epidemic and the policy responses immediately reflected social divisions. The rich were able to get tested when they wanted, and had easy access to respirators, hospital beds and well-funded medical teams. The poor did not. The prevention strategies of social-distancing and frequent hand-washing were good for prosperous suburbs. They could hardly be applied in the huge and crowded informal settlements in the world's largest cities.

As information about the epidemic piled up, other divisions came into view. Globally, men and women seemed to be infected at roughly equal rates, but more men were dying of the disease. Medical opinion suspected that the physical impact of men's higher rates of smoking and drinking – involving masculine norms of behaviour – were involved. Women were affected in other ways. The well-known medical journal *The Lancet* summarized the situation in April 2020:

Women carry a different kind of burden from COVID-19. Inequities disproportionately affect their wellbeing and economic resilience during lockdowns. Households are under strain, but child care, elderly care, and housework typically fall on women. Concerns over increased domestic violence are growing. With health services overstretched and charities under-resourced, women's sexual and reproductive health services, as well as prenatal and postnatal care, are disrupted. (*The Lancet*, 2020)

A United Nations policy brief in the same month spelt this out in more detail. In slowing economies women, who are less likely than men to have secure jobs, would lose their income faster. Lockdowns, or 'Shelter at Home' policies, were fine if the home was safe, but if the home was violent or abusive, it would be a trap. Most severe family violence, including murder, is by men assaulting their wives or partners. From early in the epidemic the number of calls to police or domestic-violence agencies in many countries began to rise. Large numbers of women are front-line workers against COVID-19, as women are about 70 per cent of the health and social service workforce. The Global Health 50/50 'data tracker' on COVID-19 in April 2020 found four countries with disaggregated data on health workers. In all four, women made up about 70 per cent of the health workers infected by the virus.

An emergency that seemed at first to have nothing to do with gender, thus turns out to have a lot to do with the situations of women and men. We can follow this further. The Internet is the key source of information about COVID-19 for huge numbers of people. But the Internet is far from gender-equal. The 2018 Wikipedia Community Engagement Insights survey found that 90 per cent of Wikipedia editors were men. Access to the Internet is also unequal. In 2015, a World Wide Web Foundation study of Internet use in nine developing nations found that women are 50 per cent less likely to use the Internet than men.

In political decision-making, including decisions about the epidemic, women continue to be the minority. Every year a 'family photo' has been taken at G20 meetings where heads of government and their senior finance and central bank representatives meet to discuss the international financial system. In 2019, two women stood among the twenty national leaders in the photo; they represented Germany and Britain. The woman Prime Minister of Britain was soon removed in a party coup. There has never been a woman head of government in modern Russia, China, France, Japan, Egypt, Nigeria, South Africa, the United States or Mexico. There has only been one each in the history of Brazil, Germany, India, Indonesia and Australia. Statistics from the Inter-Parliamentary Union showed that in 2019, 75.7 per cent of members of the world's parliaments were men.

Among senior ministers the predominance of men is even higher. In 2019, only nine countries in the world had women making up half of a national ministry (Spain, Nicaragua, Sweden, Albania, Colombia, Costa Rica, Rwanda, Canada and France). More typical figures for women in ministerial roles were 23 per cent (Fiji, India, Senegal), 12 per cent (Russia, Tuvalu, Pakistan), 6 per cent (China, Iran, Yemen) and 0 per cent (Iraq, Papua New Guinea, Thailand). The few women who do get to this level are usually given the job of running welfare or education ministries. Men keep control of taxation, investment, technology, international relations, police and the military. Every Secretary-General of the United Nations and every head of the World Bank has been a man.

Women's representation in politics has changed slowly over time, and with difficulty. French lawyer Christine Lagarde was the first woman ever to head the International Monetary Fund, appointed in 2011. The world average number of women in parliaments has increased from 10 per cent in 1995 to 24 per cent in 2019. In Australia the first woman Prime Minister, Julia Gillard, served for three years with a record eight women in ministry and five in cabinet. She was then thrown out of power in a party coup. The new right-wing government elected in 2013 had only one woman in cabinet. That cabinet minister, Julie Bishop, was Deputy Prime Minister. During an internal party leadership spill, she was the first women to stand for the top job in her own party. She garnered only 13 per cent of the vote and resigned shortly after.

What is true of politics is also true of business. Of the top 100 businesses listed on the London stock exchange in 2019 (including those that publish the mass-circulation magazines), only six had a woman as CEO. Of the 500 giant international corporations listed in *Fortune* magazine's 'Global 500' in 2019, 33 had a woman CEO. Such figures are usually presented by saying that women are now 6.6 per cent of the top business leadership around the world, and isn't that wonderful progress? It's more informative to say that men compose 93.4 per cent of that leadership.

Lower down the hierarchy, women are a substantial part of the paid workforce. They are mostly concentrated in service jobs – clerical work, call centres, cleaning, serving food, and professions connected with caring for the young and the sick, i.e. teaching and nursing. In some parts of the world, women are also valued as industrial workers, for instance in microprocessor plants, because of their supposedly 'nimble fingers'. Though the detailed division between men's and women's work varies in different parts of the world, it is common for men to predominate in heavy industry, mining, transport, indeed in most jobs that involve any machinery except a sewing machine. Worldwide, men are a large majority of the workforce in management, accountancy, law and technical professions such as engineering.

Behind the paid workforce is another form of work – unpaid domestic and care work. In all contemporary societies for which we have statistics, women do most of the cleaning, cooking and sewing, most of the work of looking after children and elders, and almost all of the work of caring for babies. (If you don't think childcare is work, you haven't done it yet!) This work is often associated with a cultural definition of women as caring, gentle, self-sacrificing and industrious, i.e. as good mothers. Being a good father is rarely associated with cutting school lunches and wiping babies' bottoms – though there are now interesting attempts to promote what in Mexico has been called *paternidad afectiva*, emotionally engaged fatherhood. Normally, fathers are supposed to be decision-makers and breadwinners, consuming the services provided by women and representing the family in the outside world.

Women as a group are less likely to be out in the public world than men, and, when they are, have fewer resources. In almost all parts of the world, men are more likely to have a paid job. Conventional measures of the economy, based on men's practices, exclude women's unpaid domestic work. By the conventional measure of paid employment, the world 'economic activity rate' for women has crept up over the decades, but is still only two-thirds of the rate for men. In 2018, the rate for men, globally, was 75.0 per cent, and for women, 48.5 per cent. The main exceptions are Scandinavia and parts of West Africa, where women's paid labour force participation rates are unusually high. But in some Arab states women's participation rates are one-quarter the rate for men, and in much of South Asia and Latin America they are about half the rate for men.

Once women are in the paid workforce, how do their wages compare? Over thirty years after the United Nations adopted the *Convention on the Elimination of All Forms of Discrimination against Women* (1979), nowhere in the world are women's earned incomes equal to men's. Women are often hired in low-wage jobs, and still receive 21 per cent less than men's average monthly wages. In some countries, the gender pay gap is much bigger. Pakistan has the largest gender pay gap at almost 51 per cent, followed by South Africa and Armenia with 30 per cent. These gaps are calculated with factor weightings to control for the clustering of women and men in particular positions in labour markets. Part of the overall gender gap in income can be explained by women being more likely to work fewer hours and more likely to be unemployed or precari-ously employed. Other reasons relate to discriminatory wage practices and to women's overrepresentation in low-paid jobs.

Therefore in economic terms most women in the world, especially women with children, are wholly or partly dependent on men. Some men believe that women who are dependent on them must be their property.

This is a common scenario in domestic violence: when dependent women don't conform to demands from their husbands or boyfriends, they are beaten. This creates a dilemma for the women, which is very familiar to domestic violence services. They can stay, and put themselves and their children at high risk of further violence; or go, and lose their home, economic support, and status in the community. If they go, certain husbands are so infuriated that they pursue and kill the wives and even the children.

Men are not beaten up by their spouses so often, but they are at risk of other forms of violence. Most assaults reported to the police, in countries with good statistics on the matter, are by men on other men. Some men are beaten, indeed some are murdered, simply because they are thought to be homosexual; and some of this violence comes from the police. Most of the prisoners in gaols are men. In the United States, which has the biggest prison system in the world, the prison population in 2016 was 1.5 million, and 93 per cent of them were men. Most deaths in combat are of men, because men make up the vast majority of the troops in armies and militias. Most industrial accidents involve men, because men are most of the workforce in dangerous industries such as construction and mining.

Men are involved disproportionately in violence partly because they have been prepared for it. Though patterns of child rearing differ between cultures, the situation in Australia is not unusual. Australian boys are steered towards competitive sports such as football, where physical dominance is celebrated – from an early age – by their fathers, by schools, and by the mass media. Boys also come under peer pressure to show bravery and toughness, and learn to fear being classified as 'sissies' or 'poofters' (a local term meaning effeminate or homosexual). Being capable of violence becomes a social resource. Working-class boys, who don't have the other resources that will lead to a professional career, become the main recruits into jobs that require the use of force: police, the military, private security, blue-collar crime, and professional sport. It is mainly young women who are recruited into the jobs that repair the consequences of violence: nursing, psychology and social work.

So far, we have listed an assortment of facts, about mass media, about politics and business, about families, and about growing up. Are these random? Modern thought about gender starts with the recognition that they are not. These facts form a pattern; they make sense in terms of the overall gender arrangements, which this book will call the 'gender order', of contemporary societies.

To notice the existence of the gender order is easy; to understand it is not. There are conflicting theories of gender (see chapters 3 and 4), and some problems are genuinely difficult to resolve. Yet we now have a rich resource of knowledge from decades of research, and a fund of practical experience from gender struggles and reforms. We have a better basis for understanding gender issues than any previous generation had.

Understanding gender

In everyday life we take gender for granted. We instantly recognize a person as a man or woman, girl or boy. We arrange everyday business around the distinction. Conventional marriages require one of each. Mixed-doubles tennis requires two of each, but most sports require one kind at a time.

Most years, the most popular television broadcast in the United States is the Super Bowl, a strikingly gendered event: large armoured men crash into each other while chasing a pointed leather bladder, and in the pauses thin women in short skirts dance and smile. Most of us cannot crash or dance nearly so well, but we do our best in other ways. As women or men we slip our feet into differently shaped shoes, button our shirts on opposite sides, get our heads clipped by different hairdressers, buy our pants in separate shops, and take them off in separate toilets.

These arrangements are so familiar that they can seem part of the order of nature. Belief that gender distinction is natural makes it scandalous when people don't follow the pattern: for instance, when people of the same gender fall in love with each other. So homosexuality is frequently declared unnatural and therefore bad, and in many jurisdictions is criminalized. But if having sex with a fellow-woman or a fellow-man is unnatural, why have a law against it? We don't provide penalties for violating the third law of thermodynamics. Anti-gay ordinances in US cities, police harassment of homosexual men in Senegal, the criminalization of women's adultery in Islamic Sharia law, the imprisonment of transsexual women for violating public order – such penalties only make sense because these matters are *not* fixed by nature.

These laws are part of an enormous social effort to channel people's behaviour. Ideas about gender-appropriate behaviour are constantly being circulated, not only by legislators but also by priests, parents, teachers, advertisers, retail mall owners, talk-show hosts and disc jockeys. Events like the Super Bowl are not just consequences of our ideas about gender difference. They also help to *create* gender divisions, by displays of exemplary masculinities and femininities.

Being a man or a woman, then, is not a pre-determined state. It is a *becoming*, a condition actively under construction. The pioneering French feminist Simone de Beauvoir put this in a famous phrase: 'One is not born, but rather becomes, a woman.' Though the positions of women and men are not simply parallel, the principle is also true for men: one is not born masculine, but has to become a man.

This process is often discussed as the development of 'gender identity'. There are some questions to raise about this concept (see chapter 6). For the moment it will serve as a name for the sense of belonging to a gender category, and what that belonging means – what kind of person we are, in consequence of being a woman or a man, or refusing to be either. These ideas are not presented to the baby as a package at the beginning of life. They develop (there is some controversy about exactly when), and are filled out in detail over a long period of years as we grow up.

As Simone de Beauvoir further recognized, the business of becoming a gendered person follows many different paths, involves many tensions and ambiguities, and sometimes produces unstable results. Part of the mystery of gender is how a pattern that on the surface appears so stark and rigid, on close examination turns out so complex and uncertain.

We cannot think of womanhood or manhood as fixed by nature. But neither should we think of them as simply imposed from outside. People construct *themselves* as masculine or feminine, and it is an active process (see chapter 6). We claim a place in the gender order – or respond to the place we have been given – by the way we conduct ourselves in everyday life. Most people do this willingly, and often take pleasure in a gender polarity. Yet gender ambiguities are not rare. There are many masculine women and feminine men. There are women in love with other women, and men in love with other men. There are women who are heads of households, and men who bring up children. There are women who are soldiers and men who are nurses. Sometimes growing up results in intermediate, blended or sharply contradictory patterns, for which we use terms like effeminate, camp, queer and transgender.

Psychological research suggests that the great majority of us combine masculine and feminine characteristics, in varying blends, rather than being all one or all the other. Gender ambiguity can be an object of fascination and desire, as well as disgust. Gender impersonations and transitions are familiar in venues from the cross-dressed actors of Shakespeare's stage to movies starring transsexual women and drag queens like *Hedwig and the Angry Inch* (2001), *Priscilla, Queen of the Desert* (2004) and *The Danish Girl* (2015).

There is certainly enough gender blending around to provoke heated opposition from movements dedicated to re-establishing 'the traditional family', 'true femininity' or 'deep masculinity'. By 1988 Pope John Paul II had become so concerned that he issued an encyclical, *On the Dignity and Vocation of Women*, reminding everyone that women were created for motherhood and their functions should not get mixed up with those of men. In a Christmas address in 2012, Pope Benedict XVI criticized gender theory directly. He argued that gender theory 'speaks of a gradual process of denaturalisation, that is a move away from nature and towards an absolute option for the decision of the feelings of the human subject'. This is a good summary of one insight from gender theory. Of course the Pope was arguing against it, saying that the church needs to demonstrate that an essential, biological nature should determine our personal and public lives. These efforts to maintain essentialist ideas about fixed womanhood and manhood are themselves strong evidence that the boundaries are none too stable.

But these are not just boundaries, they are also inequalities. Most churches and mosques are run exclusively by men, and this is part of a larger pattern. Most corporate wealth is in the hands of men, most big institutions are run by men, and most science and technology is controlled by men. In many countries, including some with very large populations, women are less likely than men to have been taught to read. For instance, 2018 adult literacy rates in India stood at 82 per cent for men and 66 per cent for women; in Nigeria, 71 per cent for men and 53 per cent for women. On a world scale, two-thirds of illiterate people are women. In countries like the United States, Australia, Italy and Turkey, middle-class women have gained full access to higher education and have made inroads into professions and middle management. But even in those countries many informal barriers operate to keep the top levels of power and wealth mostly a world of men.

There is a formidable problem of unequal respect. In many situations, including the cheerleaders at the football game, women are treated as marginal to the main action, or as just the objects of men's desire. Whole genres of humour – bimbo jokes, woman-driver jokes, mother-in-law jokes – are based on contempt for women's triviality and stupidity. A whole industry, ranging from heavy pornography and prostitution to soft-core advertising, markets women's bodies as objects of consumption by men. Equal-opportunity reforms in the workplace often run into a refusal by men to be under the authority of a woman. Not only do most religions prevent women from holding major religious office, they often treat women symbolically as a source of defilement for men.

Though men in general benefit from the inequalities of the gender order, they do not benefit equally. Indeed, many pay a considerable price, including the boys and men who depart markedly from hegemonic definitions of masculinity. They are often subject to verbal abuse and discrimination, and are sometimes the targets of violence. Social class, race, region and other factors affect the benefits gained by particular groups of men, an issue of intersectionality (see chapter 5).

Men who conform to hegemonic definitions of masculinity may also pay a price. Research on men's health shows that men as a group have a higher rate of industrial accidents than women, have a higher rate of death by violence, tend to eat a worse diet and drink more alcohol, and (not surprisingly) have more sporting injuries. In 2016 the life expectancy for men in the United States was calculated at 76 years, compared with 81 years for women. In Russia, after the restoration of capitalism, life expectancy for men was 67 years compared with 77 years for women.

Gender arrangements are at the same time sources of pleasure, recognition and identity, and sources of harm. This means that gender is inherently political, involving questions of justice. It also means that gender politics can be complicated and difficult.

Inequality and oppression in the gender order have repeatedly led to demands for reform. Movements for change include campaigns for women's right to vote, the mobilization of women in anti-colonial movements and claims for representation in post-independence governments. They include campaigns for equal pay, for women's right to own property, for women's trade unionism, for equal employment opportunity, for reproductive rights. They include campaigns for the abolition of laws against homosexuality, for the human rights of transsexual men and women and transgender people. They include campaigns against discrimination in education, against sexist media, against rape and domestic violence.

Political campaigns resisting some of these changes, or seeking counter-changes, have also arisen. The scene of gender politics currently includes anti-gay campaigns, anti-abortion ('pro-life') campaigns, a spectrum of men's movements both for and against feminism, and a complex international debate about links between feminism and global-North cultural dominance in the world. One of the most striking waves of change recently is the legalization of gay marriage. In 2015 a US Supreme Court ruling made marriage of same-sex couples legal across the United States, only 11 years after the first individual state had done so. This reform movement spread quickly in the global North, and also in Latin America. Of the 30 countries that have ended a ban on same-sex couples marrying, 23 have made this reform since 2010.

In all this history, the feminist and gay movements of the 1960s–1970s were pivotal. They did not reach their political goals, but they had a profound cultural impact. They called attention to a realm of human reality that was poorly understood, and thus created a demand for understanding as well as action. This was the historical take-off point of contemporary gender research. Political practice launched a deep, even revolutionary, change in human knowledge. This book is an attempt to map the revolution. It describes the terrain revealed by gender struggles and gender research, introduces the debates about understanding it, and offers solutions to some of the problems raised.

Defining gender

As a new awareness of issues developed, a new terminology was needed. Over the last thirty years the term 'gender' has become common in English-language discussions to describe the whole field. The term was borrowed from grammar. Ultimately it comes from an ancient word-root meaning 'to produce' (compare 'generate'), which gave rise to words in many languages meaning 'kind' or 'class' (for example 'genus'). In grammar, 'gender' eventually came to refer to a specific distinction, between classes of nouns 'corresponding more or less' – as the nineteenth-century *Oxford English Dictionary* primly noted – 'to distinctions of sex (and absence of sex) in the objects denoted'.

Grammar suggests how widespread such distinctions are in various cultures. In Indo-European and Semitic languages, nouns, adjectives and pronouns may be feminine, masculine, neuter or common gender. Not only the names for species that reproduce sexually can be gendered, but also many other words for objects, concepts and states of mind. English is a relatively un-gendered language, but English-speakers still call a ship 'she', even an oil well ('she's going to blow!'), and often masculinize an abstraction ('the rights of man').

Language does not provide a consistent framework for understanding gender. German, for instance, has 'die Frau' (the woman) feminine, but 'das Mädchen' (the girl) neuter, because all diminutives ending in '-chen' are neuter. Terror, which is neuter in English, is feminine in French ('la terreur'), and masculine in German ('der Terror'). Other languages, including Chinese, Japanese and Yoruba, do not make gender distinctions through word forms at all. A great deal depends on how a language is used. A relatively non-gendered language can still be used to name gender positions and express opinions on gender issues. On the other hand there are many communities where certain words or tones of voice are thought to belong specifically to men or women, or to express the speaker's masculinity or femininity.

In a common-sense usage in English, the term 'gender' means the cultural and psychological difference of women from men, based on a biological division between female and male. Dichotomy and difference are the substance of the idea. There are decisive objections to such a definition:

- Human life does not simply divide into two realms, nor does human character divide into two types. Our images of gender are often dichotomous, but the reality is not. Abundant evidence will be seen throughout this book.

- A definition in terms of difference means that where we cannot see difference, we cannot see gender. With such a definition we could not recognize the gendered character of lesbian or homosexual desire, based on gender similarity. We would be thrown into confusion by research which found only small psychological differences between women and men, which would seem to imply that gender had evaporated (see chapter 3).
- A definition based on dichotomy excludes the differences among women, and among men, from the concept of gender. But differences within groups may be highly relevant to the pattern of relations between women and men: for instance, the difference between violent and non-violent masculinities (see chapter 6).
- Any definition in terms of personal characteristics excludes processes which lie beyond the individual person. The creation of goods and services in a modern economy is based on shared capacities and cooperative labour – yet the products are often strongly gendered and the profit is distributed in highly gendered ways (see chapter 7). Environmental problems are connected to intensifying global production and consumption, which have gendered drivers but are neither dichotomous nor individual.

Social science provides a solution to these difficulties. The key is to move from a focus on difference to a focus on *relations*. Gender is, above all, a matter of the social relations within which individuals and groups act.

Enduring or widespread patterns among social relations are what social theory calls *structures*. In this sense, gender must be understood as a social structure. It is not an expression of biology, nor a fixed dichotomy in human life or character. It is a pattern in our social arrangements, and the everyday activities shaped by our social arrangements.

Gender is a social structure of a particular kind. It involves a specific relationship with bodies – in this the common-sense definition of gender is not mistaken. We are one of the species that reproduce sexually, some aspects of our anatomy are specialized for this purpose, and many biological processes in our bodies are affected by it (see chapter 3). What is wrong is not the attention to bodies, nor the concern with sexual reproduction. The problems come if we squeeze biological complexity and adaptability into a stark dichotomy, and then assume that cultural patterns simply express bodily difference.

Sometimes cultural patterns do express bodily difference, for instance when they celebrate first menstruation as a distinction between girl and woman. But often they do more than that, or less than that. Social practices sometimes exaggerate a distinction of female from male (e.g. maternity clothes), sometimes deny the distinction (many employment practices), sometimes mythologize it (computer games), and sometimes complicate it ('third gender' customs). So we cannot say that social arrangements routinely 'express' biological difference.

But we can say that, in all of these cases, society *addresses* bodies and *deals with* reproductive processes and differences among bodies. There is no fixed 'biological base' for the social process of gender. Rather, there is an *arena* in which human bodies with their reproductive capacities are brought into social processes. I will call this the reproductive arena (see chapter 3).

We can now define gender in a way that solves the paradoxes of difference. Gender is the structure of social relations that centres on the reproductive arena, and the set of practices that bring reproductive distinctions between bodies into social processes. To put it informally, gender concerns the way human societies deal with human bodies and their continuity, and the many consequences of that dealing in our personal lives and our collective fate. The terms used in this definition are explained more fully in chapters 3 and 5.

This definition has important consequences. Gender, like other social structures, is multidimensional. It is not just about discourse, or just about work, or just about power, or just about sexuality, but about all of these things at the same time. Gender patterns may differ strikingly from one cultural context to another, and there are certainly very different ways of thinking about them, but it is still possible to communicate between cultures about gender. The power of structures to shape individual action often makes gender appear unchanging. Yet gender arrangements are in fact always changing, as human practice creates new situations and as structures develop crisis tendencies. Finally, gender had a beginning, and gender inequality may have an end. Each of these themes will be explored in the book.

Chapter 2 discusses five notable examples of gender research, from different parts of the world. Chapter 3 looks at the question of gender difference, discusses evidence about the extent of sex differences, and considers how bodies and societies interact. Chapter 4 discusses theories of gender from all parts of the world, and the thinkers who have produced them. Chapter 5 gives an account of gender as a social structure, exploring its different dimensions, intersectionality, and change over time. Chapter 6 discusses gender in personal life, the politics of identity and intimate relationships, and how we can understand gender transitions. Chapter 7 focuses on the economic dimension of gender, globalization and organizations. Chapter 8 considers the politics of gender, both public and private, and possible futures for today's gender arrangements.

Note on sources

Most of the statistics mentioned in this chapter, such as income, economic activity rates and literacy, can be found in the online tables regularly published by the United Nations Statistics Division (see *www.uis.unesco. org*). Data cited on the COVID-19 epidemic come from Global Health 50/50 (2020) and a policy brief from the United Nations Secretary-General (2020). Figures on women's participation on the Internet came from the World Wide Web Foundation (2015) *Women's Rights Online: Translating Access into Empowerment*. Figures on parliamentary representation and numbers of ministers are from Inter-Parliamentary Union (2019), and on managers, from *Fortune* and CNBC. Background on men's health can be found in Schofield et al. (2000). Gender wage gap figures are taken from the International Labour Organization report *Global Wage Report 2018/19: What Lies Behind Gender Pay Gaps* and *World Employment Social Outlook: Trends for Women 2018* (ILO 2018). The quotation on 'woman' is from Simone de Beauvoir's *The Second Sex* (Penguin, 1972 [1949]: 295). Definitions and etymology of the word 'gender' are in *The Oxford English Dictionary*, vol. 4 (Oxford, Clarendon Press, 1933: 100).

2

Gender research: five examples

One of the best ways to understand research findings about gender is to look at the research projects themselves. In this chapter we discuss five notable studies of gender issues, coming from five continents. Some focus closely on local settings, others are more expansive. Though they deal with very different topics, they reveal some of the main concerns of gender research in general.

Case 1: Gender in high school

One of the most important tasks in social research is to take a situation that everyone thinks they understand, and illuminate it in new ways. Almost everyone has been to a school, for instance. But how well do we really understand what happens in schools? New and sometimes troubling insights emerge from the research known as school ethnography. In this approach, a researcher or research team settles down for a period in a school (or college, pre-school, or group of schools) to listen, watch, and talk. They carefully note what they observe in the everyday life of classes, corridors, playgrounds and assemblies. Typically they also conduct detailed interviews with individual students and teachers, and sometimes parents. It sounds easy, but is slow, intensive work, difficult to do well.

School ethnography has been wonderfully productive for gender research. Studies like *Learning to Labour* (England), *Frogs and Snails and Feminist Tales* (Australia), *Gender Play* (United States) and *Educated in Romance* (United States) give us rich pictures of gender-in-the-making, with insights into culture, organizations, race and class. A notable example is the study by C. J. Pascoe, vividly described in her book *Dude, You're a Fag* (2012). The setting is River High, a large public school in a fairly conservative, mainly working-class, suburban area of California – a 'middle America' environment.

Pascoe begins with a comic story that is also rather frightening. It is about an on-stage skit, written by students and performed in front of the whole school to laughter and applause, as part of an annual popularity contest to choose 'Mr Cougar', the year's top sporting hero. The two candidates Brent and Greg – who off-stage are both handsome, White, water-polo players – appear as two caricatured nerds who dance very badly. Two girls come in to dance with them but are kidnapped by a bunch of gangstas. The two boys go through a comic course of weight training, assisted by a female trainer. They throw off the mini-skirts they have been wearing, and rapidly turn into musclebound heroes. They proceed to the gangstas' hideout and, in a tough-guy confrontation, scare their opponents off. The story ends with a group of supportive Black boys dancing well, and the two heroes getting the girls.

This performance is an official school event. River High does not have a class called Gender Studies, but it surely teaches gender lessons. Notice, for instance, that the status contest is for *Mr* Cougar, there is no *Ms* Cougar. Educationists speak of the 'hidden curriculum', the lessons taught implicitly by the way the school as an institution routinely works. A sharp division between the masculine and the feminine is taken-for-granted at River High. It is clear in subject choices (the auto shop class, for instance, is almost all boys, the drama class is mainly girls). Gender division is also found in classroom materials, teachers' talk, public events, sports, dress codes, and so on. This extends to sexuality. The students are expected to sort themselves into heterosexual couples, while any other kind of sexuality is regarded with suspicion.

Pascoe speaks of the 'gender and sexuality regimes' of schools. Beyond any individuals' identities, gender exists in institutional arrangements that persist through the years while particular cohorts of students come and go. We will discuss the idea of gender regimes in chapter 5.

Brent and Greg, the heroes of the skit, establish their heroic masculinity by overcoming an inferior group of men, represented by the gangstas. At the same time they suppress an inferior form of masculinity in themselves, represented by their nerdiness. As nerds they are clumsy and weak, ridiculous in their attempts to dance, ridiculously unable to pick up weights that their female trainer can toss about. They are feminized, symbolized in the crudest way by wearing skirts. As they become muscular heroes, they drop the skirts. The skit enacts not just gender difference, but also gender hierarchy – between forms of masculinity, and between men and women. In the main plot line, only the boys play an active role, the two girls are passive objects of the action.

In the central chapter of *Dude, You're a Fag*, Pascoe explores how the hegemonic form of masculinity in River High is sustained by homophobic talk. 'Faggot' or 'fag' is American slang for a homosexual man. River High boys in their peer-groups use this hostile term constantly, and the few visibly gay boys in the school receive serious abuse and threats of violence. But as Pascoe shows in a subtle analysis of everyday interactions, the abuse isn't just homophobic. 'Fag' proves to be a very elastic term. It gets applied to weakness, femininity, incompetence, too much interest in clothes, too much academic work, or indeed anything that a group of boys want to jeer at and repudiate. *Almost anyone* can be a target, at least temporarily. 'Fag' becomes the central negative symbol in a social process of constructing a hegemonic form of masculinity. In the everyday life of the school there is a constant flow of competitive put-downs, partly joking and partly hostile, from which only those high on the masculinity prestige scale are safe.

How does a boy get to be high on this scale? Sporting success clearly helps. But the key mechanism in this school seems to be heterosexual success: the ability to get girls. Pascoe speaks of 'compulsive heterosexuality'. Sexualized banter goes on endlessly among the boys. It presupposes that males are dominant, are essentially predators, and females are expected to make themselves available. Boasting about sexual triumphs is endemic among the boys. Doubtless much of it is fantasy, but some of it is real. Pascoe illustrates this in a short case study of Chad, a self-confident, handsome and popular footballer who was happy to talk about his techniques of seduction.

For the girls, this sexuality regime is a constant pressure. The research was done before #MeToo popularized the concept of sexual harassment, but the reality is there. In school spaces, girls' bodies are subject to frequent sexualized commentary and touching by boys. Sometimes this involves physical actions that would count, legally, as assault – grabbing, pulling, rubbing with the pelvis, and so on. The dominant expression of masculinity asserts physical control over girls' bodies and movements. Most of the girls accept it, sometimes with annoyance, but usually without serious protest. They are expected to regard all this as normal boy behaviour, and to respond flirtatiously.

But there are some who do not, and here the researcher found counter-narratives. The 'Basketball Girls' are a mixed-race group who are loud, energetic, a bit aggressive, highly visible, and are understood in the school to be 'like boys'. They wear baggy clothing, are good at a sport that is coded masculine, and some are sexually assertive. They are often in trouble with school authorities, but popular among the students. In effect, Pascoe suggests, they have appropriated elements of teenage masculinity, and so have successfully claimed space and prestige in the gendered arena of the school. Masculinity is associated with male bodies, but is not *defined* by them, so can be enacted by girls and women.

There are others too who reject conventional scripts. There are the girls involved in the Gay/Straight Alliance, a recently established student club. They are more explicitly political and have a sharp critique of the school's gender order – but have had a much tougher time establishing their presence than the Basketball Girls. There is Ricky, a boy who is a talented dancer, dresses flamboyantly, and is openly gay. He has faced constant harassment and some violence. Soon after the fieldwork was over, Ricky dropped out of school. Most remarkable of all is the story of Jessie, a confident, athletic girl who is out as lesbian – which would seem to invite hostility – but is very popular and was chosen as class president and homecoming queen.

The gender regime of River High, then, is not a homogeneous space. Homophobic banter is less common among the Black boys than among the White, and is less common in mixed-gender groups than in all-boy groups. There are dominant patterns of gender, which are widely enforced, but they contain contradictions. There is resistance, and there are alternative spaces and practices. These are important conclusions, of a kind familiar in gender research. As Pascoe notes, they point to possibilities of change in the long run.

Dude, You're a Fag ends with a fascinating discussion of how the author negotiated life as a participant-observer, titled 'What If a Guy Hits on You?' Her approach was to construct a 'least-gendered identity' in order to fit into multiple scenes. It didn't always work – some comical and some tense situations resulted. Pascoe showed wit and inventiveness in keeping the project going. Anyone considering gender research should definitely read this appendix on method!

Case 2: Empire, feminism and race

Pascoe's research is focused in the person-to-person arenas of a school. The next case moves to a larger scale. We examine themes in the work of Mara Viveros, a Colombian sociologist who is one of the leading analysts of gender in Latin America.

Viveros is both a theorist and an empirical researcher. Her best-known work (Viveros 2002, 2018a) explores how masculinity is made in different Colombian communities. It explodes the myth of a homogeneous Latin American machismo, and makes a powerful argument for the importance of race in gender studies. Viveros treats race not as a fixed biological category, but as a system of social division, formed in history, operating through social stereotypes as well as violence and economic exploitation. She has written brilliantly about White masculinity and how it is expressed in politics.

In her recent work, Viveros has renewed her criticism of static models of femininity and masculinity. Yet she is interested in what is specific about social life in '*nuestra America*' – our America. She explores this by drawing on two great traditions of social thought. One is feminism, the main source of modern understandings of gender. The other is postcolonial thought, which critiques the dominant position in culture and science that is held by the global North (i.e. Western Europe and North America). Mara Viveros is one of the thinkers who has pioneered a decolonizing turn in gender studies.

Colombia is a post-colonial country with a very complex history. Indigenous settlement dates back at least ten thousand years. Diverse cultures evolved in the highlands (around the Andes) and lowlands (rivers and coasts), including some of the most complex societies on the continent. Spanish invasion in the early sixteenth century destroyed these local regimes. The colonizers installed a powerful church, and created a government and social hierarchy centred on the highlands. The lowlands became the site of a despotic economy, as the colonizers brought enslaved Africans as the labour force for export industries such as mining, sugar and tobacco.

Colombia was a battleground in the wars of independence from Spain. The republic that emerged from these struggles was dominated by a landowning class of whites or mestizos, who divided into factions and fell into civil wars. The period in the mid-twentieth century known as *la violencia* further devastated indigenous communities. Guerrilla movements in the late twentieth century sparked the longest-running civil war in recent world history. Meanwhile the Colombian economy, both legal and illegal, became tied to markets in the United States.

Viveros (2018b) tells the remarkable story of how progressive women's movements emerged in this male-dominated, highly unequal, racially divided and violent environment. The first came out of a Marxist movement that had previously assumed only industrial workers – mostly men – were the agents of social change. Women began to organize in small consciousness-raising groups, concerned to show that issues in personal life too were political.

In the 1970s, autonomy for women's groups was a hot issue internationally. It meant organizing on the basis of gender, seeing *women* rather than the working class as the agent of change. What Viveros calls 'canonical feminism' was based on the idea that in a patriarchal society, all women have interests in common. In 1981, Colombian feminists convened a continent-wide conference (*encuentro*) of feminist groups, meeting in the capital Bogotá. It was the first in a famous series of international meetings.

A main issue in the *encuentros* was the difference between 'institutional' and 'autonomous' feminism. To many activists, women's autonomy meant not only being independent of left-wing political parties, it meant being independent of *all* institutions created and controlled by men – governments, corporations, churches, and more. These groups argued that women need to create counter-power against patriarchal domination, and therefore need their own spaces, organizations and political methods.

There is a fierce logic in this position. But there is also an opposing view, that the women's movement can only be effective on society-wide issues by working in existing institutions – claiming space in parliaments, schools, government agencies, media and the economy. This strategy was followed by those feminists who went into universities and launched gender research, and those who went into government to push for women's health policies, equal opportunity, and laws against domestic violence.

Efforts of this kind in the 1990s, Viveros argues, 'institutionalized' the issue of gender in Colombian public life. Gender inequalities were now officially recognized as a problem, long-running reform programmes were set up, and research and teaching in women's studies (later, gender studies) became an accepted part of university life.

But other changes were happening at the same time. A global economic reorganization was under way that deregulated markets, privatized public assets, cut social services and lowered taxes, all in the interests of the rich. Many activist groups transformed themselves into NGOs (non-profits), to provide desperately needed community services. But when NGOs become financially dependent, and are tied up in metrics and auditing, it is likely to blunt their critique and their commitment to deep social change.

In the Colombian women's movement, the turn to NGOs sharpened an issue that had been debated since the first *encuentro*. Canonical feminism, whether institutional or autonomous, mainly developed among middle-class White or Mestiza women. Naturally, it dealt with gender issues as this group saw them. A key feature of Viveros's work is that she addresses gender relations among the socially marginalized as well as the relatively privileged, and studies social movements among Black and Indigenous women as well as White and Mestiza feminism.

Indigenous communities in Colombia were devastated by the impact of European empire, with the killings, famine, loss of land, rape, and cultural disruption that were features of colonial conquest all over the world. Indigenous communities were further damaged by the new waves of social violence in the twentieth century. It was not until the 1970s that formal indigenous political movements developed. There are more than eighty different indigenous communities in the country. When political movements did emerge, to defend land and culture and make claims for education and other resources, they followed the familiar gender pattern of Colombian public life: their leaders were men.

Women were, nevertheless, vital in their community bases, often providing local leadership. From the 1990s, grassroots indigenous women's groups became more common. They addressed issues like illiteracy, the de-valuing of women and their work, and women's exclusion from decision-making. However they could not adopt canonical feminism, which would mean publicly opposing indigenous men. That would split already poor and marginalized communities, and would challenge their own traditions.

Viveros notes that indigenous women in the region have been divided over the very concept of gender. Some think it cannot be reconciled with local cultural visions of the world based on harmony. Others think that gender awareness is essential for the transformation of society, and judge that local cosmo-visions can themselves yield a critique of the oppression of women, since oppression fractures harmony. There is a creative ferment here, and a notable challenge to orthodox ways of thinking about gender.

Africa-descendant people in Colombia form a larger group, about one-fifth of the national population, but have also been starkly oppressed. There was a history of resistance to slavery, and in the twentieth century there have been demands for full inclusion in citizenship. A modern Black political movement began in the 1970s. This was led by men, and women had difficulty having their needs recognized in the movement's agenda. But Black women were also marginalized in the new feminist movement. There was hidden 'Andino-centrism' in a movement mainly created by White and Mestiza women of the highlands, while the Black population was mainly found in the coastal lowlands.

Black women, therefore, faced multiple struggles – particularly when a brutal civil war impinged on their lives. Viveros tells the story of the Pacific coastal region, where organizations focused on Black identity at first resisted women's demands. They only gradually shifted ground, linking gender issues with the defence of community territory. This was vital when civil-war violence arrived in the region, together with illegal mining protected by paramilitary forces. Both displaced Afro-Colombian communities from their mineral-rich ancestral lands, with renewed killings and sexual violence.

Therefore Black women, rather than organizing separately, developed their activism within broad-based social movements, taking leadership positions and obliging the men of the movements to listen. Over time, the demands for gender equality have hardened. But the distinct trajectory of Afro-Colombian women's politics remains clear.

In her recent writing, Viveros reflects on the lessons for readers beyond Colombia. Indigenous and Black women's experience, she argues, challenge the model of feminism formed in the global North and circulated as if it were universally valid. Black and Indigenous women emphasize that their struggle is collective, not individual. ('Leaning In' isn't relevant!) Further, different struggles merge in their lives. Campaigns to defend communities against violence, to protect land and eco-systems against rapacious capitalism, and to achieve gender equality, are interwoven not separate.

Women's lives in the global North and the global South are connected. Global feminism is needed – but not on the old model. Viveros thinks there is a promising convergence between feminist policy work and the post-colonial recognition of different histories and different knowledge systems. Rather than a standardized global feminism, the world needs a feminism based on the acknowledgement of different experiences, promoting solidarity across borders.

Case 3: Manhood and the mines

In the late nineteenth century the fabulous wealth of the largest gold deposit in the world began to be exploited by the Dutch and British colonists in South Africa. The Witwatersrand gold deposits were immense. But the ore was low grade, so huge volumes had to be processed. The main deposits lay far below the high plateau of the Transvaal, so the mines had to go deep. The first wild gold-rushes soon turned into an organized industry dominated by large companies, with a total workforce of hundreds of thousands.

Because the price of gold on the world market was fixed, the companies' profitability depended on keeping labour costs down. Thus the industry needed a large but low-paid workforce for the dangerous conditions underground. To colonial entrepreneurs, the answer was obvious: indigenous men. So Black men, recruited from many parts of South Africa and even beyond, became the main labour force of the gold industry – and have remained so ever since.

Over a 20-year period T. Dunbar Moodie worked with partners to document the experience of the men who made up this labour force, a key group in South Africa's history. Their story is told in a remarkable piece of social history and industrial sociology, *Going for Gold* (1994). Moodie studied the company archives and government records, directed participant-observation studies, and interviewed miners, mine executives and women in the 'townships' (informal settlements) where Black workers lived. A key moment came when one of his colleagues, Vivienne Ndatshe, interviewed 40 *retired* miners in their home country, Pondoland (near the south-eastern coast). Her interviews revealed aspects of the miners' experience which changed the picture of migrant labour profoundly.

Because the mines were large-scale industrial enterprises owned by European capital, it had been easy to think of the mineworkers as 'proletarians' on the model of European urban industrial workers. But the reality was different. The racial structure of the South African workforce – Whites as managers, Blacks providing the labour – might have kept labour costs down. It also created a barrier behind which the mineworkers could sustain cultures of their own, and could exercise some informal control over their work. Most lived in all-male compounds near the mines, where they had to create their own social lives.

When the men signed on with recruiting agents – generally on contracts lasting four months to two years – and travelled hundreds of kilometres to the mines, they did not take families with them and did not intend to become city dwellers. This was not just because the wages were too low to support families in the cash economy of the cities. More importantly, the mineworkers mostly came from areas with a smallholder agricultural economy, such as Pondoland. They kept their links to that economy, and intended to return to it.

For most of them, the purpose of earning wages at the mine was to subsidize rural households run by their families, or to accumulate resources that would allow them to establish new rural households on their return – buying cattle, financing marriages, and so on. Being the wise and respected head of a self-sufficient homestead was the ideal of 'manhood' to which Mpondo migrant workers, and others, subscribed. Time in the mines was a means to this end.

This situation led to gender practices very different from those of the classic breadwinner/housewife couple. First, the men working at the mines and living in the compounds had to provide their own domestic labour, and, if sexually active, find new sexual partners. Some went to women working in nearby towns. Others created sexual and domestic partnerships, known as 'mine marriages', between older and younger men in the compounds. In such an arrangement the young man did housework and provided sexual services in exchange for gifts, guidance, protection and money from the senior man. This was a well-established if discreet custom, which lasted for decades. For the individual partners it was likely to be temporary. In due course the younger man would move on; he might in turn acquire a 'mine wife' if he became a senior man in a compound. These relationships were not taken back to the homeland.

Back in the homeland, the rural homesteads had to keep functioning while many of their men were away at the mines. This led to another significant adjustment, because the person left to run the homestead might well be a woman such as the mineworker's wife. The older Mpondo men did not define manhood, *ubudoda*, in terms of warrior virtues, but in a very different way. As one ex-miner, Msana, put it:

> Ubudoda is to help people. If somebody's children don't have books or school fees or so, then you are going to help those children while the father cannot manage. Or if there is somebody who died, you go there and talk to people there. Or, if someone is poor – has no oxen – then you can take your own oxen and plow his fields. That is ubudoda, one who helps other people. [The interviewer writes:] I ... asked whether there was not also a sort of manhood displayed by strength in fighting. Msana replied at once: 'No, that is not manhood. Such a person is called a killer.' (Moodie with Ndatshe 1994: 38)

Manhood, in this cultural setting, meant competent and benevolent management of a rural homestead, and participation in its community. Since a woman could perform these tasks, almost all the older Mpondo men logically held the view that a woman could have *ubudoda*. They were not denying that in a patriarchal society men ultimately have control. But they emphasized a conception of partnership between women and men in the building of homesteads, in which women could and often did perform masculine functions and thus participated in manhood.

But these gender arrangements, brought into existence by specific historical circumstances, were open to change. As the twentieth century wore on, the homestead agricultural economy declined. The apartheid government's policies of resettlement disrupted communities and created huge pools of displaced labour. The gold-mining industry also changed. The workers became increasingly unionized, and the mine managements abandoned old forms of paternalism and sought new ways of negotiating with workers (though they continued to foment 'tribal' jealousies). In the 1970s the old wage rates were abandoned and miners' incomes began to rise. This made it possible to support an urban household, or a non-agricultural household in the countryside, and broke the economic reciprocity between homestead and mine.

In these changed circumstances the old migrant cultures were eroded, including their distinctive gender patterns. Younger Mpondo men no longer define 'manhood' in terms of presiding over a rural homestead. They simply equate it with the biological fact of maleness – which women cannot share. 'Thus,' remarks Moodie, 'for the present generation of Mpondo, maleness and femaleness have been dichotomized again' (1994: 41). The women with manhood have disappeared from the scene.

Proletarianization has arrived at last, and with it a gender ideology closer to the European pattern. Among the younger mineworkers – more unionized, more militant and much better paid than their fathers – masculinity is increasingly associated with toughness, physical dominance and aggressiveness. This pattern of masculinity requires no reciprocity with women, who are, increasingly, left in the position of housewives dependent on a male wage earner.

There is much more in Moodie's complex and gripping book, including the labour process in the mines, sexual and domestic life in the compounds, and episodes of violence and resistance. The research provides strong evidence of people's active creation of gender patterns. It also shows the constraints under which this creation is done, the impact of economic and political forces. Different gender strategies have consequences – prosperity and poverty, dominance and dependence. Moodie gives us a sense of the powerful processes of historical change that transform gender arrangements over time.

Case 4: Bending gender

In the early 1980s a new and devastating disease was identified, eventually named 'AIDS' (acquired immune deficiency syndrome). It was soon shown to be connected with a virus (human immunodeficiency virus, HIV) that killed people indirectly, by destroying their immune systems' capacity to resist other diseases.

The global HIV/AIDS epidemic led to a massive research response, ranging from the biological studies which discovered HIV, to social science studies of the practices through which HIV is transmitted (Collyer et al. 2019). In health and illness studies, the commonest form of 'behavioural' research is surveys using questionnaires. But research of that kind, though it can yield helpful statistics, gives limited under-standing of the meanings that sexual encounters have for the partners, and the place of sexual encounters in their lives.

It is precisely that kind of understanding that is crucial for AIDS prevention strategies – which, to be successful, must involve people in protecting themselves. Therefore some researchers have turned to more sensitive and open-ended research strategies. A notable example is Gary Dowsett's *Practicing Desire* (1996). This Australian study used a traditional sociological method, the life-history, to create a vivid and moving portrait of homosexual sex in the era of AIDS.

Dowsett's study is based on interviews with 20 men. This may seem a small number, but good life-history research is remarkably complex, produces a tremendous volume of evidence and many theoretical leads, and cannot be hurried. Dowsett's study took nine years from first interviews to final publication. Each of the respondents gave a narrative of his life, talked in intimate detail about relationships and sexual practices, and discussed the communities he lived in, his jobs and workplaces, his relations with the wider world, and his connections with the HIV/AIDS epidemic. The evidence is remarkably rich, and raises important questions about gender. It is so rich, indeed, that I will discuss just one of the participants.

Huey Brown, better known as Harriet, was in his late thirties at the time of the interviews. He is a well-known figure in the homosexual networks of an urban working-class community, 'Nullangardie', which has been proletarian (in Moodie's sense) for generations. Huey's father was a truck driver, his mother a housewife. He left school at 14, and went to work at the checkout of a local supermarket. He has held a succession of unskilled jobs, mostly in cafes or hotels; at the time of the interviews he was working as a sandwich maker. He didn't have much money or education and had no professional certificate in anything. But Harriet was a formidable AIDS educator, not only organizing and fundraising for AIDS-related events, but also being an informal teacher of safe sex and an influential community mentor.

Harriet became involved in homosexual sex in adolescence, not as a result of any identity crisis or alignment with a gay community (which hardly existed in Nullangardie at the time), but simply by enjoying erotic encounters with other boys and with men. Dowsett points out that homosexuality does not necessarily exist as a well-defined opposite to heterosexuality. Among the boys and men of Nullangardie there are many sexual encounters and sexual networks which never get named, yet make an important part of sexuality as it really is.

Harriet is an enthusiast for sex, has had a very large number of partners, is skilful in many sexual techniques, adopts different positions in different sexual encounters, and gets diverse (and perverse) responses from different partners. As Dowsett remarks, this kind of evidence – certainly not confined to Harriet's case – undermines the belief that there is a single, standard pattern of male sexuality.

Like many other people, Harriet wanted stable relationships, and has had three. The first was with a jealous man who beat him severely; the third was with a pre-operative transsexual woman, which was stressful in other ways. The second, with Jim, the love of Harriet's life, lasted nine years. 'It was a husband and wife team sort of thing. I looked after him and he looked after me.' Jim took the penetrative role in sex, 'He was that straight that he just didn't like a cock near his bum.' Jim worked in the building trade, they lived together, they baby-sat Jim's nieces and nephews, and some of Jim's family accepted the relationship quite well.

Still, Harriet was no conventional wife. And as Dowsett shrewdly asks, what are we to make of Jim?

> It sounds like an ordinary suburban life, except that his partner is a drag queen with breast implants and a penchant for insertive anal intercourse with casual partners on the odd occasion! ... Whatever Jim was or is, he certainly cannot be called 'gay,' and when Harriet says: 'He [Jim] was that straight!' he means a sexually conventional male, not a heterosexually identified one. (1996: 94)

Yet after nine years Jim left Harriet – for a 16-year-old girl. There are gender practices here, but not gender boxes. The reality keeps escaping from the orthodox categories.

In some ways the most spectacular escape from the box was becoming a drag queen. In his late teens Huey began to hang out in a cross-dressing scene and became Harriet, working as a 'show girl'. In Australia, as in other countries, there is a local tradition of drag entertainment involving mime, lip-synch singing, stand-up comedy and striptease. Harriet learned the techniques of being a 'dragon', was able to pass as a woman on occasion, and even had operations to get breast implants. He acquired the camp style of humour and self-presentation which is part of the local tradition. Harriet now uses these techniques, and the local celebrity they gave him, for AIDS fundraising. But he notes a generational change. The younger men, more 'gay' than 'camp', now like beefy male strippers better than the old-style drag shows.

Hotel work and drag shows do not pay well, and in a de-industrializing economy the economic prospects of unskilled workers are not good. In his late twenties Harriet tried another form of work, prostitution. He worked in drag, and many of his customers presumed he was a woman. Some knew the score, or suspected, and for them his penis became part of the attraction. Harriet did some brothel work, but mostly worked independently on the street.

As international research shows (Chapkis 1997; Perkins and Lovejoy 2007), there are tremendous variations in the situations that sex workers face and in their level of control over the work. Harriet was right at one end of the spectrum, remaining firmly in control. He did not use narcotics, he offered only certain services, and he insisted on safe sex.

He was skilful in sexual technique, and acquired loyal customers, some of whom stayed with him after he retired from the street – and after he took off the frocks. Even so, there was risk in street work, and a price to pay. Harriet learned to keep constantly aware of where the client's hands were. After several years and two arrests, he gave it up. Even so, his sexual reputation stayed with him, and on this account he was refused a job as an outreach worker with a local AIDS service organization.

Harriet's story (this is the barest outline) repeatedly calls into question the conventional categories of gender. It is not just that Harriet crosses gender boundaries. He certainly did that, with ingenuity and persistence, as a drag artist, surgical patient, wife, prostitute and activist. Yet Harriet is a man, not a transsexual woman, and has mostly lived as a man. (In recognition of that, Dowsett writes 'Harriet ... he', and I follow this example.) There is gender perplexity also about Harriet's partners, customers and social milieu. Every player in the story seems to be surging beyond the familiar categories.

Dowsett argues that the ordinary categories of gender analysis are seriously inadequate to understand what is going on here. He mentions critiques of gender theory for being 'heterosexist', preoccupied with heterosexual relations and unable to understand people who are not heterosexual. Even when gender terms are used, in the context of homosexual sex they are transformed – for instance, Harriet's comment on 'husband and wife'.

Sexual desire and practice thus seem to act like a powerful acid dissolving familiar categories:

> But Harriet also teaches us that these gender categories are subject to deconstruction in sex itself: some like being penetrated by a fully frocked transsexual; some clients eventually do not need the drag at all; pleasure and sensation, fantasy and fixation, are the currency in a sexual economy where the sexed and gendered bodies rather than determining the sexual engagement desire to lend themselves to even further disintegration. (Dowsett 1996: 117)

Dowsett thus ponders the limits of gender analysis, and questions the concept of gender identity. It is clear that gender relations are present in most of the episodes of Harriet's life. But it is also clear that position in gender relations does not fix Harriet's (or his partners') sexual practices.

In his continuing research around the HIV/AIDS epidemic, Dowsett (2003) has argued forcefully that sexuality cannot be reduced to gender categories and must be understood in its own terms. Nevertheless, Harriet's story shows the constant interplay between gender and sexuality. Harriet's career as a sex worker rested on a gendered economy in Nullangardie which put money in the pockets of his clients – all of them men. Equally their action as clients rested on a masculine culture which regarded men as entitled to sexual gratification.

One of the lessons of this research is that we cannot treat gender relations as a mechanical system. Human action is creative, and we are always moving into historical spaces which no one has occupied before. Yet we do not create in a vacuum. We act in situations created by past actions. As shown by Harriet's sexual improvisations on materials provided by the gender order, we work on the past as we move into the future.

Case 5: Gender, marginality and forests

In South Kalimantan, the Indonesian part of the island of Borneo, the people of the Meratus Mountains live in rugged and marginal terrain. They are politically marginal to the Indonesian state, and marginal to the global economy, which was beginning to boom at the time Anna Lowenhaupt Tsing did her ethnographic work in the 1980s. Tsing's book *In the Realm of the Diamond Queen* (1993) is made up of a series of vignettes from life in the mountains.

The first vignette describes Tsing's relationship with a Kalawan woman named Uma Adang – a colourful and tireless figure in a village community who took the visiting researcher into her home, adopting her as a 'sister'. Uma Adang and her friends make theatrical formal speeches to Tsing, who reads these statements as a kind of mockery of the Indonesian state bureaucracy and Muslim orthodoxy.

Uma Adang's leadership in the community involves an assertion of authority with interesting gender dimensions. For instance, she instigates gender segregation in seating arrangements for the local meetings she convenes. This is counter to the Meratus tradition, where no such formal distinction is made. Uma Adang's practice draws from the practice of the local Muslim Banjar people. The Banjar are also a minority in the national and international economy. But they are intermediaries in the regional economy. Banjar people often dominate markets and tend to be in district-officer roles, or are police, army and other officials who routinely assert political authority over Meratus 'Dayaks' (a term used to describe the numerous ethnic groups in Kalimantan that fall outside Islam and its political sponsorship).

On the tensions of Uma Adang's leadership, Tsing remarks: 'These are not easy discrepancies to resolve, and they draw Uma Adang into a flurry of contradictions around the gender consequences of her leadership. Her leadership requires continual revision as it argues for and against local expectations about gender, ethnicity, and state power' (1993: 35).

Exchanges like these illustrate the ways in which marginality is lived and contested. Tsing is concerned with gender-differentiated responses to peripheral political status. She argues that the contestations over gender difference can also disrupt ethnic unity and spark divergent attitudes towards the state.

Tsing takes up the concept of marginality in an interesting way. Two key dynamics are visible in her account of life in the Meratus Mountains: constraint and creativity. First, the marginalization of Meratus people, particularly by state authority, is clear. Under General Suharto's army-controlled 'New Order' regime, officials conducted government in an authoritarian style similar to the Dutch colonial administration in the 1920s and 1930s. This is overlaid by another political dichotomy between Indonesia's centre and periphery, i.e. Java (where the capital is) and the other islands. The Meratus people are 'tribal' minorities peripheralized through several processes: the central government's restricting definition of citizenship; its programme for Javanese transmigration and the 'Management of Isolated Populations'; reforms of forest land title that favour the timber sector and other extractive industries; and the consistent presence of travelling military personnel.

Crucially, Tsing emphasizes a second dimension of marginality. She observes ways that marginality can be deployed as a basis for social agency. Uma Adang's self-titled 'woman's shamanism' is an example. Her spiritual teaching involves the education of her followers about symmetrical dualities (*dua-dua*) of gender (man and woman), nature (man and rice), economic organization (rich and poor) and more (Tsing 1993: 270). It is a kind of separate-but-equal approach to gender. No named duality is present in spiritual practices usually conducted by men.

Tsing argues that Northern social scientists should pay attention to the creative agency of subaltern people, and Uma Adang's practices show why. Importantly, Tsing also attends to the limits of this agency for a woman in Uma Adang's position. For instance, Uma Adang has trouble rousing other women spiritual leaders, and at times has difficulty cultivating her own audience outside the 'central proceedings' of men in community discussion.

The Meratus experience of state authority is likewise gendered. Tsing's description of conflict over fertility control concerns an encounter with the bureaucratic imperatives of the modern Indonesian state. In the 1970s and 1980s, a government-sponsored family planning programme was expanded rapidly across the country. When the programme reached South Kalimantan, resistance came from the Banjar Muslim leadership. In the smaller villages, the administration of the programme was put into the hands of local office-bearers.

In one village where at the time there was no village head, a state official reportedly told one young Meratus man, Pa'an Tini, that village elections would be held on the condition 40 women were recruited to the family planning programme. The prospect of conducting these elections attracted a group of men eager to discuss the process. Tsing argues that their enthusiasm stemmed from the wish to align with the prestige of state authority through the village elections, not from support for the cause of birth control. She observed that there was opposition when the matter of contraception was aired, but just as often misunderstanding about contraception was visible amongst these men and broader village networks.

In the end, neither the village election occurred, nor the delivery of the contraception. Instead, Pa'an Tini opted to perform the bureaucratic task in the most convenient way. He compiled a list of 40 married women to meet the nominal requirements from the central government, but did not pursue the use of contraception with those listed. He took this approach to other aspects of reporting to the state about household arrangements, for instance where family planning statistics required reporting on the 'heads' (*kepala keluarga*) of discrete families in the population. The reality of the households reported on is much more complex. For instance, a household can be formed by a brother and sister, or a combination of non-conjugal couples, while dependants in a household are highly varied. The effect of this approach to complying with state authority, Tsing notes, is that Pa'an Tini 'protected only the community envisioned in his leadership. His leadership effectively barred women from access to state-provided contraception' (1993: 111).

The political ecology of the mountainous forests of South Kalimantan is an important feature of the dynamics of marginality captured in Tsing's work. The Meratus Dayaks, like many other Dayak communities in Kalimantan, have collected forest products for world markets since before European control. Trade was regulated by court centres from the fourteenth century and in the sixteenth century by the growing Banjar Kingdom in alliance with the Muslim Javanese state of Demak. Dutch colonial rule in the eighteenth and nineteenth centuries was accompanied by a new export industry in rubber.

In the 1970s the Suharto regime pursued more direct military and economic control over these resource-rich islands. The 1975 Forestry Law made all forests property of the state. Lots of areas without trees, even towns and villages, were included in the first maps (Tsing 2004: 194). The first timber concessions divided the forests up as sites of production, focused on particular species of tree. The forest land of Kalimantan is valuable because it contains dipterocarps – giant trees that are exploited as sources of plywood for export markets. Forest concessions were legally framed in a way that assumed commercial value flowed from these specific trees, rather than from the multi-species diversity of plants and animals that the Meratus use in their shifting cultivation practices.

At the time that Anna Tsing wrote *In the Realm of the Diamond Queen*, large-scale timber extraction in Kalimantan was still relatively new. The new timber industry was operating on the greatest scale in the east of the island, but rapidly shifting south and up the Meratus Mountains. When Tsing returned to the Meratus Mountains in the late 1990s, she found that gold mining had produced devastating mercury poisoning in river ecosystems, and huge tracts of land had been assigned to logging and mining companies, and to firms producing pulp-and-paper and palm oil. Suharto's New Order was overthrown in the wake of the Asian financial crisis in 1997. However, the developmentalist model and the imposition of extractive industries in Kalimantan continued apace under the new President Habibie and his successors.

Tsing's later book *Friction: An Ethnography of Global Connection* (2004) captures the dynamics of Kalimantan as a frontier of capitalism. Tsing argues here that capitalism, science and politics strive for global connection and aspire to universal knowledge. But neither the processes of capital expansion, nor the universal claims on which they are based, make every place and everything the same. South Kalimantan is the 'frontier' Tsing uses to illustrate this point.

Uma Adang features again in the second book and her anger at the chaos of capitalist development is clear. She tells Tsing that all the trees are coming down, and remarks more than once: 'better you had brought me a bomb, so I could blow this place up' (Tsing 2004: 25). At Uma Adang's request, the two start work on a comprehensive list of plant and animal species of the local region in anticipation of further destruction.

Reflecting on this process, Tsing recalls the debates in the global North on the relation between local knowledge in the periphery and Northern conservationism. She cites the critical reflection of US ecofeminist Noël Sturgeon that ecofeminist attention to indigenous knowledge reconstitutes white privilege. This can occur through reproducing racialized, essentialist views of 'Third World' women and 'local' knowledge (Tsing 2004: 160). Rather than abandon her interest in indigenous knowledge, Tsing describes and reflects on the process of collaboration and negotiation. She, Uma Adang and other Meratus Dayaks share motivations and pleasure in the list-making.

The question of gender is not central to Tsing's second book on the Meratus Mountains, but a few sections raise questions about gender and environmental change. One concerns the stories about ecofeminism which spread through Indonesian environmental activist networks.

Tsing travelled with friends in the Indonesian environmental movement that bloomed in the late 1990s as Suharto's regime collapsed. Stories of women engaged in environmental activism, such as the Chipko movement in India where women were involved in non-violent resistance to protect forests, and the story of ecofeminism more generally, gained local attention (Tsing 2004: 236).

Tsing argues that the story of the Chipko movement established a cosmopolitan view of indigenous knowledge. It was one of a series of international stories which contributed to a new kind of environmental politics in South Kalimantan where Muslim and non-Muslim Meratus Dayaks began to collaborate. Tsing describes how young Indonesian women engaged in 'nature loving' activities were excited about gender as a new term, and wanted to know more about it. They wanted to walk forest trails without fear, and carry their own packs. The translation of these ideas illustrates that activists borrow travelling feminisms and environmentalisms for their own uses.

Tsing demonstrates that the global periphery is not a static location that stands in contrast to the dynamic core of elite-led globalization. She shows that the politics of marginality are gendered in important ways. She illustrates the possibilities for agency in the political ambitions of figures like Uma Adang. Finally, she shows how knowing and acting on environmental change poses profound challenges to society, and to the gender order.

Other notable studies might have been included in this chapter, and more will be mentioned through the book. I hope that these five show the diversity of gender dynamics, their complexity, and their power. Gender processes are at work in many issues that are not conventionally labelled 'gender issues', including environment and war. In talking about gender, we are not talking about simple differences or fixed categories. We are talking about relationships, boundaries, practices, identities and images that are actively created in social life. They come into existence in particular circumstances, shape the lives of people in profound and often contradictory ways, and are subject to historical struggle and change.

3

Sex differences and gendered bodies

At the centre of common-sense thinking about gender is the idea of natural difference between women and men. A whole industry of pop psychology tells us that women and men are naturally opposites in their thinking, emotions, and capacities. The most popular book in this genre, which assures us that men and women are like beings from different planets, has apparently sold tens of millions of copies in at least forty different languages, from Gujarati to Hebrew. Other books, and endless articles in popular magazines, tell us that men and women communicate in quite different styles, that boys and girls learn differently, that hormones make men into warriors, or that neuroscience proves that 'brain sex' rules our lives.

Most of the claims in these books are, in scientific terms, nonsense – refuted by a mass of research evidence. The US psychologist Janet Hyde (2005), the leading authority on gender difference research, points out that these pop-psychology doctrines are harmful to children's education, to women's employment rights, and to all adults' emotional relationships. Clearly we need better ways of thinking about differences and bodies. The development of gender studies now provides some of the necessary tools.

Sexual reproduction and difference

Why is there any difference at all between women's and men's bodies? Humans share with many other species, plants as well as animals, the system of sexual reproduction – a method of sustaining a species through time that allows genetic information from two individuals to be combined, rather than just one to be copied. Sex as a method of reproduction is itself a product of evolution, perhaps 400 million years old. Life forms earlier than that reproduced by cell division from one individual; many species still do so, including bacteria and rotifers. Other species, including orchids, ferns and grasses, reproduce both sexually and asexually. Gardeners exploit this when they take cuttings from a neighbour's garden. Biologists debate why sex evolved, for this odd scheme has some evolutionary disadvantages. It may have developed because sexual reproduction allows faster change, or prevents the accumulation of harmful mutations.

Sexual reproduction does not require bodies to be specialized by sex. Among earthworms, for instance, each individual is hermaphrodite, producing both sperm and ova (eggs). Thus every worm is able to perform both male and female functions. In other species, individuals produce either sperm or ova but not both. Their bodies are to some extent 'dimorphic', i.e. in a given species there are two main forms. Humans are among these species.

Genetic information encoded in DNA is carried on chromosomes, microscopic structures within the nucleus of each cell in a plant or animal. In sexual reproduction, the genetic information that is combined at fertilization comes half from a female, in the egg nucleus, and half from a male, in the sperm nucleus. Human cells usually have 46 chromosomes, which come in pairs. One pair, the so-called sex chromosomes, have particular influence in the development of the body's sexual characteristics. Females have two X chromosomes in this pair, males have one X and one Y chromosome. Under the influence of the genetic information here, given suitable environmental conditions for growth, male and female bodies develop specialized organs – wombs, testes, breasts – and certain differences in physiology, such as the balance of hormones circulating in the blood, and the menstrual cycle in women. (This is only the beginning of the science of reproductive development, which has fascinating complications and variations.)

Among mammals, females not only produce ova but also carry foetuses in a protective womb (except for monotremes such as the platypus, which lay eggs). They feed infants with milk from specialized organs – in humans, women's breasts. Among some mammal species, but not all, males have extra bulk or extra equipment: the antlers of male deer, for instance. Humans are mammals with well-differentiated reproductive systems, but modest physical differences between sexes in other respects. Human males do not have anything like antlers.

In several ways, the human species is not fully dimorphic. First, there are quite a number of intersex groups. They include females lacking a second X chromosome, males with an extra X chromosome, anomalous or contradictory hormonal patterns, and a variety of un-standard forms taken by the internal and external genitals. There is uncertainty about how common intersex conditions are: estimates range from 1 in 100 births to 1 in 5,000 births. There is continuing debate on how broad the intersex category should be, what medical or psychosocial support is needed (Ernst et al. 2018), how intersex people should be recognized in science and law and what medical terms apply (Holmes 2009).

In 2006, an international conference of endocrinologists tried to sort this out by emphasizing genetic determination, establishing new treatment protocols, and introducing the term 'Disorders of Sexual Development' (DSD) to cover all intersex categories. This term has been widely accepted inside the medical profession, but not outside. Critics have called it 'a case of epistemic injustice' (Merrick 2019): the product of decisions which were made with little input from intersex people themselves, and which stigmatize their condition as 'disorders' rather than natural variation. The DSD classification is likely to support the belief, among doctors and the parents of newborn intersex children, that surgical intervention is needed to create a body that is recognizably either a girl or a boy. There are growing numbers of life-stories told by intersex people who reject this view, and have found a path in life that falls outside the categories of 'man' or 'woman' (Harper 2007; Viloria 2017).

Second, physical differences between male and female change over the lifespan. In the early stages of development male and female bodies are relatively undifferentiated; there are only small differences between a two-year old girl and a two-year-old boy. Even the external reproductive organs – penis, clitoris, scrotum and labia – develop embryonically from a common starting point. Male and female bodies also become more similar in old age, for instance in their hormonal balance.

Third, even in early adulthood the physical characteristics of males as a group, and females as a group, overlap extensively. Height is a simple example. Adult males are on average a little taller than adult females, but the diversity of heights within each group is great, in relation to the average difference. Therefore a very large number of individual women are taller than many individual men. European-derived cultures tend not to notice this physical fact because of social custom. When a man and a woman form a couple, they usually pick partners who show the culturally-expected difference in height.

A more complex example is the brain, the topic of a great deal of recent debate on sex differences. There are some average differences in brain size and anatomy between women and men. They are less stark, and less reliably established, than aggressive popular accounts of 'brain sex' suggest. As the neuroscientist Lesley Rogers (2000: 34) put it: 'The brain does not choose neatly to be either a female or a male type. In any aspect of brain function that we can measure there is considerable overlap between females and males.' What brain differences mean for human behaviour is even more contestable. Gina Rippon's book *The Gendered Brain* (2019) tells the sad story of how, from the nineteenth to the twenty-first centuries, dubious interpretations of research findings have been turned into sexist stereotypes of fixed differences between men's and women's capacities and qualities. Those stereotypes are still being circulated. So it is useful to remember that modern neurobiology, as well as documenting brain anatomy, also reveals the 'plasticity' of the neural system: its capacity to respond to experience during childhood, and in adulthood to replace connections and develop new ones. The brain is not a hard-wired machine. Humans do have a notable capacity to learn and change.

Explaining difference: nature? culture? both?

The fact of reproductive difference between male and female humans is hardly controversial, but its significance certainly is. On this question, approaches to gender diverge sharply.

Some believe that differences of reproductive biology are directly reflected in a range of other differences: bodily strength and speed (men are stronger and faster), physical skills (men have mechanical skills, women are good at fiddly work), sexual desire (men have more powerful urges), recreational interests (women gossip, men love sport), character (men are aggressive, women are nurturant), intellect (men are rational, women have intuition), and so on.

Most arguments of this kind claim to be scientific, and some of the authors advancing them are actually biologists. From a vaguely Darwinian starting point, they deduce social facts such as human kinship loyalties, mothers' commitment to their children, husbands' sexual infidelity, women's (presumed) coyness, male bonding, and an amazing range of other things including pornography and rock music. In one of the most elaborate arguments in a genre that calls itself evolutionary psychology, David Geary in *Male, Female* (1998) tried to link psychological research on sex differences with Darwin's concept of sexual selection as a mechanism of evolution. For each topic where a sex difference can be found, Geary offered an imaginative story of how it *might* be linked to sexual selection, that is, how humans choose, win and control mates.

Biological-determinist arguments are often used to ridicule feminist ideas about the possibility of change in gender arrangements. My favourite example is the idea that men dominate in society because, with their higher levels of testosterone, they have a hormonal 'aggression advantage' in competition for top jobs. Therefore society needs patriarchy – Steven Goldberg claimed in *Why Men Rule* (1993) – to protect women from failure! However, there are also feminist arguments which treat bodies as direct sources of gender difference. US feminists in the 1980s often saw male aggression and female peacefulness as natural. The terms 'male violence' and 'male sexuality', which became common at that time, implicitly explain behaviour by bodily difference.

This approach runs into trouble on several fronts. Biological-determinist explanations of human kinship, for instance, foundered when the predictions from genetics failed to match the realities of kinship systems actually documented by anthropologists (Sahlins 1977). The explanation of gender hierarchy by a hormonal 'aggression advantage' fails when it is discovered that higher testosterone levels follow from social dominance as much as they precede it (Kemper 1990). The arguments of 'evolutionary psychology' are based on an unrealistic individualism, which takes no account of the institutions (the family, the state, the economy, etc.) involved in gender arrangements. But the most striking problem is that this whole family of arguments, though using a rhetoric of science, is actually based on speculation. Alex Dennis (2018) puts it nicely: sociobiology relies on 'a series of promissory notes' – claims that simply presume supporting evidence will appear later. Unfortunately it hasn't. Not one sex difference in psychological characteristics has actually been *shown* to result from evolutionary mechanisms.

Culture-warriors pit one or other version of biological determinism against the idea that gender difference is essentially a matter of culture or social convention. One of the earliest Women's Liberation demonstrations was a protest against gender norms. It happened at the Miss America beauty pageant at Atlantic City in 1968, a pageant that celebrated a rather narrow ideal of the way women should look. (Contrary to the usual tale, no bras were burned at this demonstration. Rather, bras and other constricting underclothes were thrown into a Freedom Trash Can.)

It is easy to find cultural images of gender: mass media are full of them. (If you haven't seen enough already, the *Shutterstock* website claims to have more than 300,000 stock gender images.) Cultural studies of gender usually treat such images in terms of a wider discourse, following the approach of Michel Foucault. (Foucault, notoriously, failed to theorize gender, though much of his writing was distinctly about men and masculinized institutions such as prisons.) Gendered bodies can be seen as the products of disciplinary practices organized by prevailing discourses – the beauty contest is a perfect example of that. Bodies are 'docile', and biology bends to the hurricane of social discipline. Men as well as women are disciplined by gender ideals. Los Angeles body-building gyms were studied by the ethnographer Alan Klein (1993) who found a whole subculture of men subjected to a fierce regime of exercise, diet and drugs to sculpt their bodies. This is an extreme case, but more moderate disciplining of men's bodies is widespread. Sport is an obvious venue and Michael Messner (2007) has shown, through a long research programme, how pervasive are gender stereotyping and gender inequality in the US sports world.

If social discipline fails to produce gendered bodies, the knife can. The silicon breast implant scandal that erupted in 2009, followed by a corporate collapse and the criminal conviction of the company's founder, made public the scale on which cosmetic surgery has been done in France and the United States. This whole industry, one might think, flies in the face of the ideology of natural difference. Research on cosmetic surgeons and their clients by Diana Dull and Candace West (1991) showed a startling solution to the cultural problem. Cosmetic surgery was considered natural for a woman, but not for a man. (The exception is penile surgery, where penis enlargement is now a considerable business.)

Cultural approaches to gender difference, though they have been very illuminating, also run into difficulties. The docility of bodies can be exaggerated. Bodies may participate in disciplinary regimes not because they are docile, but because they are active. They seek pleasure, seek experience, seek transformation. Some startling examples can be found in sadomasochist sexual subcultures (for a good, non-pornographic account, see Turley 2016). The same is surely true, in milder forms, of the whole system of fashion. Nobody compels young women to wear shoes with heels that hurt.

Focusing tightly on the signifier can make us forget the signified. What makes a symbolic structure a gender structure is the fact that its signs refer, directly or indirectly, to the way humans reproduce. Reproductive embodiment is more often emphasized in discussions of gender in the global South than in the North. As Wendy Harcourt shows in her powerful book *Body Politics in Development* (2009), a whole series of contested issues in global economic development involve troubles about bodies – in childbirth and childcare, violence, sexualization, and more.

However embodiment is relevant to understanding gender everywhere. The masculinity of industrial labour in construction or manufacturing consists in its heaviness, risk and difficulty, where men put themselves 'in harm's way', as Kris Paap (2006) puts it in her research with construction workers in the United States. These are ways that bodies are consumed: worn down, injured, sometimes killed. As Mike Donaldson (1991) remarked, 'the very destruction of the physical site of masculinity, the body, can be a method of attaining, demonstrating and perpetuating the socially masculine'.

Neither purely-biological nor purely-cultural interpretations of the gendered body are satisfactory. Can we solve these problems by holding both interpretations at the same time? In the 1970s a number of feminist theorists in the global North did exactly this, drawing a sharp distinction between 'sex' and 'gender'. Sex was the biological fact, the difference between the male and the female human animal. Gender was the social fact, the difference between masculine and feminine roles, or men's and women's personalities.

To many at the time, this two-realms model was a conceptual breakthrough. The constraints of biological difference were confined to the realm of biology itself. A broad realm of cultural life remained, where societies could choose the gender patterns they wanted. Eleanor Maccoby and Carol Jacklin, the authors of a vast and influential survey of *The Psychology of Sex Differences* (1975: 374), concluded:

> We suggest that societies have the option of minimizing, rather than maximizing, sex differences through their socialization practices. A society could, for example, devote its energies more toward moderating male aggression than toward preparing women to submit to male aggression, or toward encouraging rather than discouraging male nurturance activities.

The concept of 'androgyny' put forward by Sandra Bem (1974) and other psychologists at this time was a popular attempt to define an alternative gender pattern, a mixture of masculine and feminine characteristics.

At the high tide of liberal feminism in the 1970s, the two-realms model supported an optimistic view of change. Oppressive gender arrangements, being the products of past choices, could be abolished by fresh choices. Whole reform agendas were constructed around this principle. A notable example was the pioneering Australian national report *Girls, School and Society* (Schools Commission 1975). This described the ways girls were held back by restrictive social stereotypes, and proposed action to break down educational segregation and to widen girls' job choices. From this report flowed many projects in Australian schools encouraging girls to work in areas such as mathematics, science and technology.

However the two-realms model also ran into trouble. The idea of gender as culturally chosen difference ('sex roles') was unable to explain why one side of that difference, the masculine, was more highly valued than the other. The separation of gender from bodies ran counter to developments in feminism which were placing stronger emphasis on bodies. The philosopher Elizabeth Grosz (1994), for instance, argued that there is no consistent distinction between body and mind, and that our embodiment itself is adequate to explain our subjectivity. She suggested that bodies and minds are two aspects of the one element making up ourselves and our world, with gendered embodiment dynamically shifting over time.

If the two realms cannot be held strictly apart, perhaps they can be added together? A common-sense compromise suggests that gender differences arise from *both* biology and social norms. This additive conception underlies most discussions of gender in social psychology, where the term 'sex role' is still widely used – the phrase itself adds together a biological and a dramaturgical term.

But there are awkward problems in this approach too. The two levels of analysis are not easily comparable. It is usually assumed that biology's reality is more real than sociology's, that biological categories are more fixed. The passage from Maccoby and Jacklin quoted above continues: 'A variety of social institutions are viable within the framework set by biology.' The priority in their argument is clear: biology determines; only within its framework may humans choose. And the language of 'roles', derived from theatre, is curiously weak. The oddity of using such language for something as visceral and power-drenched as gender relations has long been recognized (Lopata and Thorne 1978).

Further, it is difficult to *add* cultural difference and biological difference because the patterns at the two levels do not match well. As we have seen, human bodies are dimorphic only in limited ways. Human behaviour and culture are hardly dimorphic at all, even in areas closely related to sexual reproduction. For instance, while few men do care work with infants, at any given time most women are not doing this work either. In current social life there is a spectrum of gender configurations that do not have biological analogues. Queer theory has emphasized this, but it is just as true in straight life. There are many different masculinities, many different femininities, and an enormous variety of ways in which gender can be enacted.

It is impossible to sustain a two-realms model of gender difference, any more than we can sustain biological or cultural determinism. It is time to look more closely at the evidence about difference itself.

Sex similarity research

In the simplified pop psychology mentioned at the start of this chapter, bodily differences and social effects are linked by the idea of character dichotomy. Women are supposed to have one set of traits, men another. Women are supposed to be nurturant, suggestible, talkative, emotional, intuitive, and sexually loyal; men are supposed to be aggressive, tough-minded, taciturn, rational, analytic, and promiscuous. These ideas have been strong in European-derived culture since the nineteenth century, when the belief that women had weaker intellects and less capacity for judgement than men was used to justify their exclusion from universities and from the vote.

The belief in character dichotomy was one of the first issues about gender to be addressed in empirical research. Starting in the 1890s, generations of psychologists have measured various traits with tests or scales, and then compared the results for women and men. The resulting body of research, long known as 'sex difference' research, is huge; this is one of the most researched topics in psychology. There is also a large parallel literature in sociology and political science, looking at group differences in attitudes and opinions, voting, violence and so forth.

The beginning of this research is described in a fascinating historical study by Rosalind Rosenberg, *Beyond Separate Spheres* (1982). The first generation of psychological researchers found, contrary to mainstream belief, that the mental capacities of men and women were substantially equal. It is an interesting fact that this finding of no difference was rapidly accepted in the mental-testing field. As psychologists developed standardized tests of general ability or intelligence (the so-called IQ tests) during the first half of the twentieth century, they incorporated the no-sex-difference finding as a given. They chose and scored test items in such a way that males and females would have equal average scores. Later attempts to find gender differences in general intelligence have come to nothing (Halpern and LaMay 2000). There is intriguing evidence that this finding – women and men are equal in intelligence – is widely accepted by the modern American public (Eagly et al. 2020).

An even more interesting fact is that this is the usual finding about other variables too. In table after table of Maccoby and Jacklin's great compendium of sex-difference research, the commonest entry in the column for the finding about difference is 'none'. Study after study, on trait after trait, compared women with men or girls with boys, and found no significant difference. In summarizing their findings, the first thing Maccoby and Jacklin (1975: 349) did was to list a series of 'Unfounded Beliefs about Sex Differences'. On the evidence they compiled, it is *not* true that girls are more social than boys, that girls are more suggestible than boys, that girls have lower self-esteem, that girls are better at rote learning and boys at higher-level cognitive processing, that boys are more analytic, that girls are more affected by heredity and boys by environment, that girls lack achievement motivation, or that girls are auditory while boys are visual. All these stories turned out to be myths.

Maccoby and Jacklin were not alone. Other reviewers too noted that the main research finding is a massive psychological *similarity* between women and men in the populations studied by psychologists. If it were not for the cultural bias of both writers and readers, we would long ago have been talking about this as 'sex similarity' research.

It is therefore intensely interesting to find that this conclusion is widely disbelieved. The acceptance of gender similarity in the field of intelligence testing turns out to have been an exception. Most people still believe in character dichotomy. Best-selling pop psychology, which works by reinforcing beliefs that readers already hold, is utterly committed to this idea. Generations of researchers in the academic world, in the teeth of the evidence from their own disciplines, have gone relentlessly on, seeking and writing about psychological gender differences. Articles about this still pour from the journals.

The gap between the main pattern *actually* found, and the widespread belief about what *should* be found, is so great that Cynthia Epstein (1988) called her admirable book about dichotomous thinking about gender, and non-dichotomous reality, *Deceptive Distinctions*. Two decades later, when she was president of the American Sociological Association, Epstein (2007) still had to argue against the conventional narrative that holds 'that men and women are naturally different and have different intelligences, physical abilities, and emotional traits'.

Why the huge reluctance to accept the evidence of similarity? Cultural background is part of the answer. Dichotomous gender symbolism is strong in European culture, so it is not surprising that when researchers look at sex and gender, what they 'see' is difference. In the usual quantitative research design, gender similarity is not a positive state. Similarity is merely the absence of proven difference (literally the null hypothesis). Since journal editors usually do not like to publish null results, the true evidence for gender similarity may be even stronger than the published research reveals.

But are these facts as solid as they seem? Conventional psychological tests may be too superficial to detect the underlying patterns of gender, lodged at a deeper level in personality. This could be true. Certainly most quantitative tests in psychology measure only immediately apparent aspects of behaviour, usually through self-report. But if the deep differences don't show up at the level of everyday life, and across a wide range of variables repeatedly fail to show up – which is what the quantitative research seems to find – then one wonders how important such deep differences can be.

A second issue is that the finding of 'no difference' is not uniform. Maccoby and Jacklin also pointed to a small number of traits where gender differences *did* show up, according to the bulk of their evidence: verbal ability, visual-spatial ability, mathematical ability, and aggressiveness. It was these findings, not the larger 'no difference' finding, which went into the textbooks, and have been emphasized by most subsequent writers.

A third issue concerns research method. Maccoby and Jacklin collected a large amount of data, mostly from hundreds of small studies with ill-defined samples. Could the many findings of 'no significant difference' reflect the methodological weakness of the individual studies? If a way could be found to combine the results of many studies, the picture might change. Exactly this became possible when a statistical procedure known as 'meta-analysis', which had mainly been used in medical research, was introduced to gender difference research in the 1980s. As the conclusions are very important, it is worth taking a moment to examine this procedure.

A meta-analysis relies on finding a large number of separate studies of the same issue. For instance, there may be many studies that have attempted to measure gender differences in aggression, or intelligence, or self-esteem. In meta-analysis the researcher first has to find all these reports in the back issues of journals. Then each study, rather than each person, is taken as one data point. A statistical analysis is then made of the whole collection of studies.

Before the studies can be combined, their findings have to be expressed on a common scale. Unless all the studies have used exactly the same measurement procedures, which rarely happens in practice, this is a difficulty. The ingenious solution is to define a common scale based on the variability of individual scores in the original studies. For each study, the difference between the average scores of women and men on the scale being used is obtained, and this is expressed as a fraction of the overall variation in people's scores found in that same study on that same test. Technically, the difference between means is divided by the mean within-group standard deviation.

For each individual study, this standardized gender difference, known as 'd', is the piece of information taken forward into the meta-analysis proper. (By an unfortunate convention, a positive d means that men as a group score higher, a negative d means that women as a group score higher.) In the next step, the average of d measures for all the studies in the meta-analysis is calculated, and the significance of its difference from zero is estimated. Then, by classifying the studies into groups (according to their date, the social group studied, the region, etc.), the way other variables condition gender difference can be examined.

The first impact of meta-analysis was to revive confidence in the existence and importance of psychological gender differences. This can be seen in Alice Eagly's *Sex Differences in Social Behavior* (1987). Even when most studies individually show non-significant differences, meta-analysis may find an effect size significantly different from zero across the whole collection of studies. A few examples from the many effect sizes reported are: +.21 across 216 studies of self-esteem (Kling et al. 1999), –.28 across 160 studies of 'care orientation' in moral choice (Jaffee and Hyde 2000), +.48 across 83 studies of aggression (Hyde 1984), and between .01 and .17 in large surveys of the frequency of sexual intercourse (Petersen and Hyde 2011).

The question then arises, what do these effect sizes mean? An effect may be significantly different from zero, which rules out pure chance, but may still be so small that it does not tell us much about the world. Here meta-analysis has its limits. By convention, an effect size of .20 is called 'small', .50 is called 'medium', and .80 is called 'large'. But there is debate about how to interpret this convention. Eagly (1987) argued that even small effects may be practically important; other meta-analysts doubt this.

As meta-analyses built up, so did a renewed scepticism about the size and scope of gender differences. Maccoby and Jacklin in the 1970s considered that 'verbal ability' was one of the traits where a difference, favouring women, was definitely established. But Hyde and McKinley (1997), reviewing meta-analyses of research since then, report effect sizes clustering around zero. Mathematics ability, another claimed area of difference, favouring men, proves to have small or very small effect sizes, between –.15 and +.22 for 242 studies, supporting the view that males and females perform similarly (Lindberg et al. 2010).

In 2005 Janet Hyde published a grand survey of meta-analyses, combining the findings of this technique across the whole field of psychology. She found 46 published meta-analyses of gender difference, which analysed over 5,000 research studies, based on the testing of about 7 million people. The research covered cognitive variables, communication, social and personality variables, psychological well-being, motor behaviours and assorted other topics. The overall finding is simply stated:

> The striking result is that 30% of the effect sizes are in the close-to-zero range, and an additional 48% are in the small range. That is, 78% of gender differences are small or close to zero. (Hyde 2005: 582, 586)

Hyde provocatively titled her paper 'The Gender Similarities Hypothesis'. It stirred controversy, and a fresh surge of meta-analyses. Ten years later another research team incorporated the new results and polished up the method. They now had 106 different meta-analyses, incorporating data from 12 million people. The results? Much the same: 'the majority of these effects were either very small (39.4%) or small (46.1%); relatively few effects were medium (11.9%), large (1.8%), or very large in size (0.8%)' (Zell et al. 2015: 13).

'Gender similarities' is hardly a hypothesis. The idea that there is a character dichotomy between women and men has been overwhelmingly, decisively, refuted. *The broad psychological similarity of men and women as groups can be regarded, on the volume of evidence supporting it, as one of the best-established generalizations in all the human sciences.*

All researchers in this field recognize that there are some traits on which gender differences do repeatedly show up. In Hyde's review they include some physical performances, for instance in throwing; some aspects of sexuality, but not all; and some aspects of aggression. What is particularly interesting is that when clear psychological gender differences *do* appear, they are likely to be specific and situational rather than generalized.

Studies of aggression often show an average gender difference, but in physical aggression more than in verbal aggression, and not in all circumstances. Bettencourt and Miller (1996) find an overall d of +.22 in experimental studies of aggression, but report that this effect depends on whether or not there are conditions of provocation. If unprovoked, men have a modest tendency to show higher levels of aggressiveness than women (mean effect size +.33); if provoked, men's and women's reactions are similar (mean effect size +.17). Hyde cites a meta-analysis of gender differences in making interruptions in conversation. The effect size varied according to the type of interruption, the size of the group talking together, and whether they were strangers or friends. She comments: 'Here, again, it is clear that gender differences can be created, erased, or reversed, depending on the context' (Hyde 2005: 589).

Meta-analysis reveals that gender differences in masculinity/femininity, as measured by tests like the famous 'Bem Sex Role Inventory', can change over time. Kristen Donnelly and Jean Twenge (2017) showed that in samples of US undergraduate students, men and women became somewhat more similar on these scales over a period of forty years, from the 1970s to the 2010s. Not, as many nervous conservatives fear, because men have become feminized: both groups' scores on the femininity scales, and men's scores on masculinity scales, changed little. It was rather because the women increased their scores markedly on masculinity scales, in the early decades of this time-span. Women's score on 'androgyny' – scoring high on both femininity and masculinity – also rose.

But has the meaning of femininity and masculinity stayed the same, over this time-span? Alice Eagly and her colleagues have unearthed a series of national public opinion polls in the United States, from 1947 to 2018, that asked respondents whether such-and-such a trait was more characteristic of men or of women. Taking the responses as measures of gender stereotypes, Eagly et al. (2020) show in a meta-analysis that there have been some significant shifts over seventy years. Belief that women have greater relationship qualities than men has increased, and so has belief in equality of competence between men and women. Belief in men's greater 'agency' qualities (decisiveness, aggressiveness, etc.) was little changed. Stereotypes have not died away, it seems, but they have been restructured – presumably in response to American women's increased workforce participation, and the particular jobs they hold.

Meta-analysis has not entirely revolutionized the study of gender difference, since the basic data collection methods remain the same. But it has certainly clarified what this body of research is saying. It tells us that across a wide range of the traits and characteristics measured by psychology, sharp gender differences are rare. Broad similarity between women and men is the main pattern. Meta-analysis adds a clearer recognition that specific and situational sex differences do appear and can be measured. Very specific skills (e.g. in one science rather than another), specific social circumstances (e.g. provocation), specific times and places (e.g. US colleges in the 1990s), and specific ways of measuring traits, all affect the extent of gender differences recorded in the research.

We thus get a picture of psychological gender differences and similarities, not as fixed, age-old constants of the species, but as the changing products of the active responses people make to a gender-structured but changing social world. With the aid of meta-analysis, psychology has gradually moved towards a way of understanding gender that has also gradually emerged in sociology.

How far can we generalize this picture? It is often observed that the modern science of psychology is largely based on white middle-class students in Psychology 101 courses in US universities – not exactly a representative sample of humanity. Given the impressive evidence of cultural and historical variations in gender arrangements (see chapters 2 and 5), we cannot assume that psychological patterns documented for the contemporary USA hold true across the world. Yet this very point, that gender differences can vary in different circumstances, has been emerging from meta-analytic research. Gender similarity research has increasing numbers of large-scale studies with better samples from the global North, and increasing numbers of studies in other parts of the world. The conclusions outlined above are a solid starting point for understanding the psychology of gender.

Social embodiment and the reproductive arena

Biological and social analysis cannot be cut apart from each other, but neither can be reduced to the other. How, then, can we understand the relation between bodies and society that is involved in gender? In this section I outline an approach that draws from discussions of gender in development (Harcourt 2016), health and illness (Connell 2012a), and studies of violence (Messerschmidt 2004); some social theory is also involved.

Our bodies are influenced by the foods we eat, sexual customs, work, war, sport, urbanization, education, medicine, and more. So, though social arrangements refer back to bodies, they also form conditions in which bodies develop and live. There is, as Celia Roberts (2000) put it, a co-construction of the biological and the social.

There are many differences among the nearly eight thousand million human bodies alive in the world. There are old and young, sick and well, plump and starving. There are differences of physical ability and disability. There are skins permanently stained with soil and skins softened with expensive creams; hands cracked from washing and hands spotless and manicured. Each body has its trajectory, each changes with maturation, childbirth, ageing. Many bodies encounter violence, starvation, disease, injury or surgery, and have to reorganize themselves to carry on; some do not survive these encounters.

Yet the tremendous multiplicity of bodies is in no sense random. Our bodies are connected through social practices, which are organized by structures including class, gender, racial division and the global economy. Large-scale structures, and personal trajectories through them, provide the conditions of new practices in which bodies are addressed and involved. Bodily processes and social structures are thus linked iteratively through time. They combine in a historical process, through which society is embodied and bodies are drawn into history. This historicity can be understood both at a micro level, in the unfolding of a conversation or a sequence of episodes in a child's growth, and at a macro level, in the dynamics of a whole gender order over decades or generations.

I call this historical process *social embodiment*. In considering the body, it could be called 'body-reflexive practice', that is, human social conduct in which bodies are both agents and objects. Bodies have a reality that cannot be reduced; they are drawn into history without ceasing to be bodies. They do not turn into signs or positions in discourse, their materiality continues to matter. As Shakespeare put it, if you prick us, do we not bleed?

Social embodiment involves personal conduct, but it is important that it also involves groups, institutions and whole complexes of institutions. Consider the body-reflexive practice that goes into making the exemplary masculinity of a sports star – for instance Steve, a champion in 'iron man' surf competitions (Connell 2000). Steve's social practice includes the training routines worked out by coaches, drawing on the professional expertise of physical education and sports medicine. It includes the practice of the sport itself, which is organized by multi-million-dollar corporations. It includes participating in publicity and getting fees from commercial media and advertisers. A major sports star, like other media figures, practically turns into a one-person corporation, employing lawyers, accountants, marketing agents, and public relations flacks. There is an elaborate social process here. Yet all of this specialized work is based on, and refers back to, Steve's bodily performances.

Gender is a specific form of social embodiment, distinctive in referencing the bodily structures and processes of human reproduction. Gender involves a cluster of social practices including sexual intercourse, birthing, care and communication, which deploy human bodies' capacities to engender, to give birth, to give milk, to give and receive pleasure, to speak and hear. We can only begin to understand gender if we understand how closely the social and the bodily processes combine. We are born in blood and pain, *and* we are born in a social order.

These bodily capacities, and the practices that realize them, constitute an arena, a bodily site where something social happens. Among the things that happen is the creation of the cultural categories 'women' and 'men', and any other gender categories that a particular society marks out. This may be called the *reproductive arena* in social life.

The idea of a reproductive arena is not the same as the old idea of a biological base, a natural mechanism that produces social effects. Sexual reproduction does not *cause* gender practices, nor provide a template for them. There are many fields where strongly gendered behaviour occurs which has no causal connection with sexual reproduction. (Football broadcasting, shoe design, futures markets, lesbian sex, Handel oratorios, the election of Popes ...) We may be one of many species that reproduce sexually, but we are the only one of them that has produced complex, historically changing social structures in which that reproductive capacity is deployed. Gender is specifically human.

Though it is often forgotten in the excitement of gender politics among adults, the reproductive arena very much concerns children. Not all sex results in pregnancy: the great majority of sexual encounters, even heterosexual ones, do not. But the fact that children do generally arrive this way, and have to be nurtured and taught, and will become the next generation of parents, matters immensely for any community that intends to last much beyond next Thursday.

As childcare illustrates, the reproductive arena is always the point of reference in gender processes, but it is far from incorporating everything that gender is about. There is a larger terrain of social life that is socially linked to the reproductive arena. We might call this the gender domain, where relations among people and groups are structured by connections to the reproductive arena. It follows from this definition that the scope and shape of the gender domain varies from one society to another, and from one period of history to another. It can be changed by deliberate action, such as pro-natalist policies that harness government, media, schools and medicine to promote population growth. De-gendering strategies in feminism, gender-neutral language in media, and equal-opportunity rules in organizations, are other examples. The movement among young people who declare themselves 'non-binary' is a personal strategy intended to escape the gender domain.

Social embodiment in the gender domain takes many forms. One of the crudest is sexual harassment, dramatized by the #MeToo movement: unwanted touching, wolf-whistles, suggestive joking, yelling from cars, ratings of one's attractiveness (that was the origin of Facebook!), online rape threats. Each one is an exercise of power directed to the body of the target. There are now hundreds of studies on the prevalence of harassment, among diverse groups – doctors in Germany, adolescents in South Africa and Spain, military personnel in the United States, passengers on public transport and tourist industry workers. The figures vary widely, because of different measures and environments, but the sheer scale of the issue emerges. A global review of research on the sexual harassment of women on public transport found prevalence rates as low as 15 per cent and as high as 95 per cent; in most countries the rates were above 40 per cent (Gekoski et al. 2017). In a large online survey of university students in the United States, 19 per cent of respondents reported an experience of sexual harassment by faculty or staff, and 30 per cent experienced harassment by other students (Wood et al. 2018). The usual pattern is that women experience much higher levels of harassment than men do. But in some studies, especially of youth, prevalence is similar; being harassed can be a widespread experience for boys (Lei et al. 2019).

The devastating human immunodeficiency virus, the agent of AIDS, was spread around the world by contacts between human bodies, usually following gendered paths. Purnima Mane and Peter Aggleton (2001), surveying the role of men in this biological process, note that men's practices in different regions are shaped by local gender orders.

The risk of transmission is highest where women have least capacity to control sexuality. Inequality and violence in relationships are often related to complicity with a power-oriented ideal of masculinity (Jewkes and Morrell 2010).

Bodies are transformed in social embodiment. Broad changes in embodiment have happened in recent history: falling numbers of children per family, lengthening expectation of life, rising average height and weight (as child nutrition and health care improve), and changing patterns of disease (e.g. polio declining, TB declined but now reviving). Such changes are structured in part by gender arrangements, now recognized as one of the 'social determinants of health and illness'. In 2017–18 women's average life expectancy worldwide was 74.7 years, men's was 70.2 years (World Bank 2020). But the gap varies between regions. The average expectation of life for women in France at that time was 85.6 years, for men 79.6, a gap that is now typical for Europe. Elsewhere the gap can be much narrower. In India, women's expectation was 70.6 years, men's 68.2. In Nigeria the figures were 55.2 and 53.5. The gender order matters, even in so elemental a matter as how long people live.

Recognizing social embodiment as a historical process allows us to understand a paradoxical aspect of gender. Many gender processes involve bodily capacities that are not gender-differentiated, that are in fact *shared* capacities of women and men. There are no gender differences in the capacity to work in an industrial economy, apart from those created by different training, the treatment of pregnancy as a disability, or the gendered design of equipment. Most production processes involve the cooperation of very large numbers of men and women in an intricate flow of work. Yet this shared labour creates the means through which gender-specific clothes, toys and other consumer goods are manufactured, mass media images of gender difference are circulated, and gender inequalities in income and wealth are produced.

Understanding social embodiment allows a clearer view of the relation between bodies and gender-related change. In sociobiology, sex role theory, liberal feminism and populist ideology, bodily difference is understood only as a conservative force. Bodies are supposed to hold back historical change and limit what social action can accomplish. We can now recognize something very different: bodies as agents in social practice are involved in the construction of the social world, the bringing-into-being of social reality, in a never-ending process of change. Bodies' needs, bodily desires and bodily capacities are at work in history. The social world is never simply reproduced, it is always being reconstituted.

Gender as a system of relations is created in this historical process, and accordingly can never be fixed, nor exactly reproduced. The vital question is not 'can gender change?' but 'in what direction is gender changing?' There are different futures towards which contemporary gender arrangements might move. We will return to this in later chapters of the book. First, we need to look at the ways gender has been theorized.

4

Gender theory and theorists: a short global history

Introduction: Raden Ajeng Kartini

Over a hundred years ago in Java, then part of the colonized Dutch East Indies, a young woman in a ruling-class Muslim family made the unusual decision to be a writer and teacher. Her name was Kartini (Raden Ajeng is a title of respect). She knew some progressive thinkers in the colony, and made contact with others in the Netherlands, especially Stella Zeehandelaar, a social democrat who put her in touch with European trends. Kartini and her sisters had an agenda for reforming Javanese society and culture, especially the position of women. Kartini was vigorously opposed to the institution of polygamy, and critical of the seclusion of women and their lack of education. Therefore she proposed to remain unmarried in order to launch a programme of action. She planned to set up a school for the daughters of the elite, to provide a model for change; and she began publishing essays and short stories.

These activities by a woman, however, were not entirely respectable in elite Javanese society. Though her father had provided a private education, neither he nor the colonial government would send her to train as a teacher in the Netherlands. Nor could she get official support for the planned school. Eventually the family arranged a good marriage for her, and she bowed to custom. She died from complications of her first childbirth, aged 25.

Kartini's letters (in Dutch) to her correspondents, which tell this story of hope and disappointment, were collected after her death, censored, and published in 1911. A little later, selections were translated into English under the sentimental title *Letters of a Javanese Princess*, and into the languages of the archipelago. (The full, tougher version is now available, see Kartini 2014.) The letters became a classic of Dutch and colonial literature, and Kartini became a heroine of Indonesian independence and Indonesian women's movements. Her work is never mentioned in the English-language literature on gender, except for regional studies.

Kartini's writing, and the way her thought has been received and ignored, raise important questions for studies of gender. She was not trying to develop a 'theory of gender' – she had much more practical goals. Yet her writing deals directly with questions that a theory of gender must address: the institution of the family, gender divisions of labour, ideologies of womanhood, and strategies of change in gender relations. She did this in the context of colonial society, opening up questions about empire, racism and the relationship between global metropole and periphery that now, more than a century later, have become key issues in feminist thought. (By 'metropole' I mean the centre on which other regions are dependent in economic, cultural or political terms.)

Discussions of gender theory usually focus only on theorists in the global North. I begin this chapter with Kartini's story to highlight the need for a more inclusive approach to knowledge.

Ideas are created in changing circumstances, by people with different backgrounds and different training. History throws different problems at them. It is not surprising that they formulate their intellectual projects in different ways. To understand theories of gender, it is necessary to encounter the intellectuals who produced them and consider the situations they faced.

Imperial Europe and its colonies

The gender theories of the European metropole are products of a secular, rationalist and sceptical culture that has taken its shape in the last century and a half. The ideas prominent now, however, have a deeper background; understanding this history helps us understand the present. The two key stories were the gradual transformation of older religious and moral discourses, and Europe's encounter with the colonized world.

Mediaeval Christianity inherited, from the saints and sages of the ancient Mediterranean world, a tradition of misogyny that to a modern reader seems not just hostile but vicious. The writings of early Christian intellectuals are peppered with sneers at women's inferiority, and warnings of the danger that women represent to the souls of men (Blamires 1992). There was, nevertheless, a counter-tradition defending women. In late mediaeval France this was brought together in a great allegory, *The Book of the City of Ladies*, by Christine de Pizan (1405). Christine refuted, point by point, the traditional abuse of women. She built an allegorical 'city' in her text which would be a safe space for women. The moral defence of womanhood was taken up in the seventeenth-century colony of Mexico by Sor Juana, a celebrated poet and essayist. Like many educated women of that time, Sor Juana could only find a safe space to work by becoming a nun. In a famous essay called *The Answer* (1691), she claimed equal respect for the work of women. The nunnery wasn't safe enough. She fell foul of misogynist church authorities and was silenced.

The counter-tradition continued in Europe. Radical Protestant groups like the Quakers in the seventeenth century defended women's right to preach, i.e. to exercise religious authority. This radical tradition was still alive at the time of the French Revolution. In 1791 the playwright Olympe de Gouges turned the revolution's declaration of the Rights of Man and of the Citizen into a declaration of the Rights of Woman and the Female Citizen. A couple of years later she was arrested and guillotined. Mary Wollstonecraft in England proposed moral reform through education in her *Vindication of the Rights of Women* (1792). The early suffrage movement in the United States was in large part a religious movement. The Seneca Falls convention in 1848, often seen as the moment when modern feminism emerged, borrowed the moralizing language of the American Declaration of Independence for its message.

Already, however, religion was being displaced by science as the major framework of intellectual life. Nineteenth-century science was actively concerned with problems about gender. Charles Darwin, the towering figure in evolutionary thought, in *The Origin of Species* (1859) made inheritance and biological selection into first-rank intellectual issues. He is not usually considered as a gender theorist, but his later work specifically addressed the choice of sexual partners and the evolutionary role of sex as a form of reproduction. This occurred at a moment in European culture when the gender division of labour, and symbolic divisions between women and men, were at an extreme. 'Darwinism' – the work of followers more than Darwin himself – popularized the idea of a biological basis for all forms of social difference, including gender division in the metropole and racial hierarchy in the expanding empires.

Gender issues ran through many early attempts by male intellectuals to formulate a science of society. The French philosopher Auguste Comte, the founder of positivism and a figure almost as influential as Darwin, gave close attention to the social function of women in the first-ever 'treatise of sociology', his *System of Positive Polity* (1851). Women were, in his view, an important base for the coming utopian society – but only if they remained in their proper sphere as comforters and nurturers of men. Comte's most distinguished follower, the British philosopher John Stuart Mill, took a more radical view in his famous essay 'The Subjection of Women' (1869). He argued for equality, and saw the basic reason for inequality not in men's moral or intellectual superiority but in physical force.

When Lester Ward wrote the first major theoretical statement in American sociology, *Dynamic Sociology or Applied Social Science* (1883), he offered a long analysis of the 'reproductive forces'. This included a critique of 'sexuo-social inequalities' such as unequal education for girls and boys. In 1879 the German labour leader August Bebel published a book *Woman under Socialism* that became a best-seller. Marx's friend Friedrich Engels wrote a long essay about gender issues, *The Origin of the Family, Private Property and the State* (1884), which became even more famous.

Why were these men concerned with gender issues? The first reason was that the 'woman question' had been placed on the agenda by an emerging movement of women, which was strong in exactly those social groups from which the new social scientists came. Women intellectuals in these generations were operating under such difficulties that they were unlikely to produce theoretical treatises themselves. They were excluded from almost all universities at the time. We hardly find a 'theory of gender' in the writings of feminist intellectuals like Harriet Martineau in Britain or Susan B. Anthony in the United States. We do find critiques of prejudice among men, and practical discussions of the suffrage, law reform and education for women.

When more theoretical writing by women developed, it was often concerned with economic issues. From South Africa came Olive Schreiner's *Woman and Labour* (1911), which analysed the 'parasitism' of bourgeois women and the refusal of bourgeois society to recognize its exploitation of working women. From Russia came Alexandra Kollontai's *The Social Basis of the Woman Question* (1909), arguing that class differences among women were so profound that there was no general 'woman question', and that working-class women should support socialism as the path towards true equality. Kollontai nevertheless argued for separate organization of women within the labour movement, and pioneered debates about sexual freedom and the reform of marriage.

The second reason was empire. The intellectuals of Paris, London, Petersburg and New York were living in the heartlands of the greatest wave of imperial expansion the world has ever known. Explorers, conquerors, missionaries and curious travellers gathered an immense fund of information about gender arrangements in the non-European world. Engels' *Origin of the Family* shows the fascination this information had for metropolitan intellectuals; early anthropology and sociology are full of it. Popular imperialism put many exotic images and fantasies of gender into circulation: polygamy, marriage by conquest, concubinage, amazon women, primitive promiscuity. In the late nineteenth and early twentieth century the news from the colonial empires was already acting alongside feminism to de-stabilize belief in a fixed gender order.

Meanwhile the peoples being colonized were not standing still. Colonialism had a massive, and often highly destructive, impact on the gender orders of colonized societies. Settler populations produced Sor Juana and Olive Schreiner, and the historical record is weighted towards the colonizers. Nevertheless by the time nineteenth-century feminism and social science crystallized in the metropole, intellectuals of colonized societies too were grappling with changing gender relations.

In Bengal – the home of a rich intellectual culture as well as the administrative centre for the British occupation of India – there was considerable debate among men about the position of women and the principle of gender equality. The famous novelist Bankimchandra Chatterjee, for example, sharply criticized men's insistence on the seclusion of women, and even argued for men doing an equal share of the housework! In Egypt, which also fell under British control after a period of self-directed modernization, gender issues were raised in a classic Islamic way by Aisha Taymour. *The Mirror of Contemplating Affairs* [Mir'at Al-Ta'mmul fi Al-Umur] (1892) examined Qur'anic texts about women as a way of raising questions about modern patriarchy. The radical Chinese writer He-Yin Zhen (1907) published sophisticated analyses of men's power, women's work and the politics of women's emancipation. Kartini's letters about education for girls were part of this widespread, though still scattered, questioning.

Already these discussions were dealing with issues we can recognize in modern gender research: power ('subjection'), sexuality ('phylogenetic forces', 'free love') and the division of labour ('parasitism'). Yet the categories of 'men' and 'women' remained absolute, in both metropolitan and colonial debates. Until they were questioned, a theory of gender could not emerge.

From Sigmund to Simone

Crucial steps were taken in the early twentieth century in central Europe. When the Viennese nerve specialist Sigmund Freud became convinced that many of his patients' troubles were psychological not physical in origin, he sought causes by exploring their emotional lives, and developed new interpretive methods to do so. His patients' talk, during long courses of therapy, gave him masses of evidence about the troubled emotional interior of bourgeois families. He documented this in intensive case histories, the most famous being 'Dora' (1905) and the 'Wolf Man' (1918). This clinical work underpinned the theoretical texts in which Freud expounded the concepts of unconscious motivation (*The Interpretation of Dreams*, 1900), childhood sexuality, the Oedipus complex and the pathways along which desire was transformed in the course of growing up (*Three Essays on the Theory of Sexuality*, 1905), and the connections between depth psychology and the wider society (*Civilization and its Discontents*, 1930).

By the 1920s, Freud's ideas had spread far beyond their first medical audience and had become a cultural force. It was clear that he had put his finger on problems that were troubling and important for European societies. Freud was no feminist, though he was probably influenced by the women's movements of the time in the problems he addressed. His first major follower, Alfred Adler, did explicitly support feminism. Adler (1927) made the critique of power-oriented masculinity a centrepiece of his version of psychoanalysis.

Psychoanalysts thus showed that the gender divisions of adulthood were not fixed from the start of life. Rather, the adult patterns were constructed in a conflict-ridden process of development over the life-course. This was a decisive shift in ideas about gender. Nineteenth-century thought, even feminism, had taken for granted the fixed characters of men and women.

The next step followed quickly. The landmark was Mathilde Vaerting's *The Dominant Sex* (1921). Vaerting, a reforming educator, was one of the first two women ever appointed to a professorship in a German university. She met an extremely hostile reaction from academic men, was thrown out of her job by the Nazi regime, and never held a university chair again. Understandably, she had a lifelong interest in the sociology of power! *The Dominant Sex* criticized the notion of a fixed masculine and feminine character on sociological grounds. Vaerting argued that masculinity and femininity basically reflected power relations. In societies where women held power, men showed the very characteristics which European bourgeois society saw as quintessentially feminine.

In developing this argument, Vaerting created the first extended social theory of gender. Her argument linked psychological patterns with social structure. She distinguished law, ideology, and the division of labour as spheres of gender domination. She even offered an amazing prediction of Men's Liberation as a sequel of feminism. Her work was rapidly translated into English, and was a focus of controversy in the 1920s. But in the European upheavals that followed, her work faded into obscurity. Like Kartini, Vaerting is hardly mentioned in English-language discussions now.

While these intellectual upheavals happened in central Europe, practical upheavals with intellectual consequences spread around the colonized and semi-colonized world. A powerful independence movement developed in India, with Mohandas Gandhi as its principal guide. Mobilization of women was an important part of this movement. Though the Ottoman Empire collapsed in the Great War, a Turkish government survived, fought off the colonial powers, and established a modernizing state under the war hero Mustafa Kemal. The Turkish republic became an important model, especially in the Muslim world. One of its features was a self-conscious emancipation of women – perhaps the first state feminism in the world.

In Egypt a second generation of feminists moved into politics as well as literary work. Huda Sharawi launched the Egyptian Feminist Union in 1923 (Badran 1988). In China, as a republic struggled to establish itself against warlords and foreign interventions, a cultural revival began, the 'Fourth of May movement'. Women writers were prominent in this, challenging Confucian doctrines and patriarchal conventions, and writing about women's experience (Ng and Wickeri 1996).

At about the same time, a new way of appropriating knowledge from the colonized world emerged – social anthropology. The Polish anthropologist Bronisław Malinowski (1927) used ethnographic information in a famous critique of psychoanalysis, arguing that the 'Oedipus complex' as described by Freud was not universal. The American anthropologist Margaret Mead's *Sex and Temperament in Three Primitive Societies* (1935), based on fieldwork in New Guinea, rejected the idea of a fixed relationship between biological sex and gendered character. Such writers gave sympathetic portraits of non-Western societies where gender arrangements functioned perfectly well, though along different lines from bourgeois life in the metropole.

This work helped to popularize the concept of 'sex roles' in the 1940s and 1950s. Social scientists assumed that people usually conform to cultural norms, and applied the principle to gender. The most influential formulation was made by the most influential sociologist of the era, the Harvard University professor Talcott Parsons (Parsons and Bales

1956). Parsons treated gender as a consequence of a social system's need for integration and stability. His much-quoted characterization of the male role as 'instrumental' and the female role as 'expressive' defined a polarity that was purely a difference of social function. Most other writers, however, presumed that the role norms reflected natural differences between women and men.

Nevertheless sex role theorists were concerned with changes in sex roles, an issue that had sharpened during the war years when women built tanks, filled shells and, at least in the Red Army, fought on the front line. Mirra Komarovsky (who later became president of the American Sociological Association, the second woman ever elected to that position) had good reason to theorize 'Cultural Contradictions and Sex Roles', a paper she published in 1946. Sex role change was also possible for men, as Helen Hacker suggested in 'The New Burdens of Masculinity' (1957). In consumer capitalism and suburban life, Hacker argued, expressive functions were being added to instrumental ones, so that men were now expected to show interpersonal skills as well as being 'sturdy oaks'.

There was a feminist colouring in some sex role discussions, including Hacker's. But the renewal of gender theory in the global North was basically the work of Simone de Beauvoir in France. *The Second Sex* (1949), the most famous of all modern feminist texts, drew on psychoanalysis, literature and the activist philosophy worked out by de Beauvoir's partner Jean-Paul Sartre, to challenge both gender domination and gender categories.

Refusing to take the polarity of masculine and feminine for granted, de Beauvoir explored how women were constituted as 'other' in the consciousness of men. Then in a remarkable series of social portraits, she explored the ways in which women could respond to this situation and constitute themselves – not escaping from gender, for that was impossible, but realizing gender differently in different life projects. This work, too, was stimulated by the upheaval of war, and de Beauvoir's topics overlapped with those of sex role research. But she saw the same topics differently, because her approach stemmed from a clear political critique of the subordination of women.

By the mid-century this was exceptional in the global metropole. Psychoanalysis had by then become a socially conservative branch of medicine, more concerned to help people conform than to criticize the culture. Sex role theory was also, in the main, a conservative approach – especially as it was applied in counselling, social work and schools. De Beauvoir's cutting edge found many admirers, but no immediate popular response.

From national liberation to Women's Liberation

While the influence of *The Second Sex* slowly spread, the greatest wave of decolonization was breaking since the decolonization of Spanish America over a century before.

The long struggle of the Indian independence movement triumphed in 1947 – though as a parting gift, the British partitioned the subcontinent, storing up war and sectarian bitterness. A couple of years later the Chinese communists won a civil war, and both Japanese and American influence in China ended. Indonesian nationalists fought off the attempt to re-impose Dutch rule at the end of the Second World War. Vietnamese nationalists and communists fought the re-imposition of French rule in Indochina, and a few years later fought the Americans, both struggles extremely violent though ultimately successful. Kenyan nationalists fought the British, Algerian nationalists fought the French, Mozambican and Angolan nationalists fought the Portuguese, and these movements too ejected the old imperial powers after much blood-letting. Other colonies were liberated by political movements without war, notably Ghana, which led the African colonies into independence; or through a complicated handover, as in Egypt.

These struggles were led by men, though in almost all cases they involved the mobilization of women, in combat as well as civil politics. The post-colonial regimes, also dominated by men, did little directly for women's emancipation but generally aimed at economic development. This gave leverage to feminist demands for the education of girls and women. A slow but very powerful education movement arose that has transformed literacy levels in the post-colonial world.

Liberation struggles in the 'third world' had a growing impact on the global North, especially on the youth movement of the 1960s. They gave a political model and a rhetoric to the new wave of feminism that erupted at the end of that decade – the Women's Liberation movement. An extraordinarily rapid mobilization of younger women occurred in the late 1960s and early 1970s, across much of the capitalist world.

The first great theoretical advance of the new feminism came from Brazil. In 1969 Heleieth Saffioti's pioneering work *Woman in Class Society* was published in São Paulo. The book presented a sophisticated Marxist-feminist account of sex as a form of social stratification. It gave a detailed account, backed with statistics, of the sexual division of labour, the political economy of the family and women's education. It took a historical approach to women's subordination and emancipation, analysed the influence of the Catholic church, and included a brilliant discussion of sexuality in Brazilian colonial society.

Saffioti was committed to socialist politics, not an autonomous women's movement (Brazil was then ruled by a right-wing military dictatorship). Her account of gender stratification highlights capitalist society's need for social control. She was influenced by structuralist Marxism from Paris, very fashionable in the 1960s. But she also used arguments from South American economists such as Celso Furtado, who were concerned with global inequality, continuing dependence, and autonomous development strategies for countries in the South.

The early Women's Liberation movement in the global North usually held a simpler, dichotomous view of power. The term 'patriarchy' was fished up from an anthropological backwater and used to name systems where men collectively oppressed women. Patriarchy, it was argued, had to be confronted by an autonomous women's movement, and the liberation of women was the cutting edge of social revolution. This view was expounded in a torrent of pamphlets and books, from Sheila Rowbotham's *Women's Liberation and the New Politics* (1969) to Robin Morgan's famous anthology *Sisterhood is Powerful* (1970) and Shulamith Firestone's *The Dialectic of Sex* (1970). Even men influenced by the new feminism began to speak this language. Calls for 'Male Liberation', in solidarity with Women's Liberation rather than against it, rapidly appeared (Sawyer 1970).

The radical movements of that time shared a belief that all systems of oppression could be overthrown. This included early theorists of Gay Liberation, who added sexual oppression to the list. Agendas for a revolution in sexuality were spelt out in Dennis Altman's *Homosexual: Oppression and Liberation* (1972) and Guy Hocquenghem's *Homosexual Desire* (1972).

By the later 1970s, however, a gender-specific view had come to prominence in the United States, Britain and Germany. This view sharply separated gender struggles from others, or saw the oppression of women as the basic social inequality. A dramatic version of this idea was presented by the US theologian Mary Daly in her book *Gyn/Ecology* (1978). Daly invented a new poetic vocabulary to express her vision of women's culture and women's anger against men. This and other critiques that focused on men's power and violence came from a current in feminism, sometimes labelled 'radical feminism', that was negative towards socialist and liberal feminists and distinctly hostile towards transsexual women.

The impulse of Women's Liberation was so powerful that it launched a whole spectrum of theories. A materialist but non-Marxist theory that focused on the division of labour, emphasizing the economic exploitation of wives by husbands, was proposed by Christine Delphy in France in a famous essay called 'The main enemy' (1970). Debate raged through the 1970s on how to theorize women's domestic labour, and whether capitalists or husbands were the main beneficiaries of women's work (Malos 1980). An environmental movement was developing alongside the new feminism. They began to merge in works like *Le féminisme ou la mort* (Feminism or death) by the French writer Françoise d'Eaubonne (1974). Mary Daly and other US authors of the late 1970s saw a close affinity between women and nature, both violated by the power of men. The current of thought that was dubbed 'ecofeminism' has broadened since (Warren 1997).

Psychoanalysis, which offered an account of the unconscious bases of gender patterns, returned to feminism in new ways. In the English-speaking world, Juliet Mitchell (1974) found in it a theory of the reproduction of class society and patriarchy. Nancy Chodorow (1978) found in it an explanation of the gender division of labour. In France, Jacques Lacan's structuralist version of psychoanalysis remained extremely influential. A number of feminists took it as a basis for formulating the psychological goals of feminism: to find a level of human reality which escaped the phallocentric structure of ordinary language and consciousness (Kristeva 1974; Irigaray 1977).

The familiar 'sex role' concept was also radicalized. This was now treated as an account of the social controls that hampered women. In the United States there was a wave of enthusiasm for the attempt by the psychologist Sandra Bem (1974) to define and measure 'androgyny' as a goal of sex role reform. A debate about the 'male sex role' and how men could break out of it, or at least bend it, began in the United States and spilled into several other countries (Pleck and Sawyer 1974). It was a Moroccan feminist, however, who produced the most interesting early research on the situation of men and the tensions within masculinity. Fatima Mernissi's *Beyond the Veil* (1975) is a pioneering feminist study of men and masculinity, set in a Muslim society.

In the 1980s a research agenda around men and masculinities crystallized in Germany, Scandinavia, and the rich English-speaking countries (Metz-Göckel and Müller 1985; Carrigan et al. 1985). Though the first impact of Women's Liberation on the academic world was the creation of Women's Studies, it was now argued that to understand gender relations we need to study the more powerful and privileged group. Many empirical studies of men's attitudes and practices were launched. Different patterns of masculinity were soon recognized, and a complex debate about the concept of 'hegemonic masculinity' began. In the following decade this research agenda became worldwide.

The nature of women's politics was also debated. It was the topic of a modern feminist classic, Julieta Kirkwood's (1986) *Ser Política en Chile* (roughly: being a politically active woman in Chile). This was written under the Pinochet dictatorship by one of the leaders of the women's resistance, and published after her death. Kirkwood observed that the problems of women had historically been seen as private issues. To transform silence into voice meant contesting both the Left's idea of gender as a 'secondary contradiction' and the Right's attempt to mobilize women in defence of 'the family'. Women as a group had to become a historical subject, capable of contesting the oppression produced by patriarchy.

The dichotomous view of gender – men here, women there – was also criticized as unrealistic, and a rapid development of sociological theories of gender followed. A young US anthropologist, Gayle Rubin (1975), blended feminism and anthropology in an abstract but influential model of 'the sex/gender system'. Feminist sociologists in several countries brought power, economics, and culture together in more complex structural theories of gender. These gave much more attention to institutions such as corporations, labour markets and states as sites of gender relations, and tried to show the contradictions, paradoxes and possibilities of change (Walby 1990; Pfau-Effinger 1998).

Governments around the world soon took note of the new women's movement. The United Nations declared 1975 to be International Women's Year, launching a series of world conferences on women. This triggered many debates and investigations, the most notable being a wide-ranging national report from India called *Towards Equality* (Committee on the Status of Women in India 1975). In 1973 the Australian government appointed a young feminist philosopher, Elizabeth Reid, as the first Women's Advisor to the Prime Minister, launching a new kind of state feminism.

The 'femocrats' of Australia, Scandinavia and Germany attempted to use bureaucratic and legal reforms to move towards gender equality across the whole society (Eisenstein 1996). Government funding was won for childcare centres, rape crisis centres and women's health centres. This created sharp debate, given that many in the Women's Liberation movement viewed the state as part of the patriarchal system. The work of feminist bureaucrats posed new intellectual questions too: how to understand the organizations where they found themselves, and how to understand the policy problems they faced.

Accordingly, new branches of feminist theory and research developed. A number of theorists re-thought the state as a gendered institution of great complexity, with possibilities of internal change (see chapter 7). Research institutes and monitoring programmes were set up, such as the Likestillingssenteret (Centre for Gender Equality) in Norway. A whole genre of feminist or feminist-inspired policy studies began to appear. To take just one field, education: there is a whole library of policy studies, from the pioneering Australian report *Girls, School and Society* (Schools Commission 1975) to the sophisticated British research in *Closing the Gender Gap* (Arnot et al. 1999) and the global picture in UNESCO's excellent *Gender and Education for All: The Leap to Equality* (2003).

In universities of the global North, the 1970s and 1980s saw a huge growth of feminist or feminist-inspired research in almost every discipline of the humanities and social sciences, and to a lesser extent in the natural sciences. In sociology, for instance, sex and gender, formerly a marginal field focused on the family, became the most active research field in the whole discipline. Feminist history grew to be a large enterprise, fuelled by the need to correct the massive biases of patriarchal history; gender was recognized as an important category of historical knowledge (Scott 1986). Feminist science studies flourished, casting new light on a form of knowledge that once was thought a perfect proof of male superiority (Harding 1986).

These innovations represented a startling success for feminism. The patriarchal monologue in culture and the sciences was interrupted almost at once. New bases for feminist thought were established in government, in universities, in the arts and in publishing. Yet Women's Liberation movement activists looked on the early stages of this triumph with distrust. They feared that bureaucratic and academic feminisms would lose their political urgency, lose touch with grassroots campaigns, and become unintelligible to working-class women.

Re-alignments: queer, intersectional, environmental

Everything that the activists feared has come to pass. Most of the academic writing about gender has become dry in style and is directed only to a specialist audience. A lot of theorizing about gender makes little reference to questions of practical policy such as girls' education, domestic violence, women's health, or employment. Increasingly, theory addressed sexual expression, personal identity, representation and language.

The main points of reference in this phase of gender studies were intellectual developments among male philosophers. Michel Foucault's studies of discourse, micro-politics and the regulation of bodies found widespread application. Jacques Derrida's influence has been more indirect, though possibly more profound. His argument on the constant deferral of meaning in language, and his technique of philosophical 'deconstruction', were read as questioning the stability of all concepts and all identities.

A book by a young US philosopher on this theme, Judith Butler's *Gender Trouble* (1990), became by far the most influential text in academic feminism in the 1990s. Butler argued that there are no fixed foundations of gender categories and therefore of feminist strategy. Gender is 'performative', bringing identities into existence through repetitive actions, rather than being the expression of some pre-existing reality. In Butler's treatment, gender radicalism consists, not of mobilization by a group called 'women', but of actions that subvert identity, disrupt gender dichotomy and displace gender norms.

This book's enormous popularity was not only due to intellectual fashion. It fed into a new kind of politics. By the 1980s, the social movements of the 1960s and 1970s in the global North had fragmented, and Women's Liberation had divided over issues of sexuality, race, and relations with the state. There continued to be gains for gender reform. In 1991, for instance, the leaders of all three major parties in Norway were women, including the Prime Minister, Gro Harlem Brundtland. But the Equal Rights Amendment in the United States was lost. Open homophobia re-emerged in many parts of the world, and received backing from the state. In 2013, for instance, Vladimir Putin's regime in Russia criminalized any action that could be interpreted by prosecutors as promoting homosexual lifestyles to youth. Forbidden actions included comprehensive sex education.

These events provoked many re-thinkings of feminism. One move was led by Black feminists in North America, who argued that White feminists' uncritical use of a unified category 'women' concealed the realities of racism. For some, including bell hooks (1984), that argument led back to the broad-spectrum radicalism of early Women's Liberation. For others it led to a kind of standpoint theory, illustrated in Patricia Hill Collins' *Black Feminist Thought* (1991). This suggested there could be multiple perspectives representing the outlook of different groups of women, especially those who were marginalized within the society of the metropole: Black feminism, Latina feminism and lesbian feminism.

In 1989 the legal scholar Kimberlé Crenshaw published a very influential article that popularized the concept of intersectionality. The idea was soon taken up by others and generalized. Intersections of gender with race, class, sexuality, age, and other social differences became major themes of research far beyond the USA. In its simpler versions, 'intersectionality' was just a way of listing the multiple identities that people might have. But the concept also offered a way of speaking about different structures of power and oppression, and how they interacted with each other. That was Crenshaw's original intention. In this sense the concept gave the politics of gender justice a better grip on the realities of social life (Misra 2018; Viveros 2018b).

The founding category of 'gender' was also re-examined. Feminist sociologists explored the micro-foundations of the gender order, looking at the way gender categories were created and affirmed in everyday interactions. 'Doing Gender', a classic paper by Candace West and Don Zimmerman (1987), crystallized this approach and had a great impact in the social sciences.

The most influential new approach, distantly influenced by Derrida, emphasized the fragility of all identity categories, and saw gender as, in principle, fluid rather than fixed. A new wave in lesbian and gay thought, which became known as queer theory, took up this idea. Its core was a critique of the cultural constraints that push people into binary identities and assume sexuality is naturally, and exclusively, heterosexual. The conventional package was labelled 'heteronormativity', and transgressions were celebrated. Cultural activism defied the norms, invented identities, played radical games with gender meanings, and set about 'queering' everything in sight. Judith Butler and *Gender Trouble* became the international icons for this movement, almost as famous as Simone de Beauvoir and *The Second Sex*. (For a wry account of these changes by a historian, see Reynolds 2002.)

There has been a reaction against the focus on identity and culture. Some Northern feminist philosophers, in a trend that has been called 'new materialism', have emphasized that actual bodies, and the material world more generally, are important (Hird 2009; for debate see Ahmed 2008). The US philosopher Jane Bennett (2010), for instance, emphasizes the continuity between human life, other forms of life, and the non-living material world. The new materialism contends that the non-human has agency too, and challenges the hierarchical thinking that divides human from non-human worlds. This connects with deepening concerns about the environment.

Ignoring embodiment is hardly a problem for feminism in the global South, where material issues such as poverty, nutrition, perinatal death, AIDS and patriarchal violence, all to do with the vulnerability of bodies, have always been central. In 1982 in Papua New Guinea there was a dam collapse at the Australian-owned Ok Tedi gold mine, pouring many tons of poisonous mine waste into the main river system of the country's south-west. The flow contaminated drinking water, killed forests and wrecked the economy that sustained around 70,000 people. Two years later, the worst industrial accident in history happened in India, when poison gas leaked from a US-owned factory in Bhopal, killing 7,000 to 10,000 people and injuring as many as 200,000 others. These were dramatic episodes in an environmental crisis spreading across the post-colonial world in the late twentieth century, as transnational corporations found cheap labour and minerals, and development-hungry governments imposed few restraints. This became a new focus for environmental feminism.

The most famous activist and writer in this movement was Vandana Shiva in India, who left a career as a nuclear physicist to campaign against ecologically destructive industries arriving in the global South. In her book *Staying Alive* (1989) Shiva described this as 'maldevelopment', involving violence against both women and nature. The industrialization of agriculture replaced traditional village farming and shrank the diversity in plant and animal life, as well as destroying human cultures.

Other feminists too criticized the masculinized ideology of economic development at all costs. Some, including the Australian activist and philosopher Val Plumwood in *Feminism and the Mastery of Nature* (1994), linked destructive development and the oppression of women to broad themes in Western culture: ideas of rationality and mastery that separated the human from the natural realm. Critics including Rosi Braidotti and Bina Agarwal thought such sweeping generalizations were unwarranted. They observed that gender inequalities pre-dated Western imperialism, and called for closer attention to the structures of property, class, caste and race that shape women's relationship to nature.

Governments, international agencies and capitalists began responding to the environmental crisis, but in problematic ways: by increasing surveillance, and trying to create market incentives. The political scientist Karen Litfin (1997) formulated a feminist critique of the way power operates through scientific knowledge and policy frameworks, such as earth satellite monitoring of the environment. The planetary gaze of satellite monitoring reflects a masculine culture of measurement and objectivity towards nature. Not only is there a masculinized ideology of development, there has also been a 'masculinization of environmentalism' (MacGregor 2009).

Global politics and post-colonial knowledge

In the 1990s and 2000s, women's studies in universities expanded to be 'gender studies' embracing lesbian, gay and transgender issues and non-feminist gender research. Journals multiplied which published research and debate about sex roles, gender, women, and eventually men: such as *al-Raida* in Lebanon, *Debate Feminista* in Mexico, *Estudos Feministos* in Brazil, and *Manushi* in India, as well as high-prestige academic journals such as *Signs* and *Gender & Society* in the United States. This has become a global field of knowledge, with research contributions coming in from all regions of the world.

The shape of this global field, however, is contested. During the 1980s Chandra Talpade Mohanty, an Indian intellectual working in the United States, formulated a critique of feminism in the global metropole. The dominant perspective, she argued, homogenized 'third world women' into a single category of victimhood – 'ignorant, poor, uneducated, tradition-bound, domestic, family-oriented, victimized, etc.' – in contrast to the supposed freedom of women in the developed world. Mohanty's brilliant essay 'Under Western eyes' (1991) became the keynote of a collection published in the United States called *Third World Women and the Politics of Feminism*. This book had a large impact, showing the global diversity of women's politics, and arguing for another kind of theory.

In 'Under Western Eyes' and her later *Feminism Without Borders* (2003), Mohanty spelled out an approach to gender that started with the historical experience of imperialism. The making and remaking of gender is interwoven with the making of race and the dynamics of global capitalism. Mohanty agrees with queer theory that there is no pre-given universal category of 'woman'. But this is for a practical, not a philosophical, reason: because systems of domination constantly divide people. Capitalism uses local gender ideologies to incorporate women's work into strategies of profit-making. This approach allows Mohanty to emphasize the practices of solidarity, the possibilities of common struggle, that can link the poor and the marginalized across differences.

Closer to deconstructionist philosophy was the work of another Indian feminist, Gayatri Chakravorty Spivak (1988). Spivak's writings on feminism are in several genres. She did not try to produce a theory of gender; indeed she seemed sceptical about any such project. Her most famous concept, 'strategic essentialism', made a criticism of identity categories, but then suggested that those categories have value for practice.

Spivak's work illustrates the tensions that arise, for intellectuals coming from the global periphery, in using concepts from the metropole. Paulin Hountondji (1997), a philosopher from Benin, has explored this issue in depth, speaking of the 'extraversion' of knowledge production in post-colonial countries. The majority world supplies lots of raw data to the mainstream economy of knowledge, but the crucial step of *theorizing* is done, overwhelmingly, in the global North. Intellectuals in the periphery are trained to look to the North for the source of their concepts, methods, equipment, training and recognition.

This is strikingly true for gender studies. Most research and university teaching on gender issues in the global South draws on concepts from Europe and the United States, and tries to combine it with local data or experience. A striking example occurred in 1984, soon after the Chinese government turned away from Maoist-era dogma, and the official All-China Federation of Women sponsored a week-long symposium on 'theoretical studies on women'. The idea of women's studies was borrowed from the United States, local statistics about the situation of women were compiled, and the result was an agenda for 'women's studies the Chinese way' (Shen 1987). But state feminism is vulnerable to changes in state policy. By 2018, Xi Jinping's heavily-masculine regime was silencing Chinese feminist voices on the Internet, using police powers to halt feminist organizing, and promoting conservative gender norms to the Chinese people.

The problem of extraversion has concerned many thinkers in the majority world. When gender research was launched in Africa in the 1970s, there was an attempt to locate it within African perspectives, while adapting ideas and methods from the metropole (Arnfred 2003). There has been a sharp debate about whether the concept of gender itself can be applied in Africa. Some have argued that gender categories did not exist, or were not significant, in pre-colonial times. Western gender categories such as 'women' are therefore an intrusion, imposed on local people by colonialism (Oyéwùmí 1997). But other scholars do see gender patterns in pre-colonial culture (Bakare-Yusuf 2003). In their view, colonialism certainly changed gender patterns, but did so by building on distinctions that already existed. In contemporary Africa, complex gender systems certainly exist and have major consequences. Among them are the patterns of economic inequality, gender-based violence and sexuality that have shaped the HIV/AIDS crisis (Ampofo et al. 2004).

Most gender theorists in the global South have worked out their ideas in negotiation with theory from the North. The Uruguayan sociologist Teresita de Barbieri found an impressive balance. In her ambitious essay 'On the Category of Gender: A Theoretical-Methodological Introduction' (1992), she offered a sociological model of gender based on the idea of social control over women's reproductive power. This control involves a wide range of processes: 'practices, symbols, representations, values, collective norms'. Building on Black feminist thought from Brazil, de Barbieri also emphasized how gender relations are interwoven with divisions of race and class. She argued persuasively that gender research needed to include men. In the years after her paper was published, research on men and masculinities indeed became one of the features of Latin American gender studies (Madrid et al. 2020).

Even more ambitious is the work of Bina Agarwal in India, who has a claim to be the most important modern theorist of gender. An economist by profession, Agarwal has been involved as a public intellectual in development policy debates. She has drawn together feminist studies of states, communities and households around Asia (Agarwal 1988). She is a patient empirical researcher, and her great book *A Field of One's Own* (1994) analyses the changing relations of women and men to the land in different regions of South Asia, via the intricate politics of families and livelihoods in rural society.

In another major book, *Gender and Green Governance* (2010), Agarwal explores the conditions under which women's participation in forest management improves environmental and social outcomes. She uses quantitative and qualitative data to illustrate common patterns, as well as the differences in women's participation connected to class, caste, age and region. Nearly half the world's population still live in rural areas, including the majority of the world's poor. The careful treatment of rural economies is not the only reason Agarwal's work is important. Her approach connecting environmental issues to social justice and land rights is a major contribution to modern environmental thought.

Most gender theories have assumed well-integrated gender orders, with norms and hierarchies all complete. Yet thinking about the societies of the global periphery raises the question of how gender orders might be *dis*-integrated, how gender relations might *lack* order. Amina Mama (1997), a leading feminist thinker from Africa, argues that high levels of gender-based violence in contemporary African societies are connected to the gendered violence of colonialism. Mai Ghoussoub (2000) speaks of deep cultural disturbance in the Arab world around the position and identities of men, 'a chaotic quest for a definition of modern masculinity'. Discussing masculinities and femininities in the 'water wars' in Bolivia, Nina Laurie (2011) forcefully argues that research on globalization in the South cannot presume a consolidated gender order. Here, the research on masculinities can be helpful. In an important historical study, Robert Morrell (2001) showed how the British settlers in Natal, South Africa, constructed – in schools, the state, and paramilitary forces – a hegemonic masculinity suited to imposing a racial, economic and social hierarchy on the colony. It was imposed only with difficulty, and with recurring violence.

It is unlikely that theory can work exactly the same way in different regions. The world is not being blended into one soup, as popular theories of globalization suppose. But we certainly do not live in a mosaic world where each culture is intact and separate. If such a world ever existed, five centuries of imperialism and a world economy have put paid to it. We need ways of talking to each other across distances and boundaries, in gender studies as in other fields.

In *Re-orienting Western Feminisms: Women's Diversity in a Postcolonial World* (1998), the Australian sociologist Chilla Bulbeck describes this problem and considers what is involved in moving feminist thought beyond Eurocentrism. To respond to the post-colonial and neo-colonial world is not just a matter of adding a critique of racism. It needs what Bulbeck calls a 'world-traveller perspective': learning to see oneself as others do, learning to respect other experiences, and learning to work in coalitions. In the past, we should note, being a world-traveller was a costly privilege. Now, it is a necessary attitude.

Gender studies as a field of knowledge and education has spread, diversified, and flourished on a world scale. But in recent years attacks on gender-equity policies and gender theory have become more intense and more organized, by right-wing parties, governments and churches (see chapter 8). The US historian Joan Scott (2016) may be right that the church's war on gender in the long run is a losing war. In the short run, however, gender studies as a field of knowledge is under challenge to a degree not seen since the 1970s. With the rise of authoritarian populism in many countries – including India, Brazil and the United States – we can expect gender research and activism to remain highly contested.

5

Gender relations

Gender as a social structure

The simplest way to recognize the social dimension of gender is to speak of 'gender roles' or 'sex roles', assuming that people's behaviour follows a script or a norm. The metaphor of a role is a familiar one – as Shakespeare said, 'all the world's a stage'. We constantly see actors playing highly gendered roles on stage and on screen. The idea of gender roles in everyday life can be regarded as a first approximation, useful for some purposes. It certainly calls attention to how gender is learned, a question that will be examined in chapter 6.

But this is only a first approximation. There are serious weaknesses in role theory as a general approach to social life. It gives little grip on questions of social inequality, power, or prejudice. (We don't comfortably speak of social class or race roles.) It gives little grip on the complexities of intersectionality, to be discussed later in this chapter. Finally, role theory suggests that it will be easy to reform social arrangements, since all we need to do is re-write the scripts. But gender inequalities, like class and race inequalities, are tough to dismantle.

We need more powerful concepts to understand the intractability of social relations, resistances to reform, and the circumstances in which major change becomes possible. Such concepts have been available since the time of Mathilde Vaerting, discussed in chapter 4. The key move is to recognize gender as a *social structure*. This concept expresses the large-scale patterns in relationships among people and groups, and the persistence of those patterns through time. It is most easily understood through examples.

The research projects discussed in chapter 2 include two studies of organizations, Pascoe's study of an American high school and Moodie's study of South African mines. Each of these organizations had a regular set of arrangements about gender. These arrangements defined who did what work (e.g. only men became underground mineworkers); what social divisions were recognized (e.g. how a girl was positioned on-stage); how emotional relations were conducted (e.g. the 'mine wives'); and how these institutions were related to others (e.g. the families of the students).

These arrangements can be called the *gender regime* of an institution. Research has mapped the gender regimes of a very wide range of organizations: schools, offices, factories, armies, police forces, sporting clubs. Some years ago I was part of a research team that looked at gender arrangements in ten public-sector workplaces in Australia. Though the ten sites were very varied – their jobs ranged from high-level policy-making right through to sewage disposal – we found well-defined gender regimes in all of them (Connell 2006a). Most managers and technical workers were men, most clerical workers and human service workers were women. At the same time, changes were happening. Masculinized industrial jobs were being automated, the 'secretary' job was disappearing, and the equal opportunity principle was being accepted. A middle-aged man in the study summed up this change (Connell 2006b: 446):

> I would like to think we are a little bit more enlightened now. I think it has been proven that women can do just about any job that a male can do, that there is no male-dominated industries as such – maybe the construction industry is. But I think that from an Agency viewpoint, and even from a workplace viewpoint now, it is accepted that we have got women [professional staff], they can come in and do just as good a job as what men can do.

That reform was real. Yet at the grassroots level, every agency in the study still had definite gender divisions.

When Pascoe went into River High and found that the 'shop' (mechanical arts) students were almost all boys, she was not exactly surprised. Nor was Moodie astonished to find an all-male workforce at the Witwatersrand gold mines. The gender regimes of these organizations connect with wider patterns across a whole economy, which also endure over time. I call these wider patterns the *gender order* of an industry, a country, a region. The gender regimes of particular institutions usually correspond to the broad gender order, but may vary from it. Change often starts in one sector of society and takes time to seep through into others.

When we look at the gender regime of an institution or the gender order of a larger social formation, we are basically looking at a set of social relationships, that is, ways that people, groups and organizations are connected and divided. A simple definition of 'gender relations' is the social relationships that arise in and around the reproductive arena defined in chapter 3.

Gender relations are continuously constructed in everyday life. This point is well established by ethnomethodology, a type of sociological research concerned with what people presuppose in their everyday conduct. West and Zimmerman (1987), in the celebrated article mentioned in chapter 4, analysed how gender emerges in routine inter- actions. People engaging in everyday conduct – across the spectrum from conversation and housework to economic exchanges – are held accountable in terms of their presumed 'sex category' as man or woman. The conduct they produce in response to this accountability is not a product of gender. It is gender itself.

In that sense we make our own gender. But we are not free to make it just as we like. Our gender practice is powerfully shaped by the gender order around us. That is what West and Zimmerman imply when they say we are 'held accountable' for our gendered conduct. The gender order, in turn, is the product of a previous social process. We can imagine it geologically, as the deposit that previous social actions and social actors have laid down through time.

A structure of relations does not mechanically decide how people or groups act. (That is the error of social determinism, and it is no more defensible than biological determinism.) People act creatively and transform situations. Yet they are never acting in a void. A social structure defines what is intractable in their situations: what are the real possibilities for action, what are the limits to those possibilities, and what consequences flow from their actions. For instance, in a patriarchal gender order, women may be denied advanced education and entry to professional jobs, while men may be cut off from emotional connections with children. Both patterns have consequences that will echo through many people's lives, including the children's. Structures have powerful effects on what changes are possible. Because they do, they are likely to be contested. This is the basis of gender politics, to be explored in chapter 8.

Four dimensions of gender relations

Both research and practical experience show that we need a concept of gender as social structure. How do we make that abstract idea concrete? Is there, perhaps, a key to the whole thing, an underlying principle that makes sense of the whole domain of gender?

Many of the Women's Liberation activists and theorists discussed in chapter 4 thought there was such a key: power. The basic pattern of gender was dominance for men, subordination for women. Others have thought in the same style, but with different definitions of the vital key. The key might be evolution, hormones, men's physical strength, women's childbearing, the universality of the family, the need for social reproduction, the demands of capitalism, identity, colonial conquest, or something else again.

Since no ultimate cause can be decisively proved – or for that matter disproved – it would be arbitrary to accept any of these as the single solution. We should notice their diversity. This strongly suggests that the idea of *one* underlying logic for gender is too simple. Perhaps we need to think of gender as a complex structure with more than one dimension.

Certain theorists have suggested exactly this. When the pioneering British feminist Juliet Mitchell published her article 'Women: The longest revolution' in 1966, she argued that women's oppression involves not one, but four structures: production, reproduction, socialization and sexuality. In *Gender and Power* (Connell 1987), I defined three structures of gender relations: power, production, and cathexis (emotional attachment). In *Theorizing Patriarchy* (1990) the British sociologist Sylvia Walby distinguished six structures: paid employment, household production, culture, sexuality, violence and the state. The Indian economist Bina Agarwal (1997) argued that gender relations are constituted in four arenas: the household/family, the market, the community and the state.

There are good reasons for these moves towards a more complex view of gender relations. Gender orders and gender regimes change unevenly, with some areas of social life moving faster than others. A gender division of labour may fade away, as happened to keyboard work, so the feminine job category 'secretary' has mostly gone – but the masculine 'boss', connected with power, has stayed. Songbooks and film catalogues are filled with tear-jerkers about the emotional demands of the gendered heart in conflict with the obligations of careers, families and war.

Conflicts appear at an institutional level too. For instance, liberal states define both men and women as citizens, that is, as alike. But the dominant sexual code in the same countries defines men and women as opposites. Conventional ideologies define women primarily as wives-and-mothers, belonging in a private sphere. Put all this together, and women in the public domain – trying to exercise their rights as citizens – have an uphill battle to have their authority recognized. A striking example is the failure of the highly-qualified Hillary Clinton in the US presidential election of 2016, defeated by a property magnate and media personality with no governmental experience at all. There were other factors at play, such as Clinton's links with an unpopular corporate elite and Trump's persistent appeal to racism. But the successful discrediting of the first woman to have a real chance of being elected President of the United States is a notable fact.

Even more revealing is the story of Julia Gillard, Prime Minister of Australia from 2010 to 2013, the first woman in that role. Conservative public figures and the main opposition party bitterly opposed Gillard. The hostility was often expressed by references to her being an unmarried woman. Media made frequent comments on Gillard's physical appearance and clothes, political cartoons against her featured sexualized imagery, and right-wing radio presenters made violent comments against her. In October 2012 she gave a passionate speech in Parliament accusing the aggressive male opposition leader of sexism. The fifteen-minute video of the speech attracted global attention and is now known as the 'Misogyny Speech'. In July 2013, with an election looming and her poll numbers down, Gillard's own party dumped her.

So there are strong reasons to acknowledge complexity *within* the structure of gender relations, as well as recognizing intersectionality with class and race. This chapter outlines a four-dimensional model of gender as a social structure. This model distinguishes (1) power relations, including violence and state authority; (2) economic relations, including production, circulation and consumption; (3) relations of cathexis, i.e. emotional attachment and antagonism; and (4) symbolic relations, including communication and representation.

This four-fold model emerges from a reading of modern research on gender and from the experience of social movements. As I noted above there are other ways of mapping the dimensions, so this framework is not definitive; but it is concise and it seems to be useful. It is practical as a research tool, and it can be helpful in understanding gender relations, and struggles to change them, on both large and small scales.

1. Power relations

The power dimension of gender was central to the concept of patriarchy – to the idea of men as a dominant sex class, to the analysis of rape as an assertion of men's power over women, and to the critique of media images of women as passive. The authority of husbands over wives, and fathers over daughters, is institutionalized in patriarchal gender orders. Such authority is still accepted in many social contexts, even in modified forms such as the idea of the father as head of the household.

The continuing relevance of power is indicated by statistics of violence and abuse. For instance, in Australia 17 per cent of women reported having been victims of physical or sexual abuse from a partner since the age of 15, according to 2016 national data, a far higher proportion than men at 6 per cent (Australian Bureau of Statistics 2017). A well-known multi-country study by the World Health Organization (WHO, 2013) found that between 15 per cent (Japan) and 71 per cent (Ethiopia) of women had experienced physical or sexual violence by an intimate partner at some point in their lives. Worldwide, about 35 per cent of all women have been subject to one or other of these forms of violence.

Gendered violence, also called gender-based violence, takes many forms. They range from being harassed, intimidated or threatened, through slapping and beating, to rape, torture and murder. There is quite a large criminological literature on this (Carrington 2015; DeKeseredy and Hall-Sanchez 2018). The contours vary across the world scene. There are dowry deaths of young wives in one region; so-called 'honour killings' – better understood as patriarchal murders – in another. In a third, where divorce rates are high, numbers of women are assaulted or killed by angry husbands during the course of a separation.

Patriarchal power is not only a matter of direct control of women by individual men, it is also realized impersonally through the state. A famous article by Catharine MacKinnon (1983) analysed court procedure in US rape cases. Independent of any personal bias of the judge, the procedures by which rape charges were tried effectively placed the woman making the charge on trial, rather than the accused man. The woman's sexual history, marital situation and motives in laying a charge were all under scrutiny. Despite attempts at reform, it can still be a damaging experience for a woman to bring rape or harassment charges. The #MeToo movement of 2017–18 has found this.

Power relations are organized in a different way in bureaucracy, but that too is gendered. Clare Burton (1987), an Australian social scientist who served in government as an equal opportunity commissioner, spoke of the 'mobilization of masculine bias' in selection and promotion of staff. By this she meant the tendency, in organizations dominated by men, to favour procedures that favour men. Since men do control most large-scale organizations in the world, this is a far-reaching process producing gender inequality. Armies are basically bureaucracies that specialize in violence. Men rather than women control the means of force in every corner of the contemporary world.

An important complexity in gendered power relations was addressed by Gay Liberation. Here the focus was on gendered power that oppressed a specific group of *men*, through criminalization, police harassment, economic discrimination, violence and cultural pressure. This argument laid the foundation for the broader study of gendered power relations among men. Again, the patterns of violence are illuminating. Homophobic assaults and killings of gay men, and episodes of public violence that erupt from masculinity challenges, both establish power relations between groups of men (Tomsen 2013).

Power can be more indirect. The approach popularized by Foucault doubts that there is a unified agency of power in society; rather, power is widely dispersed and operates intimately, constituting subjects within the logic of a given discourse. Many feminist as well as gay theorists saw here a way of understanding how hierarchies of gender and sexuality gain a grip in people's lives. The discourse of fashion and beauty, for instance, positions women as consumers, subjects them to humiliating tests of acceptability, and is responsible for much unhappiness, ill health, and even some deaths by starvation in countries with giant food surpluses, when girls' dieting turns into out-of-control anorexia.

The most sweeping exercise of power in the last 500 years, however, is not captured by concepts like bureaucracy or discourse. This is the creation of global empires, the invasion of indigenous land by imperial powers, and the domination of the post-colonial world by economic and military superpowers. As Valentine Mudimbe (1994: 140) wrote of the Congo, 'to establish itself, the new power was obliged to construct a new society'. Indigenous societies were pulverized, enslaved, displaced or exploited. Imperial conquest was a gendered process – think of all those masculine conquistadors and explorers – and indigenous gender orders were transformed by plantation economies, missions, and relocations. Colonizing forces seized women's bodies as well as the land. A social hierarchy that fused gender and race became a core feature of colonial societies. It persists in the world today.

Power is constantly contested. Domestic patriarchy may be quietly softened by the women of a household. Oppressive laws have sparked public campaigns for reform, including the most famous of feminist campaigns, the struggle for the suffrage. As the women of Hull House in Chicago sang, a hundred years ago:

Let us sing as we go, Votes for Women!
Though the way may be hard,
Tho' the battle be long,

Yet our triumph is sure –
Put your heart into song:
Into cheering and song – Votes for Women!

(Cassano et al. 2019)

Discursive power too can be contested and transformed. This is shown in the remarkable work of the Australian educator Bronwyn Davies. In *Shards of Glass* (1993) Davies shows how teachers in the classroom can help children and youth gain control of gender discourses, and learn to manoeuvre among gendered identities. Colonizing power too was always contested, and women played an important part in colonial liberation struggles. Contemporary women's activism is found in every part of the world, and campaigns in different countries have been increasingly connected (Moghadam 2005). As well as a concept of inequalities of power, then, we need a concept of equal power – an idea of gender democracy.

2. Economic relations

In the classic ethnographies written about colonized peoples by European anthropologists, there is typically a passage that describes differences in the work done by men and by women. The 'sexual division of labour' was the first dimension of gender to be clearly recognized in social science. Thus, as anthropology described the Aboriginal communities of inland Australia, hunting wallabies and kangaroos was undertaken by men, collecting root vegetables, seeds and small animals was done by women.

Gender divisions of labour are indeed common, and have even been thought a cultural universal found in all societies. They are found in radically new contexts as well as 'traditional' ones. For instance, in computing – which has only existed as an industry since the 1950s and was at first not strongly gendered – a division of labour emerged in which engineering (hardware and software) was defined as men's work while data entry was women's work. More recently online computer gaming has gone through a similar change, becoming strongly masculinized over time.

Such divisions have effects beyond the workplace. Where men are a large majority in engineering and mechanical trades, and women a large majority in arts-based and human service jobs, there is likely to be a corresponding division in education systems. The students in high school and technical college courses on engineering and computing are mainly boys, while enrolments in fine arts and food preparation are mainly girls. As the British researchers Madeleine Arnot, Miriam David and Gaby Weiner show in *Closing the Gender Gap* (1999), the classic study of gender in a whole school system, strong differences in fields of study have survived despite the closing of gender differences in school retention rates.

Before we believe gender divisions of labour are universal and therefore 'natural', two major complications should be considered. First, anthropologists have often been summarizing a cultural norm or preference, rather than documenting actual work. The fine detail of the same studies often shows some women who look after cattle, act as head of household or show up for the cane-cutting, and some men who collect seeds, do the weeding or weaving, cook, or look after the children. There can be plenty of overlap in actual work done, whatever the norms say.

Second, while gender divisions of labour are common, there is not exactly the same division in different cultures, or at different points of time. The same task may be women's work in one community and men's work in another. Farm work such as digging, planting and weeding is an important example. Change occurs, sometimes fast. In the two World Wars of the twentieth century, belligerent governments mobilized millions of women to do factory work formerly done by men – hence the famous American image of Rosie the Riveter. The Soviet Union in the desperate war against Hitler sent hundreds of thousands of young women to do soldiers' work in combat zones – including snipers, tank commanders, artillerists, combat medics, and the women's regiments of the Red Air Force. Their story is told in Svetlana Alexievich's (1985) astonishing documentary novel *The Unwomanly Face of War*, based on years of emotional interviews with veterans who survived this most murderous of front lines. It was a scandalous book, because the obsessive official re-telling of the war as a narrative of heroic men had completely repressed women's experience. It helped win Alexievich the Nobel Prize.

There is more to the division of labour than differences between jobs. Feminist thinkers have repeatedly pointed to the very large amount of work that is done *outside* paid jobs, which is still essential work. This includes childcare, housework, cooking, care of the sick and elderly, gardening, the work that keeps clubs, churches and political parties running, and the learning that students do in schools and colleges. As the British sociologist Miriam Glucksmann (2000) puts it, we have to take into account the *total* social division of labour.

In the history of the European middle classes, a division grew up between a sphere of life defined by money transactions, employment, and the accumulation of capital, and a sphere of personal and domestic life characterized by kinship and emotion. In this division the economy was culturally defined as men's world (regardless of the presence of women in it), while the domestic sphere was defined as women's world (regardless of the presence of men in it). This division is still implied when people talk about work/life balance or the tensions between job and home.

The Norwegian sociologist Øystein Holter (2005) argues that this division is the structural basis of the modern gender order in capitalist countries. His point is not only that our notions of 'masculinity' and 'femininity' are closely connected with this division. Just as important, the social relations that govern work in these two spheres are different. In the economy, work is done for pay, labour-power is bought and sold, and the products of labour are placed on a market. In the home, work is also being done: housework, cooking and childcare are serious work, even with vacuum cleaners and microwave ovens. But this work is done for love or mutual obligation. The products of labour are a gift, and the logic of gift-exchange prevails. From these structural differences, Holter argues, flow characteristically different experiences for men and women, and our ideas about the different natures of men and women.

On a world scale, gender divisions of labour mean that women and men are differently located in a *gendered accumulation process*. Maria Mies (1986), the German theorist who formulated this concept on the basis of her experience in India, suggested that the global economy developed through a double process of colonization and 'housewifization'. Women in the colonized world, formerly full participants in local non-capitalist economies, were increasingly pressed into the housewife pattern of dependence on a male breadwinner. Over three decades after Mies wrote, the picture looks more complex. There is more recognition of the significance of women's paid work. More and more women have entered professions such as medicine and law. Yet large gaps in overall income reflect the fact that large numbers of women have entered the wage economy only as an insecure, unskilled labour force.

This became a stark issue in the COVID-19 pandemic in 2020. Many women workers in precarious employment were on the front line against this deadly infection. They included hospital cleaners, domestic workers, carers for the elderly and the sick, nurse's aides, as well as the garment workers manufacturing masks and protective clothing that were suddenly needed in huge amounts. The demand for women's labour included mothers suddenly having to do care work for their children in lockdowns, as the schools and childcare centres closed.

3. Emotional relations

The importance of emotional attachment in human life was made clear a hundred years ago by Sigmund Freud. Borrowing ideas from literature and neurology but mainly learning from his own patients, Freud showed how charges of emotion – both positive and negative – were attached, in the unconscious mind, to images of other people.[1] His famous analysis of the Oedipus complex, the psychological residue of a young child's powerful emotions towards mother and father, showed how important the patterning of these attachments might be. Feminist writers, from Simone de Beauvoir on, have emphasized that emotional relations are part of a larger whole: they are structured in gender terms.

Emotional commitments may be favourable or hostile towards the object. Prejudice against women (misogyny), or against homosexuals (homophobia), are familiar patterns of negative cathexis. Emotional commitments are often, as Freud emphasized, both strongly loving and strongly hostile at once. He called that pattern 'ambivalence', and it is a useful idea for understanding the complexities of gender relations.

A major arena of emotional attachment is sexuality. Anthropological and historical studies made it clear long ago that sexual relations involve culturally formed relationships, not simple biological reflexes (Caplan 1987). This does not mean that sexuality can be reduced to gender, as Gary Dowsett (2003) cautions in relation to the HIV/AIDS epidemic. It does mean that sexuality is often organized on the basis of gender.

The hegemonic pattern of gender in the global North assumes that sexual attraction works across genders, i.e. involves one man and one woman. As Frank Sinatra's dreadful 1955 hit put it,

> Love and marriage, love and marriage,
> Go together like a horse and carriage ...

Here cathexis is simply presumed to be cross-gender; same-gender or homosexual cathexis is excluded. This distinction is so culturally important that it is commonly taken as defining different kinds of people, 'homosexuals' and 'heterosexuals'. The recent political struggles about marriage equality are about whether this difference should be enforced by law. Certain biologists have gone looking for a homosexual gene to

---

1 This idea was called 'cathexis' by Freud's English translators, and I use this expression too. For careful definitions, see the very useful dictionary *The Language of Psycho-Analysis* by Laplanche and Pontalis (1973).

explain the difference, but no such thing has been found. Curiously, no one has gone looking for a heterosexual gene.

Cross-cultural research shows that many societies do not make these distinctions, or do not make them in the same way. In classical Greece, the hegemonic pattern of sexuality included strong attachments among men, especially between older men and male youth. The 'Sambia', a community in Papua New Guinea described by Gilbert Herdt in *Guardians of the Flutes* (1981), treat same-gender sexuality as a ritual practice that all men are involved in at a particular stage of life. From a European point of view, all Sambia men are homosexuals at one age, and all switch over to become heterosexuals at another. That is absurd, of course. From a Sambia point of view, they are simply following the normal development of masculinity.

In the contemporary global North, households are supposed to be formed on the basis of romantic love, that is, a strong individual attachment between two partners. This ideal is the basis of most television soaps and Hollywood weepies. Its impact is confirmed by research with numerous groups of young people, including the American university students described by Dorothy Holland and Margaret Eisenhart in *Educated in Romance* (1990). More recently, Averil Clarke studied the pursuit of romantic relationships by college-educated African-American women in *Inequalities of Love* (2011). Compared to their White and Hispanic counterparts, college-educated Black women's lives include less concern with marriage, more unwanted pregnancy, abortion and unwed childbearing. Clarke argues that social inequalities are produced not just through the economy but also through the pursuit of romantic love and the formation of households.

As the model of romantic love has spread around the world via mass media and missionary religion, it comes into conflict with other ways of forming new households – notably with arranged marriages that represent alliances between kinship groups. This conflict too is a familiar topic in fiction and films. For instance, the self-conscious search for new ways of defining emotional relationships and sexual partnership is the central theme of the Indian writer Sharanya Manivannan's short stories, in her ironically-titled collection *The High Priestess Never Marries* (2016).

Most households have another strong form of cathexis: between parent and child. This relationship too is likely to be strongly gendered, where there is a gender division of domestic labour. In a familiar pattern, care for young children is the business of women, especially mothers, and strong emotional bonds result; while fathers as breadwinners are expected to be emotionally distant. But this pattern too is under challenge, with new 'engaged fatherhood' ideals spreading (see chapter

6). Taga Futoshi's (2007) study of the discourse of fatherhood in contemporary Japan shows how difficult the resulting emotional dilemmas can be. Whichever way fathers turn, the result can be conflict and a sense of guilt.

Emotional relations are also found in the workplace. This is not just a matter of office romances or workplace sexual harassment. Emotion can be part of the work itself. Arlie Hochschild's classic book *The Managed Heart* (1983) analysed jobs in the US economy where producing a particular emotional relationship with a customer is central. These are, typically, gender-typed jobs. Hochschild's main examples are airline hostesses, where workers are trained to produce sympathy and induce relaxation; and telephone debt collectors, where workers must display aggression and induce fear. Hochschild argued that this kind of labour is becoming more common with the expansion of service industries. If so, alienated relations based on commercialized feelings and gender stereotypes will be increasingly important in modern life.

Hostile emotional relationships are important too, and the hostility is not only symbolic: it can be violent. Stephen Tomsen's (2013) study of homophobic killings in Australia shows two major patterns of conduct. One is gang attacks in public places by young men who go looking for homosexual men to punish, regarding them as gender deviants or perverts. This kind of violence depends on mutual encouragement in the group. The other pattern is killings by individuals in private. Some of these involve a violent response to a sexual approach (and perhaps to the killer's own ambivalent desire) which is felt to be a threat to masculinity. Both patterns may result in killings of extreme brutality, an indication of the strong emotions involved.

4. Symbolic relations

All social practice involves interpreting the world: we live in a universe of meanings. At the same time, meanings bear the traces of the social processes by which they were made. Cultural patterns reflect particular social interests and grow from specific ways of life.

This is true of gender symbolism. Whenever we speak of 'a woman' or 'a man', we call into play a tremendous system of understandings, implications, overtones and allusions that have accumulated through our cultural history. The meanings of these words are far richer than the biological categories of male and female. When the Papua New Guinea highland community studied by the celebrated anthropologist Marilyn Strathern (1978) say 'our clan is a clan of men', they do not mean that the clan consists entirely of males. When an American football coach yells at his losing team that they are 'a bunch of women', he does not mean they can now get pregnant. But both speakers are saying something meaningful in their contexts.

The study of cultural representations of gender, gendered attitudes, imagery and language, has been one of the most active areas of gender research, especially in the rich countries of the global North. It is not so central in the developing world, where questions of poverty, power and economic change have higher priority. But even here it is relevant, as we see in Superna Bhaskaran's *Made in India* (2004), a lively discussion of beauty pageants and Barbie-doll femininity, discrimination against homosexuals, and gender images in Indian media.

The best-known theory of how gender symbolism is structured comes from the French psychoanalyst Jacques Lacan. Lacan's analysis of the phallus as master-symbol led to a view of language as 'phallocentric': a system in which the place of authority, the privileged subjectivity, is always the masculine. The potentially infinite play of meaning in language is fixed by a phallic point of reference. In that case, culture itself embodies the 'law of the father'. And if that is so, the only way to contest patriarchal meanings is to escape known forms of language. Hence French feminist thinkers such as Xavière Gauthier (1981) developed an interest in women's writing as an oppositional practice that, to exist at all, had to subvert the conventions of culture.

By the 1990s, escape from phallocentrism and from rigid dichotomies of masculine and feminine became a key form of gender politics in the global North. Queer theory's critique of 'heteronormativity' leads to a strategy of cultural disruption. In queer writing and politics there is an energetic celebration of diversity in sexual identities and self-presentations, taking pleasure in disrupting familiar gender categories (e.g. Bauer et al. 2007). In the new century, there was a vigorous assertion of 'non-binary' gender identities, especially in the United States. This created turbulence and backlash, not only in mainstream institutions and politics but also in feminism and in gay and lesbian groups.

Though language – speech and writing – is the most analysed site of symbolic gender relations, it is not the only one. Gender symbolism can also be found in dress, makeup, gesture, photography, film and electronic media, and in more impersonal forms of culture such as the built environment.

Rosa Linda Fregoso's *The Bronze Screen* (1993) illustrates some complexities of these cultural processes. She studied films produced by Chicana/Chicano film-makers about communities of Mexican affiliation in the south-western USA, outside the Anglo Hollywood orbit. Chicano (men) film-makers, Fregoso observes, have not demeaned their women characters, but they have not given them an active role in discourse. Only with the advent of woman film-makers was there exploration of generational difference, language, religion and relationships from women's standpoints.

Elizabeth Ault (2013) makes a stronger criticism of *The Wire* (HBO, 2002–8), the acclaimed television crime drama set in Baltimore. Though *The Wire* is distinctive in giving attention to the structural dimensions of urban politics, especially class and race, like most crime dramas it is mainly focused on men. Ault argues that the few portrayals of African-American mothers in the drama exhibit a view of Black motherhood as irresponsible, irrational and emasculating.

Gender symbolism is frequently deployed in times of struggle. 'The United States Army *builds* MEN', declared a First World War recruiting poster, depicting fine Aryan types of the craftsman, the sportsman and the crusader knight: 'Apply nearest recruiting office'. Any young men who did apply would have found themselves not in a crusade but in a war of industrial slaughter by machine-guns and artillery. The anti-apartheid movement in South Africa also put symbolism of masculinity into play, as the formidable union movement constructed masculinity on a 'worker' model. A more ambiguous role was played by the Zulu-nationalist Inkatha movement, which tried to mobilize men around a 'warrior' image but stood for a conservative social order. In the aftermath of the armed struggle, the 'young lions' of the African National Congress's guerrilla forces lost their social respect, and often fell into unemployment and violent crime (Xaba 2001; Waetjen 2004).

Symbolic expressions of gender change over time, though not evenly. In an extended analysis of survey data from Germany and Japan, Ulrich Mohwald (2002) shows a shift of attitudes in both countries towards gender equality. However the course of events was different. The breadwinner/housewife model, formerly unknown in Japan, was constructed in the late nineteenth and early twentieth century as a middle-class ideal. Following the Second World War, Japanese women endorsed both legal equality *and* this unequal nuclear-family model. Another shift of opinion followed the Women's Liberation movement, with increasing value placed on women's careers and sharing work in the home. In Japan this shift occurred in the attitudes of all generations. In Germany, however, the shift away from traditional gender attitudes involved a generational split – it mainly happened in the younger generation.

Intersectionality

The four dimensions of gender just discussed are not separate institutions, and in real-life contexts they constantly interweave and condition each other. No economic division, for instance, could be sustained very long without symbolic justification. Birgit Pfau-Effinger's (1998) very sophisticated cross-national analysis of gender arrangements in European labour markets depends on this point. Different cultural models of gender, she argues, underpin different divisions of labour.

Further, the structures of gender are interwoven with other social structures. Fregoso's analysis of gender in Chicana/o film presupposes the structure of ethnic inequality in the United States – which has been strikingly re-emphasized by the Trump presidency. Hochschild's analysis of gendered emotional labour, and Pringle's analysis of secretarial work (see chapter 7), presuppose a class structure where groups of workers depend on capitalist corporations for their livelihood, and must deliver certain kinds of labour to get their wages.

This kind of interweaving has been discussed in recent social science under the name of 'intersectionality'. American lawyer Kimberlé Crenshaw (1989) coined this term while involved in struggles for the rights of Black women in US courts. Crenshaw argued that attending to gender or race *separately* could not capture these women's experiences, nor their legal needs. It was important to highlight the combination of gender and race as sources of disadvantage.

The concept has now been taken up internationally, and to many it is a defining feature of gender analysis today. Most intersectional analyses highlight the importance of race, but also recognize sexuality and class alongside gender. Sometimes other social divisions such as religion, national origin or generation are added. The Australian environmental philosopher Val Plumwood (1994) has suggested that nature too needs to be incorporated in feminist thought as a category alongside race, class and gender.

There is a question about how many intersections should be pursued. They could be multiplied almost indefinitely. This is not the only problem. 'Intersection' is a metaphor from geometry, and easily pictures social structures as stacks of categories, like bookshelves or boxes. There is a risk, then, that intersectional analyses will be static. Joya Misra's (2018) review of intersectional sociology in the United States shows that this can be avoided. An excellent example of a dynamic intersectional analysis is Mara Viveros's (2018b) account of social movements in Colombia, discussed in chapter 2 above.

We might best think of intersectionality not as a fixed theory, but as a broad approach to research and activism that emphasizes there are always multiple social inequalities and social justice struggles. There are varying types of intersectional research: some focus on complexities within categories, some on relations between different structures, some on the instability of the categories themselves. The approach does give a grip on complexities of power. Good intersectional analyses will illuminate how multiple inequalities produce real social situations.

Ethnicity, for instance, is constantly defined through gender relations. The notion of an extended family is central to racial and ethnic rhetoric: 'our kith and kin', as the British used to say; 'brothers born of warrior stock', in the language of Zulu nationalism in South Africa (Waetjen and Maré 2001). Jill Vickers (1994) noted that male-dominated ethnic-nationalist movements usually lay heavy emphasis on women's reproductive powers. Women are 'mothers of the nation', or the nation itself is conceived as a mother in need of protection by her sons. The same tones can be heard today in the White-supremacist and anti-immigrant rhetoric of right-wing parties in Europe, the USA and Australia, and in Hindu-supremacist ethno-nationalism in India.

For many purposes it is important to treat gender as a structure in its own right. But we must remember that gender relations always work in context, always interact with other dynamics in social life.

Crisis tendencies and change

Why do gender relations, and the structures that organize them, change? Most explanations have focused on external pressures: new technology, urban life, mass communications, secularism, or just 'modernization'. It is true that broad social forces can alter gender patterns. But gender relations also have internal tendencies towards change.

Theorists who emphasize that gender is constructed discursively may also argue that the results are fluid. The uncertain and contested character of the category 'women' is a central theme in feminist and queer theorizing influenced by Butler and Spivak. Meanings in discourse are not fixed, and if Derrida's argument is accepted, cannot be fixed in any final way. Many theorists have drawn the conclusion there is no fixed connection between discursive identities and the bodies to which those identities refer. People with male bodies can enact femininity, people with female bodies can enact masculinity. Gender identities can be played with, taken up and abandoned, unpacked and recombined. There would seem to be inherent instability in gender.

These ideas have been extremely influential, especially in the global North, but the idea of a generalized instability has also been criticized. The new materialism mentioned in chapter 4 rejects an over-emphasis on discourse. There is a material world, which has its own determining power. Social scientists notice that in some historical situations gender identities and relations change slowly, while in other situations they change explosively. Sylvia Walby's *Gender Transformations* (1997) suggests that distinct 'rounds' of restructuring can be identified in the global North. Gender boundaries seem to have hardened, not weakened, in Iran and some Arab countries in the last generation (Moghadam 2013).

A concept of generalized instability does not explain why some people would want to change gender arrangements, while others would resist. That can be explained better in terms of structural thinking about inequality, intersectionality, and the politics of social justice.

Can structural thinking account for change? The key ideas here come from German critical theory, especially the work of Jürgen Habermas (1976). Structures of inequality develop crisis tendencies, that is, internal contradictions that undermine current patterns, and force change in the structure itself. This concept allows us to distinguish periods when pressures for change are only gradually building, from periods when they erupt into actual crisis and force rapid change. The analysis of structure allows us to identify interests that can be mobilized for and against change.

Crisis tendencies can be identified in each of the four dimensions of gender relations defined earlier in this chapter. We will illustrate just one of them, economic relations. The division of labour has been the site of massive change. Through the second half of the twentieth century, more and more of women's labour was incorporated into the market economy. As we noted in chapter 1, the global labour force participation rate for women in 2018 was 48.5 per cent; significantly below the rate for men, but still a major part of the paid workforce. In rich countries this historical change took the form of growth in married women's workforce participation rates, i.e. movement from unpaid to paid work, especially in the service sector. In developing economies, the change took the form of an even more massive move into cities, into market-based agriculture and into factory work such as the clothing industry.

In recent years the overall gender gap in labour force participation has remained constant. This gap does not mean than women do less work than men. Women do most of the domestic work and childcare as well as a part of waged labour. Women and men, as a whole, make roughly equal contributions to total social labour. There is an underlying contradiction between this, and the gendered appropriation of the products of social labour. The gendered appropriation is seen in the markedly unequal incomes of women and men as groups, the better conditions and career prospects that men generally have, and the patriarchal inheritance of wealth and power, as seen in corporate dynasties from the Rockefellers to the Koch brothers.

Women have a general interest in changing this, so may become active in community organizing, in workers' unions, in producer cooperatives

or environmental campaigns. But the turbulence of the gendered accumulation process, and its intersection with class relations, affect this.
Economically privileged women, who are usually the most influential in
politics, have an interest in resisting economic reforms that cut deeply
into gender inequalities, because that would disturb the corporate system
from which they benefit. So we do not see many rich women in their fur
coats standing on the picket lines to support strikes of fast-food workers.
Some critics, such as Hester Eisenstein in *Feminism Seduced* (2009),
see the liberal feminism of the global North as deeply complicit with
corporate capitalism.

The concept of crisis tendencies is not applicable everywhere. To
speak of contradiction presumes a coherent gender order within which
opposing tendencies arise. But what if the gender order itself has been
smashed? That is exactly what happened in imperial conquest, with the
arrival of the colonizing powers and the disruption or destruction of
local gender orders. As noted in chapter 4, a consolidated gender order
cannot be presumed in the colonized or post-colonial world. Gender
structures are not necessarily coherent, bounded systems. They may be
patchworks and heaps of fragments rather than well-oiled machines –
yet still shape people's lives.

The contemporary global economy, too, restructures local gender
orders. Evidence about this has emerged in research on motherhood. In
Nicaragua, following the election of a right-wing government in 1990,
a market agenda drove public sector cuts, privatized state agencies and
reduced social services. Julie Cupples' (2005) interviews with single
mothers in the town of Matagalpa showed these changes reflected in
mothers' loss of dignity and greater difficulty in making ends meet. But
the women of Matagalpa responded actively. With the growth of an
informal economy, they moved into employment, however precarious,
more confidently than the men – often reducing or abandoning their
housework commitments to do so. Needing to care for children obliged
the women to generate a family income. Over time, Cupples argues,
paid work became consolidated as part of women's identity. Being a
breadwinner is now part of motherhood, rather than being opposed
to it.

The ideas in this chapter, together with the analysis of embodiment
in chapter 3, yield a concept of gender itself. Gender is the way human
reproductive bodies enter history, and the changing way social processes,
unfolding through time, deal with birth and generational continuity.
Gender is a *social* process, a dynamic of change quite different from
biological evolution. It does not imply heteronormativity, does not
require that all women should be married mothers nor that all men
should be fathers with mortgages and lawnmowers. Humans have an

enormous range of possibilities in relationship, pleasure and work. What our biological and social continuity require, above all, is provision for childcare and education. It is not often put like this, but children and history are the crux of gender analysis.

6

Personal life

For most of us, being a boy or a girl is a taken-for-granted part of growing up. In adulthood, being a woman or a man is an ordinary part of the way we conduct family life and sexual relationships, the way we present ourselves in everyday situations, and the way we see ourselves. This chapter examines how gender emerges and becomes an ordinary fact in this intimate realm of life. The chapter also examines tensions in this realm – because for some of us, growing up gendered is not simple at all.

Socialization and psychoanalysis

When sex role theory provided the main framework of gender research in English-speaking countries of the global North, in the 1950s and 1960s, there was a straightforward account of how people acquired gender, which ran like this. Babies were labelled as either girls or boys. The boy babies were expected to behave rougher and tougher, to be more demanding and vigorous. In time they were given toy guns and footballs. The girl babies were expected to be more passive and compliant, also more decorative. As they grew older they were dressed in frilly clothes, given dolls and makeup kits, told to take care of their appearance and be polite and agreeable.

Put more formally, sex roles were thought to be acquired by socialization. Various agencies of socialization, notably the family, the school, the peer group and the mass media, took the growing child in hand. Through many small interactions, these agencies conveyed to the girl or the boy the social norms or expectations for behaviour. Roles could be acquired in a lump by imitating role models, such as a father as a role model for a boy, or they could be learned piece by piece. Compliance with the norms would lead to rewards, or positive sanctions: smiles from mother, approval from friends, success in the dating game, appointment to a good job. Nonconformity or deviance would lead to negative sanctions, all the way from receiving frowns to getting beaten or sent to prison.

With this mixture of positive and negative reinforcement, it was thought, most children would learn the behaviours and develop the traits that their culture thought appropriate for women or for men. They would internalize the norms. As socialized members of society, they would in their turn apply negative sanctions to deviants, and teach the norms to the next generation. The process could go wrong, for instance if fathers disappeared from families and boys lacked role models. This would probably lead to juvenile delinquency or worse.

There is some value in this story of how gender is acquired. It identifies institutions, such as the family and the media, that do have gender regimes and do influence children. But there are also severe problems with this story.

First, it is far too monolithic. The world does not consist of neatly separated cultures, each one internally homogeneous. Cultures have been smashed, fragmented and reorganized by conquest, colonization, migration, and contemporary globalization. The model ignores power relations, and mistakes what is dominant for what is normative. Actual societies are not unanimous about what gender patterns to approve: indeed opinions can be sharply divided. There are always multiple patterns of masculinity and femininity that complicate the picture of learning.

Second, the socialization model supposes that learning gender is a matter of acquiring traits, that is, regularities of character that will produce regularities of behaviour. Sex role theory, basically, is a social version of the difference model of gender discussed in chapter 3. But as the research examined there shows, major differences in traits between women and men (or between girls and boys) are rare.

Third, the socialization model pictures the learner as passive and the agencies of socialization as active. In real life, gender learning does not look like this. There is a whole research literature about life in schools – including C. J. Pascoe's *Dude, You're a Fag* discussed in chapter 2 – showing that gender learning is turbulent and active. Barrie Thorne's classic description of California elementary schools in *Gender Play*

(1993) is a perfect example. The boys and girls in these schools do not lie back and let the gender norms wash over them. They are constantly busy. They sometimes accept gender divisions supplied by adults and sometimes reject them. They set up their own gender divisions in the playground, and then disrupt them. They explore gendered self-presentations, as when the older girls put on lip gloss. They complain, joke, fantasize and ask questions about gender.

The socialization model misses the pleasure that is obvious in much gender learning. It also misses the resistance which many young people offer to hegemonic definitions of gender. The model misses the difficulty of constructing identities and working out patterns of conduct in a gender order marked by power, violence and alienated sexuality. James Messerschmidt's *Flesh and Blood* (2004), with vivid studies of the lives of American youth who got into trouble with the law through violence, is full of evidence of this difficulty, and shows the resistance and the divergent life-courses that result.

Fourth, the socialization model recognizes just one dimension of learning – towards or away from the sex role norms. This makes it hard to understand the shifts of direction that appear in a young person's life, coming apparently from nowhere. There can be a shift of attachment from mother to father, a new level of aggression, a sudden burst of sexual activity. A young person may vehemently reject gender stereotypes, criticize their political or human inadequacy, and search for something different.

The turbulent character of human development is better understood by psychoanalysis. Freud's case studies emphasized conflict and contradiction. Freud recognized that a person is often developing in different directions at the same time, at unconscious and conscious levels. Psychoanalytic ideas have changed over the last century, and contemporary schools of psychoanalysis remain deeply divided, but in virtually all of them this insight remains important.

In Freud's account, gender development centred on the Oedipus complex. This is the psychological pattern that grows out of an emotional crisis in middle childhood, when the child's sexual desire, focused for the moment on mother and father, is repressed. In Freud's argument, this crisis sets up an unconscious pattern of motivation, different for boys and girls, that continues to influence their mental life from the shadows. In the normal case, Freud thought, the oedipal pattern of development leads to adult heterosexual attraction. Psychoanalysis thus offered an explanation of how a conventional gender pattern is transmitted from generation to generation with apparent ease, shaping the strongest desires of adult men and women. But the theory also showed that this effect was achieved through emotional contradictions and crises which *could* lead along other paths. Thus *non*-normative gender development could also be understood.

Psychoanalysis has always been controversial, and its influence in social science has declined. Many psychologists are completely sceptical of these ideas. There is a curious tendency for psychoanalytic movements to turn into cult-like celebrations of a great founder, in which imaginative ideas become rigid dogmas. Yet there are powerful insights here. We can still learn from psychoanalysis that the development of gender is a contradictory process, not a smooth one; that it involves bodily desires and obscure emotions; and that it has varied and sometimes paradoxical outcomes in personal lives.

Gender identity

Perhaps the commonest way people now talk about gender is in terms of identity. This became a key concept in gender studies quite recently, and it is worth knowing its history.

'Identity' is an old philosophical and legal term, originally meaning 'sameness'. It referred to something remaining stable over time, or two things being equivalent. In time, the word acquired a psychological meaning. The most famous version was presented in the psychoanalyst Erik Erikson's book *Childhood and Society*. This interpreted a range of modern personal, social and political problems as difficulties in achieving identity. 'The study of identity, then, becomes as strategic in our time as the study of sexuality was in Freud's time' (Erikson 1950: 242).

But where Freud had focused on unconscious forces, Erikson emphasized the conscious agency of the mind, the ego. To Erikson, 'identity' meant the coherence of the psychological mechanisms by which the ego handles the pressures that impinge on it. The question 'who am I?' is answered by the ego's success in mastering the trials and tribulations of psychological development, especially in adolescence. As Erikson's ideas were popularized, 'identity' came to mean a person's psychological core, a stable sense of self. Articles in popular magazines began agonizing over how teenagers achieved identity, or failed to.

Erikson did not have *gender* particularly in mind. This turn was made by the American psychiatrist Robert Stoller (1968), an early researcher on transsexuality. Stoller altered Erikson's concept in two ways. First, the 'core gender identity' that Stoller saw as the basis of adult personality was supposed to be formed very early in life, not in adolescence. Second, where Erikson referred to the integration of the ego as a whole, Stoller focused on one aspect of the person: their involvement in gender relations. Stoller assumed that the integration of the personality as a whole *was* largely focused on the sense of being a man or woman, boy or girl. But we could speak just as meaningfully of racial identity, generational identity, national identity or class identity. Stoller's model thus led unexpectedly towards a conception of identity as plural rather than unitary.

Stoller's work became influential partly because American feminism too emphasized gender in the rearing of children. Nancy Chodorow in *The Reproduction of Mothering* (1978) linked the adult gender division of labour – caring for infants being defined as women's work – with the children's paths of development. Girls and boys, Chodorow argued, face different emotional situations in early childhood. Girls, brought up by a parent of their own gender, form less distinct ego boundaries. When they grow up, they have a stronger motivation for nurturing children. Boys, pushed towards separation from the mother, typically have an earlier break in development. They have more difficulty in establishing gender identity, and maintain stronger boundaries to the self in adulthood.

Though it has been well established that men can 'mother' (Risman 1986), in most contemporary societies, not many of them do. But are the reasons psychological, as Chodorow thought? Scandinavian countries made an economic reform – paid leave for fathers of very young children – and this has been successful in changing behaviour (Holter 2003).

There has also been more recognition that we do not find a simple male/female dichotomy in adult personalities, as chapter 3 showed. Since the 1970s there has been a broad shift in gender analysis from a dichotomous picture of gender to a more plural one. One reason is the growing evidence of diversity in real-life gender patterns. Diversity between societies, and between different situations, is clearly shown when research from different countries is brought together (e.g. Enarson and Pease 2016; Kulkarni 2019). There is considerable evidence that there are multiple masculinities within the same society, even within the same institution, peer group or workplace. Sofia Aboim writes of *Plural Masculinities* (2010), and, like other recent researchers, lays emphasis on the hybrid character of actual masculinities.

The idea of gender identity has remained popular, partly because of the rise of discursive approaches to gender. The result was to de-emphasize material, bodily and institutional constraints in the picture of gender. The new theoretical language was easily interpreted to mean that gender is malleable, fluid, easily modified – indeed, that gender identity can be chosen.

The concept of 'identity' has now come to mean people defining who they are in terms of difference from other people. This is closely related to the idea of identity politics as it developed in the United States. In this model of politics, one becomes part of a social movement by acknowledging or claiming the distinctive identity (as Black, as a woman, as lesbian, etc.) that the movement represents. How far this model corresponds to the realities of social movements is debatable. In practice, radical movements may be more concerned with economic justice or ending racist violence than with expressing identity. But 'identity' has become the most popular way of talking about social difference and diversity.

The queer politics that emerged in the global North in the 1990s has a paradoxical relationship with this concept. On the one hand, queer theorists challenged universalizing concepts like 'woman' and 'gay', seeing them as forms of constraint rather than bases of liberation. Queer activists challenged taken-for-granted communities by emphasizing their diversity: for instance, highlighting the presence of Black lesbians in White-dominated lesbian communities.

On the other hand, the queer movement did grow out of lesbian and gay networks, and has produced the biggest and brightest new identity concept in gender politics. This is 'LGBT', a term that came into use in the United States in the 1990s and has since spread around the world. It originated as 'LGB' – lesbian, gay and bisexual – listing the groups in homosexual politics who, in the afterglow of the 1970s liberation movements, came to be seen as identity groups demanding civil rights. In the 1990s, transgender groups (themselves far from homogeneous) were included by adding the 'T'. The logic is not immediately obvious: L, G and B are defined by sexual object-choice, T is not defined by sexuality at all. Queer theory might see them all as defying the heteronormative order. But the main political effect was to avoid referring to stigmatized sexuality at all, in favour of an identity-based, *non*-gendered 'LGBT community'. These euphemisms are now standard in journalism and human rights work, and they have been successfully exported to other countries. Back in the USA it was soon thought the list was not inclusive enough. So more groups have been added: queer (Q), intersex (I), asexual (A) and others. There is no logical limit to this.

Queer theorists' scepticism about identity concepts is supported by social research from quite different points of view. Here is an example. Arne Nilsson's (1998) beautifully crafted study of homosexual history in the Swedish city of Göteborg identifies three ways of being a homosexual man: 'so', commonly a bit effeminate; 'real men', often working-class youth; and '*fjollor*', flamboyant queens. Three well-chosen identities, perhaps? But Nilsson also shows how the patterns grew out of the social structure of this industrial and maritime city. Among the conditions shaping men's sexuality were crowded housing, a sharp gender division of labour, high density of men in public spaces, a non-respectable working-class street life, connections to other cities via the shipping trade, patterns of policing, and the poverty of many young men who might enter homosexual relationships for a period and then move on.

These conditions changed. The 1950s saw rising affluence in Sweden, suburban housing for the working class, the growth of a welfare state, and moral panics about the seduction of youth. A sharper cultural distinction between heterosexual and homosexual men followed the increasing privacy of sexual conduct itself. Thus, the configurations of sexuality which might easily be read as identities were dependent on historically transitory social conditions, and for many participants lasted only a limited period of their lives.

Is it actively misleading to use the term 'identity' for a pattern of gender or sexual practice? The philosopher Guy Hocquenghem (1972), one of the most brilliant theorists of Gay Liberation, argued that homosexual desire is in principle anarchic, it does not reveal a personal unity. It is desire that has escaped being 'oedipalized', that is, organized by the patriarchal gender order. On Hocquenghem's argument, homosexuality is the opposite of an identity, it is desire and practice that cannot be welded into a unity.

Strikingly, a great deal of *heterosexual* desire also fails to be oedipalized. Heterosexual desire, too, is often perverse, transitory, and pushes against fixed positions and bounded identities. Lynne Segal points out in *Straight Sex* (1994: 254–5) that 'Sexual relations are perhaps the most fraught and troubling of all social relations precisely because, especially when heterosexual, they so often threaten rather than confirm gender polarity.' It is in sexuality that heterosexual men are most likely to experience dependence, uncertainty, passivity and – quite simply – shared experience with women.

We might also ask, is a unified identity really so desirable? To weld one's personality into a united whole is to refuse internal diversity and openness, perhaps to refuse change. Major reform in gender relations may well require some loss of self-coherence as part of the process. Barbara Risman (1998) found something like this in her study of 'fair families' in the United States, where people were trying to create gender-equal households. She called her book *Gender Vertigo*. Reshaping intimate relations on principles of equality is possible, but can be very difficult to sustain.

Bodies, death and fate

Most psychological discussions ignore the power dimension of gender. But this is as important in intimate life as it is on the larger scale. My partner Pam Benton died of breast cancer. Breast cancer is almost entirely a women's disease. The medical specialists who treated it, however, were mostly men. Like other elite professional men, most had built a conservative, upper-class masculinity.

Early in the treatment, Pam was referred to a prominent Sydney oncologist. Oncology is specialization in cancer, especially in its treatment through chemotherapy, the use of toxic drugs. This gentleman announced his opinion that if women would use their breasts for what they were intended for, they would not have so much trouble. Pam was furious and refused to be treated by him.

There is, as the oncologist well knew, research evidence that rates of breast cancer are lower in women who have had babies early in life and have breast-fed. That is impersonal fact. Yet we might ask why researchers were concerned with that particular piece of background rather than with stress, or cancer-causing chemicals in the environment. Worse, the oncologist made this research finding into a gender insult by his bland presumption that what women are 'for' is bearing babies. To him, if women had a different pattern of life, they were asking for what they got.

The story suggests how intimate gender politics is. Some issues about power and inequality are mundane, such as who does the dishes and who writes the shopping list. Some issues are life-and-death, such as how cancer treatment is done. Pam was an activist in the women's movement. She could see the gender politics in cancer medicine, and was not willing to be put down yet again by privileged men.

The first tumour, which Pam discovered through routine screening, was so advanced that it required a mastectomy, surgical removal of the whole breast. This is a frightening (though not in itself life-threatening) operation which leaves a long scar where the breast has been. Recovering from the operation, Pam made contact with the support services officially available to mastectomy patients. The main services were: supply of an artificial breast, in the appropriate size to replace the one that was lost; visits from women who came to give grooming and dress advice so that the patient could present an attractive feminine appearance to the world; and advice on how to restore family normality, overcome a husband's expected sexual disgust at a mutilated body, and deal with children's anxiety about their mother being taken away from them.

This, too, is political. It is about placing women back in the culture of heterosexual femininity. It is about denying that normality has been rent. It is about holding women responsible for other people's emotional needs. And – not least – it is about restoring normal services to men.

But this politics operates at so deep a level of emotion that it is hardly perceptible as politics unless one is already conscious of gender issues. Many women dedicate their lives to making a family and seeing it through the life-cycle. Having an attractive or at least presentable body is an important part of mainstream Australian culture's definition of femininity. Women who are shocked by a major operation, and terrified by discovering they have a deadly disease, are unlikely to revolt against stereotyping, especially when it is presented to them by other women as a form of care.

These things happened in the 1990s and cancer medicine has evolved since then. There are now more women in the medical profession, and some services have taken note of the criticisms. Yet the political dimension remains, for instance in the rise of cosmetic surgery as an adjunct to cancer treatment.

Gender politics constantly has this elemental, intimate character. That is one reason why change in gender relations can be threatening, to many women as well as many men. Impending changes can upset people's cherished images of themselves, their personal relationships, their social embodiment and their everyday habits.

Here are some brief examples of intimate politics from other parts of the world. One comes from Costa Rica in Central America, a beautiful hilly country that is a banana and coffee exporter, vulnerable to price fluctuations. The Latin American debt crisis of the 1980s drove the economy into a neoliberal restructuring, in which many men became unemployed. Susan Mannon (2006) interviewed middle-aged married people in an urban area and her report tells the story of one couple who lived through these events.

Cecilia and Antonio had set up their household on a breadwinner/housewife basis. Antonio was a low-paid, unskilled public sector worker. The gender division of labour was not imposed on Cecilia; she was an active participant in creating demarcations between family tasks. But economic need drove change. As inflation gripped, Cecilia, like other married women, returned to the money economy. She did this first by renting out a room in their house, thus commodifying her domestic work. The sharp breadwinner/housewife division began to blur by Cecilia expanding her labour. Antonio did not do housework, but held on to authority in the family, with support from patriarchal norms in the society around. Cecilia did not use her new economic strength in challenging his position, which might have disrupted the social position of respectability that she was trying to protect. Patience and love won out.

In a moving book called *Breaking Ranks* (2010), Matthew Gutmann and Catherine Lutz present the lives of six veterans of the US military forces involved in the invasion and occupation of Iraq. The five men and one woman tell about growing up and entering the armed forces. Their stories sound very familiar: families where boys play war games and various male relatives have served as soldiers, communities where military recruiters offer a way out of poverty, and mass media that glamorize nationalism and combat. The US military now recruits women, and Tina, the woman in this group, had been an athlete and was recruited via the military training corps in her school.

All six, however, became dissenters and active opponents of the war. There were different pathways, but in Gutmann and Lutz's account, it was not political debates that mattered most. Rather it was the raw, embodied experience of a heavily-armed force facing an insurrection, that disrupted conventional loyalties and self-images. Front-line troops witnessed the killing and wounding of local people, the widespread destruction in a poor, occupied country, and the gap between the reality on the ground and the glossy official optimism.

Anna Temkina (2008) reports a life-history study of sexuality among middle-class women in St Petersburg in the post-Soviet era. Different sexual scripts could be distinguished in their stories. The women who had grown up in the Soviet period had lives organized by marriage. They usually placed themselves in a passive position in their narratives, describing themselves as objects of men's desire – all reasonably in accord with Soviet gender ideology. Their sexual lives, Temkina observes, were ruled by others and by the surrounding conditions. We might say that these women experienced gender as their collective fate.

But this was not the dominant story among younger women, who grew up in the post-communist transition and under the new capitalist regime. These women describe themselves as having agency in their sexual lives. They are more likely to emphasize seeking their own pleasure, or using their sexuality to gain benefits, i.e. bargaining with men. Making more conscious choices about contraception and relationships, they are more inclined to see their lives as personal projects than as an unavoidable collective fate. Still, they are not outside history. As Russia rolled back the limited Soviet-era emancipation of women, neo-traditionalist ideologies of gender emerged. A new public patriarchy was constructed, centred on Vladimir Putin, whose public displays of masculinity are famous.

When the Women's Liberation movement said 'the personal is political', they were making a point that still holds good. Gender politics are present in our most intimate relationships and decisions. The complexities are many, the price of change can be high, and sometimes one just gets tired. But this intimate politics is part of the reality of gender, even in dramatic large-scale changes.

Gender projects and active learning

To understand how gender is made real in personal life, we must recognize that growing up has many contradictions, and that learners are active, not passive. We must recognize the agency of bodies in the social world, since the active learner is embodied. We must recognize the power of the institutions that shape the learner's world. We must give an account of the gender competencies that young people learn, and the different life projects they create. And we must recognize historical change, that runs through the whole process.

The pleasures involved in learning gender are in part bodily pleasures, pride in the body's appearance and performance as well as sexual pleasure itself. Bodily changes such as first period, first ejaculation, the 'breaking' of a boy's voice, the development of a girl's breasts, are usually important. Yet their meanings remain ambiguous until they are given definition by a culture's gender symbolism.

Because gender practice involves bodies but is not biologically determined, the learned behaviour may be hostile to bodies' physical well-being. Young men in rich countries such as the United States and Australia, enacting their fresh-minted masculinities on the roads, die in appalling numbers in traffic accidents, at a rate four times higher than young women. A large number of adolescent girls and young women start dieting in an attempt to maintain their heterosexual attractiveness and for some, this escalates into life-threatening anorexia.

In poorer countries the circumstances are different but the stakes are also very high. In the Palestinian confrontation with Israeli military occupation, most of the front-line resistance has been carried out by very young men and boys. As Julie Peteet (1994) showed in a terrifying ethnography of the first *intifada*, being beaten or arrested by the Israeli army and police became a rite of passage into masculinity for Palestinian youth. Some of them were killed.

Embodied learners encounter the gender regimes of the institutions around them. The socialization model was right about the importance of the family, the school and the media in children's lives, but failed to recognize the complex gender regimes of these institutions. In a school, teachers and other adult workers show the children a range of different patterns of masculinity and femininity. Differences in masculinities among teachers in Britain are clearly shown in Máirtín Mac an Ghaill's (1994) study of upper secondary schooling. In Julie Bettie's (2003) ethnography of a high school in California, the focus is on femininities, and the race/ethnic hierarchies among the girls clearly affect the making of gender. This is intersectionality (chapter 5) at ground level.

The diversity of gender patterns among children and youth shows through clearly in research that looks across multiple social groups. An excellent example is Stephen Frosh, Ann Phoenix and Rob Pattman's *Young Masculinities* (2002), a report on 11- to 14-year-old boys in 12 secondary schools across London. They show that race is prominent in London boys' stereotypes of masculinity – Afro-Caribbean boys are considered high in masculinity and Asian boys are considered low. Relationships with schools are ambivalent: boys both desire academic success and reject it as feminine. Above all, this study shows that diversity in the boys' lives exists in tension with 'canonical narratives' of masculinity that admire physical toughness, sports skills and hetero-sexuality. All boys acknowledge this hegemonic masculinity but most do not fully inhabit it. Rather, their adolescence is marked by complex negotiations with definitions of gender. They may criticize some versions of masculinity as too tough, while rejecting others as too effeminate.

A good part of young people's learning about gender is acquiring gender competence. Young people learn how to navigate the local gender order and the gender regimes of the institutions they deal with. They learn how to inhabit a certain gender position and produce a certain gender enactment. Young people also learn how to distance themselves from a given gender stereotype, how to joke about their own performance. Most boys and girls fail to match gender ideals of appearance, skill or achievement, but most of them still cope! I hope the same can be said for adults.

Active learning means a commitment of oneself in a particular direction. The learner does not simply absorb what is to be learned, but engages with it, moving forward in life. The pleasure in gender learning is the pleasure of creativity and movement. Such learning can occur at any moment in everyday life when a person encounters gender relations. A lovely piece of research showing this is Wendy Luttrell's *Schoolsmart and Motherwise* (1997). Her interviews with African-American and White working-class women in adult education programmes in the United States, looking back at their personal histories, revealed a lifelong process of learning gender. It continues even in old age, as the amazing Simone de Beauvoir was the first to point out.

Gender learning is often casual but over time it takes definite shapes. What is learned is connected with other pieces of learning. Children learn about, and create in their own lives, the configurations of gender practice that we call 'femininity' and 'masculinity'.

Gender configurations, being patterns of activity, are not static. Masculinity and femininity can be considered as projects, to use a concept from Simone's partner Jean-Paul Sartre (1968). These are patterns of a life-course moving from the present into the future, bringing new realities into existence. Parts 4 and 5 of *The Second Sex* are an extraordinary mapping of life projects for women as they existed in European society and history: from childhood to sexual initiation, to life as a lesbian, a married woman, a mother, a prostitute etc., and then into old age.

Social science adds two vital elements to this philosophical conception. First, it details the cultural, institutional and economic circumstances in which gender projects are formed. Second, it shows the collective, social character of the projects themselves. It is usually the *shared* trajectories of gender formation that researchers pick up when they describe 'masculinities' or 'femininities' in their research.

Gender projects can be turbulent and may involve heavy costs. Any life trajectory involves moments in which commitments to a gender pattern are made, or new resolutions of gender issues are achieved. Let us consider some cases from around the world.

One is an early study of men in the Australian environmental movement (Connell 1995). Most of these men grew up in homes with a conventional gender division of labour, and in childhood and adolescence they began to make a commitment to hegemonic masculinity. But this moment of engagement was followed by a moment of negation, as they started to distance themselves from the conventional pathway, for a variety of reasons including family conflict. Most went on, in the counter-culture or in the green movement, to meet and work with feminists. They were obliged to confront gender issues head-on. This was a moment of separation from hegemonic masculinity. Some then moved on to a moment of contestation, starting a political project of reforming masculinity and committing themselves to gender equality.

A generation later, many more men have gone down this path. There is now both research and strategic debate about changing masculinities and environmental issues. Martin Hultman and Paul Pulé's *Ecological Masculinities* (2018) provides an overview. Involvement in a social movement is not the only way masculinities can change. Geographical mobility and cultural context may also have an effect, as Karla Elliott shows in *Young Men Navigating Contemporary Masculinities* (2020). Her closely-observed interviews with young men in contemporary Berlin, a city notable for diversity and experimental ways of life, reveal a number of pathways towards more 'open' and egalitarian conceptions of masculinity. Elliott argues that change is fostered in the cultural and social margins, but is possible also for the more privileged.

As gender orders change, new trajectories for both women and men become possible. This can be seen in Chilla Bulbeck's three-generation study in Australia, *Living Feminism* (1997). Younger women do not constantly face the same impasses as women of earlier generations.

Belief in gender equality has certainly spread among younger men in many countries too. An example is a national study of men in Germany by Paul Zulehner and Rainer Volz (1998). In this survey, men below the age of 50 endorsed a gender-equal model of family life, and rejected 'traditional' norms, far more often than men above 50. The large international survey known as IMAGES (Promundo 2015) suggests this pattern is a common one. Changed beliefs can be expressed in action. For instance, younger fathers are usually more involved in childcare than older fathers, though this is not uniform between countries.

We should not assume that 'traditional' masculinities are fixed forever in the same posture. As the South African psychologist Kopano Ratele (2014) observes of debates about Black African men, traditions of masculinity are multiple, and are constantly being re-worked. Tradition can be claimed by power-holders to bolster their own position, but tradition can also be used in other ways. Ratele gives the charming example of the traditional-style marriage of two young gay men in KwaZulu Natal, held in 2013 with two hundred guests: a creative use of an old-established social form.

But we should not assume, either, that closed, power-oriented and patriarchal masculinities have evaporated. They are still present, and may have great influence. Here is a notable example. In Chile, the first country to adopt a neoliberal agenda, market economics and dictatorship consolidated the power of an existing ruling class. In a close-focus study of the way this class reproduces itself through time, Sebastián Madrid (2016) examined masculinity in elite private schools, through life-history interviews with 41 of their former pupils.

Madrid found a pattern that one of his interviewees, Germán, called 'diversity without diversity'. There are differences within the Chilean ruling class: three kinds of schools, families with old money vs families with new money, differences of religion, and so on. Differences in masculinity arose, with a competition for hegemony between 'Golden Boys' who followed the schools' agenda, and the disruptive 'Death Row' boys who revelled in partying, sports and fights. But all were, as Germán put it, in the top 2 per cent of the social pyramid. They lived in the same bubble, as another interviewee remarked. And most of them, after leaving school, lived in continuing affluence and sometimes considerable power.

Shared class privilege shaped the boys' sexuality. Towards women of their own class, they learned to cultivate respect and distance: relationships here meant marriage. Towards other women, another ethic applied. Interviewees mentioned the practice of *chaneo*, where elite boys formed short, casual liaisons with working-class women. These sexual encounters gave great prestige in the boys' peer groups, though they had to be concealed from school authorities and parents.

Such studies of elite masculinities or femininities are not common, but they do exist, and they are important. They demonstrate that the active, creative learning of gender does not necessarily lead towards openness and equality. Gender projects *may* be directed towards the making and re-making of privilege.

Gender transitions

Different cultures have classified people in different ways. There are not only the two groups women and men; there may also be third genders, or subdivisions of two – for instance, different social positions for women before and after menopause – that seem to multiply the gender categories in which people may live.

This question has intrigued researchers. There is an ethnographic literature about the 'two-spirit' people of indigenous cultures in the south-western region of North America (Williams 1986). Two-spirit people have male bodies, a social position closer to that of women than of men, and great spiritual power. Javanese society traditionally provided a space for '*banci*', people with male bodies and women's dress, who typically have straight men as sexual partners. In Brazil there are *travesti*, often in poverty and making their living as sex workers, who are physically male but feel themselves feminine, and have sex with men within a sexual culture that makes a strong distinction between the insertive and the receptive partner. In South Asia there is a variety of gender-crossing groups. The best-known are the *hijra*, whose lives are shaped by caste and kinship, religion and poverty as well as by individual gender projects, and who have a ritual role in local society (Reddy 2006).

These groups are all different from each other, and it is debatable whether the idea of a 'third gender' helps to understand them. Certainly such patterns can change, a fact well shown in Thailand (Jackson 1997). Even within the gender order of the global North, supposedly binary, there are a number of ways people move across the boundaries between man and woman.

People who somehow live across gender boundaries, who don't just dip in and out, have fascinated researchers. From the early days of sexuality and gender studies, such folk have appeared in the pages of reports as a kind of intriguing monster. Richard von Krafft-Ebing, whose disdainful *Psychopathia Sexualis* (1886) was both a founding text of medico-legal sexology and an under-the-counter best-seller, collected lurid cases of 'mental hermaphroditism'. The genial Havelock Ellis devoted over a hundred pages of his *Studies in the Psychology of Sex* (1928) to 'Eonism', his term for thorough-going gender inversion, named after the Chevalier d'Éon, a French aristocrat who had at different times presented as a man and as a woman. Even the great Sigmund Freud (1911) did it: his discussion of the case of Dr Schreber examines gender-change beliefs in a case of psychosis.

Many years later transsexuals, as such people came to be called in the 1950s, still appeared to psychiatrists and sociologists as a kind of natural experiment exposing the mechanisms of the gender system. We now have a good understanding of how transsexualism came to be defined as a medical syndrome in the global North, and the controversy among doctors that resulted (Stryker 2008). Interested readers will find many of the key documents in the first edition of Susan Stryker and Stephen Whittle's admirable *Transgender Studies Reader* (2006).

The rise of performative theories of gender sparked great interest in gender variations and fluidity. By changing the performative actions, many people thought, we should be able to create non-normative gender, or even escape gender altogether. This version of queer theory influenced a transgender movement that emerged in the United States in the 1990s. It emphasized the instability of gender boundaries, rejected the 'binary' of male vs female, and argued for the fluidity of gender identity. 'Transgender' and 'trans' have become umbrella terms for a variety of identities and projects, rather than names for specific groups (for a recent review see Pearce et al. 2019).

Viviane Namaste in *Invisible Lives* (2000) challenged this transgender discourse. She argued that the real-life experiences, subjectivities and needs of transsexual men and women were being erased by queer theory as well as by government agencies. Simply accessing health care and social services, as Namaste's research in Canada showed, can be very difficult. Yet state agencies, and institutions more widely, are vitally important for transsexual women. How they are treated by the police, schools and hospitals really matters. Namaste's studies in her important book *Sex Change, Social Change* (2011) show the multiple struggles for recognition, livelihood and safety that have been carried on – in prisons, in the media, in universities, in social services and in human rights forums.

Namaste's argument links to the realities of gender-crossing lives in the global South, such as those of *hijra* groups in South Asia. Most groups who live across gender boundaries are exposed to stigma, poverty and violence, often severe. They have been targets of death squads engaged in 'social cleansing' in Christian Central America. They are subject to severe repression in some, though not all, Islamic countries (more on this shortly). The narratives of their lives, recorded in researchers' interviews and in autobiographies such as the South African collection *Trans* (Morgan et al. 2009), emphasize the *intransigence* of gender rather than its fluidity. These gender projects have continuity over time – however wrong in terms of conventional social embodiment they may seem.

An example from Latin America shows the social realities involved. Fernando Serrano-Amaya's (2018) profound study of sexual politics and social upheaval in Colombia includes the life-story of Zoraya, a *chica trans* activist in the Caribbean coastal region. Zoraya was brought up as a boy in a working-class family. She left school at 13, about the time she found the social world of *travestis*. The family tried to wrench her out of this milieu by force; the effort failed. Zoraya learnt the trade of hairdressing, and like others in her family she has moved around the region looking for work and avoiding the worst violence. Colombia was going through a long-running, complex and bitter civil war. Zoraya has often faced death threats or actual violence, and she has learnt impressive survival skills: how to negotiate, how to joke, how to fight back physically, and how to judge the moment to escape. Serrano-Amaya's narrative includes the dramatic story of how Zoraya survived for a time in a village controlled by an armed right-wing paramilitary group, accustomed to killing and usually hostile to social deviance. Her resilience is truly remarkable.

What exactly is involved in transition? There are excellent studies and moving autobiographies of transsexual men (Rubin 2003; Nery 2011). However I will focus on the situation of transsexual women, who have attracted most of the attention and controversy. I should say that this is also my own situation, so there is an element of autobiography here.

Transition generally starts with an experience of contradictory embodiment. Transsexual women describe this experience in varying ways: as having a man's body and a woman's body at the same time, or one emerging from the other, or – the traditional one – being trapped in the wrong body. These figures of speech have aroused scorn, but they do highlight the importance of social embodiment. Transsexuality is best understood, not as a syndrome or as a discursive position, but as a bundle of life trajectories that arise from contradictions in social embodiment. Transsexual women's narratives speak sometimes of a dramatic moment, sometimes of a gradually growing awareness, in either case recognizing as a *fact* about oneself, being a woman despite having a male body.

But this recognizing is a fearful thing, because the central contradiction in transsexuality is so powerful. This fact is at odds with what other people *know* – such as Zoraya's family insisting she was a boy – which the transsexual woman knows too. And there is no walking away from this terror: gender is intransigent, both as a structure of the society and as a structure of personal life. Some transsexual women try to keep the contradiction inside their skins, and ride out the terror. Some kill themselves; it is not known how many, but there are certainly high rates of what the psychologists call 'suicidal ideation' – that is, thinking about it – and actual attempted suicide. Moving towards transition is an attempt to end this precarious practice and achieve a settlement.

Because the contradiction is one of embodiment, transition usually involves modifications to the body. This is done with medical help, in rich countries and in the privileged classes of other countries. Poor people may have no alternative to black-market hormones and amateur surgery. Either way the process is traumatic; Claudine Griggs (1996) has written a superb narrative of her reassignment surgery, that makes this clear. Though media and scholarly attention have focused obsessively on the surgery, that is only a part of the medical treatment, and medical treatment is only part of transition. A huge amount of other work has to be done: raising funds; getting personal support, post-operative care and legal documentation; finding housing; dealing with relationship crises; dealing with a workplace or finding work; dealing with bodily changes; gaining social recognition; and dealing with hostility. Zoraya for instance learned a feminine trade, migrated to find work and safety, learned to negotiate and fight. She won at least partial recognition, and later campaigned for recognition for others.

Transsexual women follow varied strategies in dealing with families, employers and other relationships. Research in the United States has shown contrasting workplace strategies (Schilt and Wiswall 2008; Catherine Connell 2010). Some conceal their stories – the 'stealth' strategy – while others are not only open about their transition, but contest sexist beliefs and practices. These studies had mainly middle-class samples. Working-class transsexual women often have no alternative but to survive by sex work.

As Harriet (chapter 2) found, there is a certain clientele of straight men who are excited by transsexual bodies. But this does not mean they respect them. Roberta Perkins' presentation of the voices of transsexual women in Sydney, in her pioneering study of trans lives, includes Naomi, a stripper who remarked:

> I think men have a definite dislike for women in general, that's why women are raped and bashed, and strippers are up there to provide an outlet for this dislike by the yelling of profanities at them. Transsexuals are lower down than women according to men, and look how many men sexually abuse transsexuals. (Perkins 1983: 73)

Sex work is a precarious milieu, exposing transsexual women to high levels of HIV infection and violence.

The work of gender transition engages all the dimensions of the gender order, it is not only about sexuality or identity. It is structured by gender inequalities: the process is not the same for transsexual women and transsexual men. Transsexual women shed the patriarchal dividend that generally accrues to men in labour markets, families, professions, etc. A small but illuminating econometric study by Kristen Schilt and Matthew Wiswall (2008) in the United States found there was an economic penalty in transition for both men and women. But transsexual men eventually were better paid after transition than before, while transsexual women lost, on average, nearly one-third of their income.

In gender transition, a great deal rests on the responses of others. Transition puts marriages at acute risk: a wife's position in the gender order is seriously challenged, and may be traumatically undermined, by a husband's moves towards transition. (The legalizing of 'gay marriage' eases this problem, for some.) With transsexual women's children, too, relationships may end at transition. Responses from the wider environment are also important. Sunni Islam, like Catholic Christianity, is negative towards transition. But the highest religious authority in Shi'ite Islam, the Iranian ayatollah Khomeini, issued a *fatwa* (religious ruling) approving the principle of gender transition. This ruling has become famous. In the Islamic republic of Iran, therefore, transsexual women have a legal existence. They live constrained lives, like other women in this patriarchal gender order, but they do have a degree of legitimacy (Najmabadi 2014).

In the 1970s, some radical feminists in the United States and Britain strongly rejected transsexual women. For a time this was taken to be the standard feminist view. Attitudes in the women's movement gradually changed towards inclusiveness, which is the usual position now. Transsexual lives can be made harder, as Namaste says, by denial of recognition from institutions or movements. Yet these lives do show the potential for change in the historical process of social embodiment. At the very least, they enrich the project of gender justice that feminism has launched.

7

Work, economy and globalization

Most discussions of gender focus on issues in personal life, from sexualities to identities. That is understandable: gender problems often come to a head in person-to-person relationships. But to grasp what happens at this level we must also take into account institutions, economies, ideologies and governments. This chapter examines gender in the gritty material world of work and organizational life, starting with gendered labour processes, and working up the scale to the global economy.

Gendered labour

The Canadian researchers Pat Armstrong and Hugh Armstrong began a chapter of their *Theorising Women's Work* (1990: 57) with these remarks:

> Although some feminist theorists focused on what women and men think, others began their analyses of women's work by concentrating on what women and men actually do. They looked at the jobs women have in the labour force, at the work they perform in the household, and at the relationship between these two kinds of work.

I will follow this excellent advice. The richest information about gendered labour comes from close-focus studies, often combining ethnographic observation in workplaces with detailed interviews with the workers.

Some of the best studies focus not on women but on men. A classic is Cynthia Cockburn's book *Brothers* (1983), a study of masculinity among printing workers in England. Cockburn traced how young men entering the compositors' trade were trained by the older workers, not only in the technical skills, but much more broadly in the rituals, jokes, view of the world, and sense of brotherhood that went to make up a masculinized occupational culture. This culture had formed when compositors had to manipulate dirty metal type at speed in a factory-like workplace. It was sustained through a dramatic technological change, in which the job came to be done on keyboards in an office-like environment. The old culture remained valuable to the workers in conflicts with the bosses; it also continued to exclude women.

The same approach can be taken to heavy industry. This was done by a high-powered Canadian team studying a large steel plant in Hamilton, Ontario. Stelco had been a strongly masculinized workplace, with a local culture not too different from the printing shop: sexualized joking, male bonding (in the language of the period), and of course men-only facilities such as toilets. But here an attempt was being made, supported by the union, to break down gender exclusion and bring women workers into steelmaking. The mixed response from the men is vividly described in the book *Recasting Steel Labour* (Corman et al. 1993). The campaign was, ultimately, undermined not by the workers but by the bosses, who downsized the plant in the face of deregulation and global competition.

Workplace studies of masculinity have also been done in the global South, for instance the project with South African gold miners discussed in chapter 2 (Moodie 1994). Such research continued to diversify in the new century. There is some fascinating work on firefighters in Sweden and Britain, looking at the role of technology, traditions of masculine heroism, and the unpleasant tactics of harassment and exclusion through which firefighting has been preserved as a men's domain (Baigent 2016; Ericson and Mellström 2016). Kris Paap's *Working Construction* (2006) looked at the building industry in the United States, asking 'why white working-class men put themselves – and the labor movement – in harm's way'. This is not a metaphor. Industrial accidents are common in construction. Generally, heavy labour wears down the worker's body over a working life. A respected model of working-class masculinity accepts this as the price to be paid for being a breadwinner and supporting a family.

Studies of women's occupations, too, have used close-focus methods. In cases such as nursing and early childhood education, cultural definitions of femininity influenced the way an occupation was constructed. In other cases they did not. Factory labour, for instance, is not usually coded feminine. But there have always been women in cotton mills and other factories since the dawn of the industrial revolution.

In Britain at almost the same time as Cockburn's study of men in printing, Miriam Glucksmann published *Women on the Line* (1982). This was based on seven months' participant-observation when the author became one of the workers in a motor vehicle component assembly plant. Glucksmann's report gives vivid pictures of the bosses, daily life on the production line, and how life on the job connected with home life. In this plant there was a rigid gender division of labour. Women were employed only in the low-paid routine jobs. Their promotion was blocked, while men could get twice the wage for doing easier jobs. 'It was obvious that the only qualification you needed for a better job was to be a man.' The women were disillusioned about men, and supported each other in daily conflicts with male supervisors. But their poverty, fatigue, household demands, and the gender segregation of working-class life in Britain made effective organizing almost impossible.

Secretarial work also involves gender hierarchy, but this story is more tangled. In the mid-twentieth century being a secretary was archetypal 'women's work', as the Australian sociologist Rosemary Pringle shows in her book *Secretaries Talk* (1989). It didn't start that way. Being a clerk in an office was originally a man's job, as described in Herman Melville's grim short story 'Bartleby the Scrivener' (1853). With the advent of the typewriter and the growing scale of office work, clerical work increasingly involved women. The specific occupational role of secretary evolved as a combination of keyboard and filing skills with organizational know-how. It also, crucially, included the emotion work of managing social relations in the office, projecting glamour, and looking after the male manager's personal business. This is the secretary as shown in numberless Hollywood comedies and romances from *The Office Wife* in 1930 onward (though fifty years later the office wife revolted in the movie *9 to 5*).

Women continue to do such work today, re-named 'administrative assistant' or 'personal assistant'. The US Census found that between 2006 and 2010, 96 per cent of the 4 million workers with jobs that fell under the category 'secretaries and administrative assistants' were women. But with the advent of the personal computer and word processing programs, clerical labour is once again being done on a large scale by men. Nowadays it is commonly mixed with other tasks rather than treated as a separate job. A corporate executive may read and answer a couple of hundred e-mails and text messages in a day. Academics, male or female, typically spend hours each day in front of a computer screen doing multiple forms of clerical work.

A theme repeatedly shown in the ethnographies is the relationship between gender in the workplace and gender in the home. In the bread-winner–housewife couple, each of these patterns is defined by the other, and the overall division of labour takes a clear-cut masculine-vs-feminine shape. When in 1971 the English researchers Jan and Raymond Pahl published 'a study of career and family relationships in the middle class', they called it *Managers and their Wives*. Readers could assume that all of the managers were men and none of the wives were managers.

Several decades later, Judy Wajcman (1998) published her research about a new generation in the same country. Women managers had now appeared: that much had changed. Yet the most poignant material in Wajcman's study reveals their struggle to succeed in corporations that still assumed managers had wives to look after their homes. Under the pressure of long hours and intensive work practices, the women had to arrange their domestic lives to suit the corporation – hiring other women to do the housework, doing a double shift themselves, or remaining single.

The fact that some managers hired other women for domestic labour is an important issue. Several generations earlier, middle-class English families would *normally* hire working-class women as cooks, maids or housekeepers. Ruling-class households would have both men and women servants in an elaborate, gender-divided hierarchy (as pictured in the nostalgic television series *Upstairs Downstairs*). Working-class households were unlikely to have servants but might have a variety of adults – grandparents, grown children, other relatives, boarders – living under the same roof. The two-adult 'nuclear family' is far from being the universal template.

In the important theoretical text on gender mentioned in chapter 4, Teresita de Barbieri (1992) presented women's domestic service as one of the significant economic and political complexities of Latin American gender orders. Employer–employee tensions between women make it hard to establish solidarity on gender lines, and create zones of uncertainty as the economy evolves. As social inequality has risen in recent decades in China, domestic servants known by the euphemism *baomu* ('protecting mother') have reappeared in large numbers. They are often poor women migrating from the countryside; their story is well told in Yan Hairong's *New Masters, New Servants* (2008). An international trade in domestic labour has also developed. Peruvian women go to Chile, Filipina women travel in very large numbers to East and South Asia, while other women travel from Moldava in Eastern Europe to domestic service in Turkey (Chang and Ling 2000; Keough 2006).

There are also men who migrate to do this work. Cleaning, cooking, and caring for the elderly have no necessary connection with female bodies. (Nor, apart from breast-feeding, does caring for young children, though it is widely assumed this is a natural task for women.) Ester Gallo and Francesca Scrinzi (2016) spent many years studying migrants in Italy who do this kind of work, and their report on migrant men is very illuminating. Local men as well as local women are their employers. Men are quite capable of care work and some take great pride in it, though others treat it in strict economic terms as just a job. Doing stereotypically women's work may involve a re-working of conventional ideas about masculinity.

Workplace gender inequalities have often been entrenched in law. In a famous case in the Australian industrial court in 1919, which set wage standards across the country, the judge determined that women's basic wage would be 54 per cent of the basic wage for men. It was assumed that only men had a family to support, and employers should not be burdened with unnecessary costs. A whole century of struggle by working-class women for equal pay followed. The women's basic wage was officially raised by the court to 75 per cent of the men's rate in 1949, and finally to 100 per cent in 1969. Equal pay for equal work was achieved – in legal principle. But in practice, a gender gap in wage rates continued. It still exists fifty years after the Equal Pay Case decision. So the struggle continues (Risse 2019).

The ethnographic studies of gendered labour sometimes show divisions between men's and women's work that are deeply entrenched and hard to shift: Glucksmann's factory study is a case in point. But in other cases, change is prominent. Printing and secretarial work have been changed by tremendous technological shifts; middle management and some professional roles have opened up to women; paid domestic labour has changed from a highly personal form of dependence to a market-based service industry.

Even in occupations that are strongly gender-typed, there are often some workers of the 'wrong' gender. Their experience may be very helpful in understanding the pressures and tensions of gendered work. The US sociologist Christine Williams developed this idea in an influential book *Gender Differences at Work: Women and Men in Nontraditional Occupations* (1989). Williams' interviews included men working as nurses, and women working in the US Marine force. She found that the two situations were not equivalent. It was not just a question of being a minority in a gendered occupation: position in the larger gender order also mattered. Men in nursing, for instance, are more likely to get promotion into nursing management than their numbers would suggest.

There are also studies of occupations that are not gender-typed to the extent secretarial work, nursing, printing and military forces have been. Both men and women are present in large numbers in teaching, restaurant service and retail. Does this mean that gender is absent from working life in teaching, restaurant service and retail? Far from it. Gender is likely to shape the conditions of employment: it is more common for women's jobs to be part-time or insecure, partly because of the pressure on women to do childcare. Gender often influences specialization within an occupation. In the education sector, one of the largest, women generally predominate in kindergarten and elementary school teaching, men predominate in higher education teaching, with secondary school teaching balanced between. To give the figures for just one country: in Italy in 2017, women were 95.6 per cent of teachers in primary schools, 70.2 per cent of teachers at secondary (high) schools, and 37.1 per cent of teachers in tertiary education, i.e. colleges and universities (OECD 2020). These differences between sectors are found in most countries, though the overall balance of women and men in the teaching workforce may be higher or lower. Within high schools and universities, men are more likely to be in engineering and mathematics departments, women in humanities and performing arts. There are complex contours in gendered work.

Finally, it is useful to think about *not* having an occupation: that is, being unemployed. That condition may itself have a gendered meaning. To be 'unemployed' one must first be in the labour force, prepared to take a job. Though women's rate of labour force participation has risen in most parts of the world, it is still well below that of men, as noted in chapter 1. The classic photographs of unemployed workers' marches from the Great Depression of the 1930s are overwhelmingly pictures of men. That seems to be usual in economic downturns. At other times, however, unemployment rates for men and women are broadly similar. When *under*-employment is added in, from an economist's point of view women may have a higher rate of under-utilized labour than men do.

Further, what one does as an unemployed worker may be gendered. In a fascinating study of an unemployed workers' movement in Argentina, Cecilia Espinosa (2013) shows how women were expected, as well as doing domestic work in their homes, to do it for the movement. They were expected to staff the canteen, do the childcare, and so on. A maternalist construction of femininity in the broader society carried over into unemployment. It was only when the women *piqueteras* began to articulate gender grievances and organize separately, that the movement as a whole was pushed to a declaration for gender equality.

Gendered corporations and markets

The corporation is the key institution of the worldwide capitalist economy. There were 7.4 million corporations in the United States in 2010, according to taxation statistics. Most were small, but more than 2,000 held assets of $2.5 billion each. Transnational corporations are the main players in the international economy. The biggest have workforces in the hundreds of thousands: both Foxconn and Volkswagen had over 660,000 employees in 2018 while Walmart had 2.2 million. They have profits (and sometimes losses) in the tens of billions, Apple making $260 billion profit in 2019. The larger TNCs have annual revenues bigger than the entire national product of small countries.

Corporations are gendered institutions, with a gendered history. 'Companies' of merchants in early modern Europe were entirely composed of men. When ownership began to be divided up and turned into a kind of commodity itself, with the creation of joint-stock companies and the first stock exchanges, these too were socially defined as men's institutions. These facts only came into focus when the new feminism challenged conventional economic and organization theory. The change is marked by the work of Rosabeth Kanter in the United States, whose book *Men and Women of the Corporation* appeared in 1977. Kanter criticized the absence of gender awareness in organization research, and showed how the gender regimes of the organizations themselves shaped men's and women's careers, rather than any gender differences in personality.

Over the next three decades, social research on corporate life built up. Some of the studies have already been mentioned: Hochschild's (1983) research on emotion work in airlines and debt agencies, and Pringle's (1989) study of secretaries. Some of the best research has focused on manual workers in large-scale industries, as shown in the last section.

Gender divisions are also strong in corporate agriculture, which is now transforming rural life across the world. A fascinating oral-history study in Chile by Heidi Tinsman (2000) describes the export-oriented fruit industry created under the Pinochet dictatorship. The companies engaged in this business recruited women workers on a large scale. Some surprises followed. When rural women had command of an income, and were able to make shopping trips and purchasing decisions with their own money, it changed the balance of power with their husbands. The segregated work groups created by the employers provided an alternative to domestic isolation, and led to new connections among women. In both ways the process eroded the dictatorship's patriarchal ideology, which defined women basically as mothers.

As this research built up, a theory of gendered organizations emerged (Acker 1990). The key idea was that gender discrimination is not an accidental feature of bureaucracy, which can be fixed by changing a few attitudes. Gender is a structural feature of corporate and bureaucratic life, linked to gender relations in other sectors of society. Gender shapes job definitions, understandings of 'merit' and promotion, management techniques, marketing and a whole lot more (Mills and Tancred 1992).

The analysis of gender in workplaces has become steadily more sophisticated since those beginnings. There is increasing attention to informal gender relations: the #MeToo movement against sexual harassment dramatized one aspect of this. It is increasingly recognized that gender in organizations is not a rigid structure but a dynamic one. Gender is produced and constantly negotiated in organizational processes (Gherardi and Poggio 2001; Martin 2003).

In the United States significant numbers of women have now reached middle management, and there is a familiar image of the 'glass ceiling' which blocks them from getting right to the top. As early as 1991 the US Congress set up a 21-person Glass Ceiling Commission to investigate the problem (Glass Ceiling Commission 1995). They found that among the biggest corporations in the United States at the time, 97 per cent of senior managers were White, and 95 to 97 per cent were men. Of the top 1,000 companies, two had women CEOs. This was thought to be progress.

Gender issues are usually thought to be about women, but with imbalances on this scale, the idea gradually dawned that these were issues about men. Managerial masculinities emerged as a research field in the 1990s, and that is still an active field of study. It is clear, for instance, that managerial masculinities change over time. The British historian Michael Roper, in a fascinating book called *Masculinity and the British Organization Man since 1945* (1994), traced changes in British manufacturing firms. An older generation of managers had a hands-on relation with the production process, identified themselves closely with the firm and the quality of the product, and took a paternalistic interest in the engineering workers. With the growing power of finance capital in the British economy, a new cadre of managers appeared. They are also men, but are more oriented to accountancy and profit, less interested in the technology and the product, and not much interested in the workers. A more generic and ruthless managerial masculinity has taken over.

Capitalist economies are turbulent: markets expand and collapse, industries rise and fall, corporations restructure themselves in search of profit. The deregulated, globalized economy of the twenty-first century is more open to individual promotion for a minority of women. But it also fosters a more aggressive masculinity in management, with shorter time-horizons and astonishing rewards. The ten highest-paid CEOs in US corporations are each paid more than $50 million per year, mostly as bonuses and stock options rather than as regular wages. Many other top managers of large companies get more than $10 million per year. This is the background to corporate indifference to, or active denial of, environmental problems. There is a huge personal advantage for top managers in focusing on short-term profit and stock market price.

A competitive masculinity also appears in financial markets; its form too is subject to change. Caitlin Zaloom (2006) conducted a lively ethnographic study of commodity-trading 'pits' in Chicago and London with an open-outcry method of doing business, where physical presence mattered. She found a hyper-aggressive form of masculinity, focused on self-promotion and winning in direct competitions. But the digitalization of these markets changed the noisy pits into silent computer screens, bringing in new forms of technical knowledge and requiring more advanced education. That dramatically changed the expression of masculinity in the arena of trading in financial products.

When Rosabeth Kanter studied women in corporations in the 1970s, she found that social pressures tended to reinforce traditional femininity. When Judy Wajcman interviewed women managers in the 1990s, in the study mentioned above, she found they were under heavy pressure in the other direction. They had to work the long hours, fight in the office wars, put pressure on their subordinates, and focus on profit. Wajcman found no truth in the widespread belief that women coming into management would bring a more caring, nurturing or humane style to the job. It is not surprising that she called her book *Managing like a Man*.

As economic relations become internationalized, what are the implications for managerial masculinity? A disturbing answer is given by an international merger of finance companies in Scandinavia, where gender orders are among the most egalitarian on earth. Janne Tienari and colleagues (2005) conducted interviews with the top executives of the merged firm, and found a remarkable situation. A large majority of the senior managers were men, and they did not want to hear about gender-equality problems. They took management to be naturally men's business, 'constructed according to the core family and male-breadwinner model'. The researchers concluded that the conditions of transnational business intensify the discourse of managerial masculinity as competitive, mobile and work-driven. This is strong enough to override the Scandinavian countries' public commitment to principles of gender equality.

What about the situation lower down, among the people who do the bulk of the corporations' work? Here gender relations are more diverse, as corporations have assembled large and socially complex workforces. Racial hierarchies, sexualization and class distinctions all influence workplace masculinities and femininities. Heidi Gottfried's *Gender, Work, and Economy* (2013) assembles a mass of evidence on how much manufacturing now depends on women's low-wage, precarious labour in a geographically dispersed assembly line. This can be dangerous. The risk was horribly shown in 2013 by the Rana Plaza clothing factory collapse in Bangladesh with a death toll of 1,219, most of them women.

What of the institutions that represent workers' interests in battles with corporate power – the unions? Here too we find mostly patriarchal organizations. There have been some remarkable episodes of industrial organizing among women. One was the world-famous London match-girls' strike in 1888. Another was the 1968 women's strike at the Ford car plant in Dagenham in outer London – not quite so famous, but well dramatized in the film *Made in Dagenham*. Despite these events, for generations union membership was mainly composed of men, and union leadership overwhelmingly composed of men. It has taken a long struggle to establish a voice for women through the unions, even in a country like Australia where both unionism and feminism have been strong (Franzway 2001). Resistance from men who embody an old, combative style of working-class masculinity, to whom women were hardly legitimate members of the workforce, has been a constant problem.

Yet as economies have changed, women have been a rising proportion of union membership. Three recent presidents of the Australian Council of Trade Unions (the unions' peak organization in this country) have been women, and a former union lawyer, Julia Gillard, became Prime Minister in 2010. Research by an Australian/US team (Franzway and Fonow 2011) traces feminist politics in the international arena of labour movements, and sees this, for all its difficulties, as a hopeful arena for change.

Theorizing the gendered economy

Much of the research on gendered labour and gendered corporations was framed by debates about the relationship between class and gender. European socialist thinkers in the nineteenth century, notably Engels and Bebel, raised the question of women's relation to capitalism. The orthodox view taken by socialist men, then and since, was that women's emancipation depended on the workers' movement. Class struggle was primary, and other forms of oppression such as patriarchy, racism and colonialism could not be resolved until the capitalist mode of production was replaced by socialism. A significant number of socialist women accepted this doctrine. But it created a dilemma for activists confronting gender-based violence, unequal pay and other injustices, who were trying to organize women to transform gender relations. Were they supposed to wait around until working-class men rose in revolt? Many arguments about reconciling feminist and socialist ideas have followed.

One approach takes the concept of the capitalist mode of production as its starting-point. In Marxist theory this mode of production has a fundamental class division between capitalists who own the means of production and workers who own only their own labour-power. Theorists asked how this system persisted through time. This might be explained by culture and ideology, fitting people into their economic slots. Alternatively, the key could be found in the labour required to reproduce the workforce and the social relations of capitalism. Reproductive labour could include infant and child care, shopping and cooking meals, providing sexual services, and so on. As much of this seemed to be done free of charge by wives in families, it could be understood economically as a transfer of value from women to employers. Thus capitalism indirectly exploited women. A vigorous debate arose about this analysis, known as the 'domestic labour' debate. A Wages for Housework movement arose to claim back the value of the free gift, though this did not last. Increasingly the discussion moved on to *paid* reproductive work and its connection to gender norms and more complex divisions of labour (Malos 1980; Luxton 2006).

Another approach refused to give priority to class analysis, seeing both capitalism and patriarchy as full-scale systems which might support each other or be in conflict. This became known as 'dual systems' theory. It was particularly attractive to those who saw patriarchy as an economic structure in its own right. In a famous essay, the French feminist Christine Delphy (1970) pointed out that the bulk of women's unpaid labour occurs within family relationships; that the family is a production unit; and that its output is normally placed on the market by men, who accumulate the benefits as their own property. Delphy argued that there is a patriarchal mode of production distinct from capitalism, in which women as a class are exploited. Radically, this implies that *husbands* can be seen as a class of exploiters. Delphy's work referenced small businesses, especially farms, in France, but the basic idea has wider application. In many countries men's accumulated shares in pension funds are much larger than women's accumulated funds. A recent report from the OECD (2019) found there was a 'gender gap' in pension incomes for people over 65 in *every* country that reported statistics. That is a telling sign of the economic benefits men have assembled over a working life.

Chapter 1 cited figures showing women's average wages, worldwide, are 21 per cent less than men's average wages. These figures compare the median earnings of full-time employed men and women. 'Gender gaps' also exist in the numbers who are in the paid workforce in the first place, and then in the kind of employment they mostly have. A number of different processes contribute to the surplus of resources made available to men. This surplus can be called the *patriarchal dividend*: the benefits to men as a group from maintaining an unequal gender order. This is an important structural feature of any gendered economy.

The patriarchal dividend is the benefit to men as a group. Some men get more of it than others, other men get less, or even none, depending on their location in the social order. The gendered accumulation process in advanced capitalism delivers to the most fortunate men dividends in the realm of fantasy – consider the fortunes of Jeff Bezos ($131 billion), Bill Gates ($97 billion) and Warren Buffet ($83 billion), the three richest humans in 2019. By contrast, an unemployed working-class man may draw no patriarchal dividend in an economic sense at all. Specific groups of men are excluded from parts of the patriarchal dividend, on lines of race, caste and religion. In most parts of the world homosexual men too are excluded from the authority and respect attached to men who embody hegemonic forms of masculinity; though they may, and in rich countries often do, share men's general economic advantages over women.

Some women, by being married to wealthy men or inheriting fortunes from their fathers, also draw a dividend from the gendered accumulation process. That is, they live on a profit stream partly generated by other women's underpaid work. Even women who earn wages, provided they are above average, are able to benefit from poor women doing the housework and childcare. An earlier section of this chapter noticed the growth of migrant domestic labour. This trade has allowed many middle-class women to move into professional or business careers, without putting pressure on middle-class men to raise their share of domestic labour.

The situation addressed by gender theorists fifty years ago has certainly not remained the same. This is well illustrated by changes in Japan. The Japanese economic miracle of the postwar years centred on powerful manufacturing corporations – Toyota, Sony, Honda and their like – which offered male employees lifelong security and popularized the conformist *sarariiman* (salaryman) model of middle-class masculinity. Ethnographic research showed a sharp gender hierarchy in Japanese corporate life, with male managers offered permanency and promotion, women subordinated in secretarial work and expected to leave on marriage (Ogasawara 1998). This regime, Heidi Gottfried (2015) argues, rested on a reproductive bargain. The Japanese state promoted a gender order where women ran the home, following *ryosai kenbo*, the ideology of 'good wife, wise mother', while men achieved security as bread-winners in the corporate world.

But this was always, in part, an illusion. Japanese capitalism rested on a large half-hidden world of non-standard employment with much less security. When expansion faltered, housewives were urged back into the workforce. Towards the turn of the century, Gottfried suggests, the scale of precarious employment grew and the reproductive bargain unravelled. We know from the research of Taga Futoshi and others, that this was the moment when the salaryman model of masculinity was seriously challenged, and more diverse and caring patterns of masculinity were explored (Roberson and Suzuki 2003).

From the 1970s, intensifying in the 1980s, a package of changes in capitalist economies spread globally: deregulation and internationali-zation of markets, privatization of public assets and services, reduction of taxes, rising power of finance, and increased reliance on computers and electronic communication. These pressures broke up tightly-regulated national economies such as Japan's, and led many theorists to think a new phase of capitalism had arrived. Pamela Odih, for instance, in *Gender and Work in Capitalist Economies* (2007), pictures a shift from Fordist Times, where the tightly-controlled production line and the full-time breadwinner were the paradigm; to Post-Fordist Times marked by flexible labour, just-in-time production and precarious jobs; and then to Global Times where production processes are parcelled out across global assembly lines and jobs migrate to where the labour is cheapest.

Gathering themes from recent feminist thought on several continents, the German sociologist Ilse Lenz (2017) argues that if we are prepared to speak of flexibilized capitalism, we could equally speak of a flexibilized gender order. Among the indicators: the multiplication of gender categories, the fragmentation of labour markets, the advent of more women to political authority, and the greater variety of family forms. At a global level too, there is more recognition of diversity among modern gender orders. These trends are not uniform, and they are opposed by powerful forces, but it is hard to deny their relevance. The older and simpler models of patriarchy now have to be re-thought in new historical conditions.

These debates concern economies as they are, but feminist thought also concerns economies as they should be. Alternatives to capitalist development have been explored by Australian economic geographers Kathy Gibson and Julie Graham (who, before Graham's death, wrote together under the name J. K. Gibson-Graham). In their book *The End of Capitalism (As We Knew It)*, Gibson-Graham (1996) argued that what we usually understand as a 'capitalist system' is in fact an assemblage of capitalist and non-capitalist enterprises, finance and property relations. Non-market relations and practices survive alongside commodified ones.

In their last article written together, Gibson-Graham outlined an ethics of belonging in the time of the Anthropocene, seeking new 'assemblages that are experimenting with new practices of living and being together' (Gibson-Graham 2011: 4). This was not just theoretical. They researched local initiatives such as employee-owned businesses that contribute to local sustainability, alternative currency projects in the United States, and a fresh produce cooperative in Australia. These examples illustrate less exploitative connections to the non-human world, and more sustainable development pathways.

Globalization

Connections between gender activists in different parts of the world are not new. Kartini in Java, at the beginning of the twentieth century, could rely on support from women in the Netherlands (chapter 4). International women's organizations have existed for more than a century, such as the Women's International League for Peace and Freedom, founded during the First World War and still going today.

There has been much more attention to this question since the United Nations Decade for Women (1975–85). A series of high-profile world conferences on women created a global forum for these concerns and crystallized a policy agenda around women's interests (Bulbeck 1988). This reflects an important reality in gender relations today. There are significant features of the gender order which cannot be understood locally, which require analysis on a global scale.

The process that Sarah Radcliffe et al. (2004) call 'the transnationalization of gender' is happening in all the dimensions of gender relations defined in chapter 5, including the economic. This is hardly surprising in a time when large percentages of national economies are owned by transnational capital, large sections of industry are dependent on foreign trade, and major investment decisions are made by transnational corporations.

Imperial conquest, neo-colonialism and the current world systems of power, investment, trade and communication have brought very diverse cultures and communities in contact with each other. Consequently their gender orders have interacted. This has often been a violent and disruptive process. Local gender arrangements were overthrown by slavery, indentured labour, land seizure and resettlement. Empires assaulted local gender arrangements which did not fit the colonizers' cultural templates or economic interests. Missionaries, for instance, tried to stamp out the indigenous gender-crossing traditions in North America, and what they saw as women's lasciviousness in Polynesia. The 'muu-muu' dresses sold to thousands of tourists in Hawai'i are far from being an indigenous tradition: they are the legacy of colonial religious authorities' attempts to cover up women's bodies from necks to ankles. Women's traditional rights to own land in Hawai'i were practically obliterated by the islands' American colonizers, in a process that transformed communal landholding into a system of private property in the hands of men (Stauffer 2004).

In the contemporary world, disruptions of gender orders still occur in episodes of violence, including invasions, insurrections and civil wars. Masculine violence is sustained by a global trade in weapons, all the way from handguns to fighter jets. Some of this is secretive, some is illegal, and governments report armaments deals in different ways, so it is difficult to get exact figures. Nevertheless the key research agency monitoring the situation, the Stockholm International Peace Research Institute (2020), reports that the global arms trade in 2017 amounted to *at least* $95 billion. Probably more.

An essay by Mai Ghoussoub (2000) on masculinity in Arab media, especially in Egypt, illustrates the turbulence of large-scale changes in gender relations. She starts with two strange episodes: rumours about an Israeli-invented chewing gum that makes Arab men impotent; and the sudden popularity of mediaeval courtship manuals that celebrate sex in the name of Islam. Ghoussoub argues there is a deep cultural disturbance about masculinity in the post-colonial Middle East. The context is slow economic modernization, political turbulence, and the military weakness of Arab states in the face of Israel and the United States. The increasing economic and social status of women in Arabic-speaking societies has posed dilemmas for men whose identities are still founded in patriarchal gender ideologies.

Imperialism certainly affected gender arrangements among the colonized – but also among the colonizers. Ashis Nandy (1987) shows that British rule in India changed masculinities among the British rulers, promoting simplified, power-oriented ways of being a man. The imperial pioneer and conqueror became a masculine model echoing in educational agendas in the homeland, such as the Boy Scout movement. This was founded by General Robert Baden-Powell, a British military officer who had commanded troops in frontier wars, and drew on that experience for the cultivation of manliness among British boys.

Empire and globalization created new institutions operating on a world scale, including transnational corporations, global markets, global media and transnational states (discussed in chapter 8). These institutions all have internal gender regimes, and each gender regime has its gender dynamic – interests, gender politics, and processes of change. World-spanning institutions thus created new arenas for gender formation and gender dynamics.

The term 'globalization' first came into use to describe an economic strategy for manufacturing and finance corporations in the global North. They could grow by moving beyond their national origins into markets in other regions. Though the trend had begun decades earlier, by the 1980s corporate executives and business journalists were thinking of markets as being in principle global. From that idea followed the popular belief that culture too was becoming homogeneous, or at least hybridized, across the world.

Corporations operating in global markets, such as Toyota, Microsoft, Shell, Glencore Xstrata and Allianz, are now the most powerful business organizations on the planet. They typically have a strong, though complex, gender division of labour in their workforces, and a strongly masculinized management culture. Below this level, there is now a wide spread of medium-sized corporations that operate internationally and form networks beyond the control of national governments and their policies.

How transnational businesses work as organizations, and the use they make of gender, is illuminated by Juanita Elias's (2008) study of the garment sector in Malaysia. This industry depends on a low-wage workforce mainly composed of women. Factory management is done by local men who deploy family networks and political connections to recruit women workers. These men promote an ideology of docile, productive femininity for their workers. At this level, the firms are still Taylorist and authoritarian. However, overall investment and international trade is in the hands of elite managers. These are also men, but they come from outside Malaysia. Their working world is very different. They have an ideology of 'teamwork' and make heavy use of computers, the Internet, and corporate intranets. These men maintain a close connection with the corporate world of the global North.

In the industrialized countries of the global North, large corporations formerly provided relatively secure employment for a mostly male workforce in a primary labour market. Under the neoliberal ideology and business-friendly governments of recent decades, these firms have become more tightly controlled through computerized management systems, but their workforces have become less secure and more diverse. Many of their operations are outsourced to smaller companies. The smaller companies that supply the majors or operate in the niches they leave open, often operate in secondary or informal labour markets, which provide low wages and no security of employment. It is these firms that account for most of women's industrial employment.

Multinational media corporations circulate film, video, music and news on a very large scale. So do corporate media that rely on user-generated content (Facebook, Instagram). All contain a massive supply of gender images and circulate gender meanings, and most of these are far from gender-equal. The Internet has a huge supply of pornographic sites that present women as objects of male desire and consumption. The celebrity culture that is a staple of media for women does much the same, insisting on heterosexual couples as the ideal to be admired. Sports programming for men presents a monotonous diet of aggressive, muscular masculinity. The modest excursions into change offered by programmes such as *Queer Eye for the Straight Guy* seem marginal in comparison.

International markets – capital, commodity, service and labour markets – have an increasing reach into local economies. Like international media, they are now weakly regulated. Research has shown the gendered character of markets as social institutions, with an aggressive and often misogynist culture in areas such as commodities, energy, stock and futures trading. Here is a passage from an interview with an Australian finance company executive, one of the few women who actually worked as a trader in the 'very macho culture of the dealing room' (Connell 2012b):

> In the dealing rooms, oh, full of the macho bravado, and the liar's-poker type environments. Where, you know, they're [saying] how big their positions are – the bragging, the womanizing, the whole bit. And all of which is entirely forgiven because they make a load of money … it attracts a certain type of person. [How did you survive in this environment?] I ran a futures book. Futures isn't sexy these days, but they were [then] at the sexy end of the market, they were sophisticated, and people didn't really understand what you were doing. … So they could have thought I was a green tree frog, I knew I was making money. So to that extent the simplicity of the performance criteria goes your way. But the culture was very very hostile. … You'd get the whole kit-and-caboodle, you know: the nude posters went up, and all this sort of stuff, the comment on everything you wore, and everything you did.

International state institutions will be discussed in chapter 8, but here we should note that some of the most important are directly concerned with economic affairs. They include the International Labour Organization (formed as far back as 1919), UN agencies such as the World Bank and the International Monetary Fund, and the Organisation for Economic Co-operation and Development. There are also regional unions of states, some tight and some loose: the European Union (which at one stage was called the European Economic Community), the African Union, Mercosur and others. None of these has uncontested power over the global economy, but most can bring pressures to bear that influence the economic dimension of gender.

We cannot assume a coherent global gender system, as earlier theories of universal patriarchy did. There is still enormous diversity in local gender orders. But the links between them, through the economic processes and transnational institutions just outlined, are important. Since the 2007–8 global financial crisis there has been a political backlash, with the rise of nationalist parties drumming on the theme of 'border protection'. Regimes that want to build walls, material or symbolic, range from the Orbán government in Hungary to the Trump administration in the United States. Yet their economies continue to depend on global trade, global media and global flows of finance. Their gender orders will continue to be linked.

8

Gender politics

If change in gender relations is always possible, as chapter 5 showed, then it can become the goal of social action. This is a simple definition of gender politics – the struggle to alter a gender order, or to resist change. This chapter will consider the many forms taken by gender politics, and the stakes for which people contest. This means looking at the central institution in politics, the state, in terms of its gender regimes and policies; and at the global arenas in which some of the major issues in gender politics are now fought out.

Forms of gender politics

Historically the most important movement in gender politics has been feminism. Feminist awareness and feminist campaigns are the source of most of the research discussed in chapter 3, most of the gender theories discussed in chapter 4, most of the problems discussed in chapters 6 and 7, and most of the political agendas discussed in this chapter.

Not all political movements among women are feminist. Raka Ray's (1999) study of women's politics in India gives a clear example. The Communist Party of India (Marxist), the long-term governing party in the province of West Bengal, established a women's organization called Paschim Banga Ganatantrik Mahila Samiti. This functioned mainly to implement the official line coming down from the male leadership of the Party – a line that insisted on solidarity between working-class women and men, not on the specific interests of women. Consequently the women of the Samiti, while working for women's economic and educational advance, shied away from anything that implied a direct challenge to men. They did not, for instance, make a public issue of men's violence against women, though that has been a central issue for feminists all over India.

This pattern is not peculiar to India. Postwar Japan, for instance, saw a remarkable growth of women's organizations. Women had gained the vote, and in the 1950s and 1960s were an important constituency. As Tanaka Kazuko (1977) describes, political parties controlled by men set up women's auxiliaries to claim this constituency. There were also big state-based women's organizations. But these organizations were tied to a patriarchal political system. When the Women's Liberation movement erupted, it represented a radical break. As in the United States and Europe, the claim for *autonomous* women's organization was a vital move. From that, the shape of modern gender politics has developed.

Gay Liberation, emerging in the United States at almost the same time, similarly involved autonomous organization. The movement linked personal and structural issues, and its public demonstrations, like those of Women's Liberation, produced emotions of exhilaration and common purpose. Lesbian and gay politics, however, involved also the process of 'coming out'. Making a declaration to oneself, family, friends and workmates that one belongs to a stigmatized group can be difficult, and takes time. Everyday life has to be realigned from its conventional heterosexual forms. Here the collective process depended on change in personal life; though as movements grew, they also supported personal change.

Homosexual politics had a further complication because a gender division ran through it. Lesbians and gay men are not in the same economic, social or political situation. In some countries the laws that criminalized homosexual sex for men ignored women. So did some gay male activists. Gay Liberation itself was mainly a men's movement – though the iconic action with which it began, the 1969 'Stonewall' anti-police rising in New York, was led by transsexual and transvestite sex workers.

A decade after the emergence of Gay Liberation, homosexual men's politics was transformed by the HIV/AIDS epidemic. A whole new set of relationships with doctors, science and the state had to be negotiated, at the same time dealing with a hostile symbolic politics about infection, pollution and uncleanness. Both jobs had to be done in a context of illness, bereavement and fear. Gay communities in wealthy countries not only survived this crisis, but also responded in new ways, creating AIDS support organizations and the 'safe sex' strategy (Kippax et al. 1993).

In poor countries, men who have sex with men usually lack economic resources, and may also face homophobic governments. This is a serious problem in Africa, which has the highest burden of HIV infection and illness. Governments in Senegal, Zimbabwe and Uganda have made homosexual men targets for blame and persecution, which has disrupted AIDS prevention work. They are not alone in their hostility to homosexuality, which is found in other regions especially among right-wing parties and fundamentalist religious groups.

In the 2010s, with the HIV epidemic partly mitigated by safer sex and antiretroviral drugs, the focus of gay politics in the global North shifted to achieving marriage equality. Legislative reforms removing the requirement that a legal marriage must be heterosexual have become more common. In the United States, for instance, marriage of same-sex couples became legal in one state in 2003, then in more states as public opinion shifted in favour, and finally was made legal nationally by a Supreme Court decision in 2015.

The 'gay marriage' issue called out a mobilization of conservative gender politics. Such an event is not exactly new; the women's suffrage movement was met with strong resistance a century ago. As Mala Htun's (2003) study makes clear, the intransigence of the Catholic church blocked the legalization of abortion across Latin America for a generation. (The entirely predictable outcome is that rich women can get safe abortions, poor women cannot.) Some women's groups have fought against feminism, such as REAL Women of Canada, a conservative lobby group that idealizes the 'traditional' family and campaigns against abortion, gay rights and universal access to childcare. Small 'father's rights' groups have arisen in a number of countries, which are fiercely hostile to feminism, and accuse divorce courts of being biased against men.

Since about 2010 this kind of politics has acquired a new level of ideological coherence and international organization. In Europe ultra-conservatives in the Catholic church launched a movement that attacked 'gender theory', 'gender ideology' or simply 'gender'. The target of these attacks is a caricature, made up from bits of queer theory, radical feminism and American individualism. But the caricature has been effective as politics, since it creates a moral panic about several targets of conservative fears: gay men, lesbians, feminists, sex education and women's reproductive rights. All these are seen as examples of the sinful decadence of the modern world. 'Anti-gender' and 'religious freedom' campaigns have been mounted since 2010 in a number of countries, from France, Hungary and Colombia to Australia, opposing women's and gay rights and targeting gender studies in schools and universities. In the United States fundamentalist Protestant churches and conservative militants in the Republican Party have launched attacks on transgender rights and gay marriage, and renewed their attempts to roll back women's abortion rights. (For background see Bracke and Paternotte 2016; Garbagnoli and Prearo 2017.)

Usually, however, the defence of patriarchal gender orders has not required new social movements. It has been accomplished by already-existing institutions: the state, the corporations, the media, and religious hierarchies. Most of the world's mass media are persistently anti-feminist, some of them, including the Murdoch media empire, vehemently hostile. For the most part no explicit campaign is needed. Everyday sexist practice, such as the media's trivialization and sexualization of women, and the routine functioning of institutions, does the job.

Take, for example, military forces, which are easily recognized as patriarchal institutions. Research in a number of countries – Germany (Seifert 1993), the United States (Barrett 1996), Turkey (Sinclair-Webb 2000) and others – documents an oppressive but efficient regime designed to produce a narrowly defined hegemonic masculinity, emphasizing physical hardness, conformity and a sense of elite membership. Similar patterns are found in other uniformed services such as police and firefighters (formerly known as 'firemen'). This can be a problem in bushfires, epidemics or tsunamis, when other human capacities such as empathy and caregiving are needed. Recent research on masculinities in disaster situations finds that strongly contrasting masculinities do emerge (Enarson and Pease 2016).

Institutions like armies, police forces and most churches reproduce gender hierarchies through their ordinary daily operations. Patriarchal trends can also emerge indirectly. British social scientist Sherilyn MacGregor (2009: 128) argues that the rise of a technocratic approach to climate change signals a 'masculinization of environmentalism'. Climate change is understood as a techno-scientific problem best addressed through technological innovation, and increasingly as a security issue that may require militarized responses. Alternatively, it may be seen as a problem requiring hyper-active entrepreneurship. The billionaire Richard Branson's career as a 'green capitalist' illustrates this. With immense publicity, he has supported biofuels, announced a Virgin Earth Challenge to create new technologies, held a conference on Creating Climate Wealth, and so on. Branson and other celebrity entrepreneurs perform an 'already-existing, virulent, muscular neoliberal, masculinist subjectivity reworked to fit the green capitalist agenda' (Prudham 2009: 1607).

Not all men defend patriarchy. Indeed, a 2009 CBS News Poll reported that 58 per cent of American men identified as feminist, and a smaller proportion (34 per cent) believed that a strong women's movement is still needed. Opinion poll data are not very robust by themselves, but there is something substantial behind these figures. The last generation has seen the emergence of social movements among heterosexual men, in a variety of countries, who support gender equality in practical ways. Tina Sideris (2005) describes a grassroots example in South Africa, where since the end of apartheid there has been an official commitment to gender equality, in tension with longstanding local patriarchies. A group of men in the rural Nkomazi region near the border with Mozambique are trying to move to a more respectful and gender-equal practice in their lives. All are married, with children. They have been renegotiating the gender division of labour in their households, and adopting nonviolence. But they find it difficult to shift the meaning of masculinity away from being a head of household. In the Nkomazi gender regime, the authority dimension of gender seems hardest to shift.

That is an informal movement, but organized groups campaigning for gender justice have also emerged, in the United States, Scandinavia, Germany, Chile, Mexico, India and other countries. There is an international network of such men's movements and NGOs, called MenEngage (*www.menengage.org*). Research and action programmes intended to reduce violence against women, and support engaged fatherhood, are now found in many countries and have support from the United Nations (Lang et al. 2008). Most remain small, compared to the scale of the problems.

A central feature of modern gender politics is the struggle against gender-based violence. Shelters for battered women began to be established in the early 1970s. 'Reclaim the Night' protests have been held since 1975. The first was held in Philadelphia in response to the murder of Susan Alexander Speeth whilst walking home alone. These marches are often, though not always, organized and attended by women only, and involve a speak-out or candlelight vigil. In Canada in 2011, public protests called SlutWalks were organized in response to a Toronto Police officer's advice that to remain safe 'women should avoid dressing like sluts'. SlutWalks spread to cities including London, Chicago, Philadelphia, Bhopal, Delhi and São Paulo (Borah and Nandi 2012).

In 2012 a huge outcry followed the gang-rape and murder of a young woman, Jyoti Singh, a crime committed on a bus in New Delhi. Five of the perpetrators were convicted, one as a juvenile, and years later the four adult men were hanged. In 2017, in the United States, the #MeToo movement began to spread through Twitter and other social media, in protest against workplace sexual harassment and sexual violence. Though originally about mass media figures such as Harvey Weinstein, who was convicted of crimes in 2020, the movement rapidly spread to other industries and other countries.

It is doubtful whether public outcry against gender-based violence has done much to change its prevalence. As the COVID-19 epidemic spread globally in 2020, women's advocates warned that closing workplaces and confining people to their homes was extremely likely to drive up the level of domestic violence against women. The inertia of institutions, the massive economic inequalities between women and men, and the persistence of patriarchal gender ideologies make this likely.

Gendered states

Most of the world's presidents, prime ministers, cabinet ministers, generals and civil service managers are men. Women gained legal status, and the right to vote, later than men. Though most governments today declare they are committed to gender equality, in practice things are different. A detailed survey has found that 'In much of the world, states continue to uphold laws that restrict women's ability to work, inherit, sign contracts, or act autonomously in the public sphere' (Htun et al. 2019: 194). These researchers found, remarkably, only four countries that have *no* laws that limit women's rights or contribute to workplace discrimination against women. It is usual for governments to maintain some restrictions on women, even now.

In the 1970s and 1980s, feminists in the global North made a number of attempts to theorize the state as a patriarchal institution. The main themes were: the state is the core of power relations in gender, through laws, police and military force; the state has a well-marked internal gender regime, that generally privileges men; the state makes policies with gender effects, for instance reproducing economic inequality; the state defines gender categories and relations, such as marriage; the state is the key target in gender politics; and the state as the core of gendered power is liable to crisis and change (Connell 1990).

These conclusions were drawn from both research and practical experience, and they have a certain solidity and realism. Some activists and theorists go further and see the state as always patriarchal, violent and oppressive. This has been a theme in feminist peace movements, environmentalism, struggles for abortion rights, and anti-violence work, including the shelter movement. Their rejection of the state is understandable: in some fields at least, state power in the hands of men and state controls over women are very hard to shift.

But there are other ways of viewing the state. In the light of women's changing position in Scandinavian countries, the Norwegian political scientist and labour politician Helga Hernes (1987) formulated the idea of the 'women-friendly state'. If feminist organizing from below met a positive response from above, she argued, the state could be a means towards a society of gender equality. This idea became popular since it picked up a strategy being pursued in a number of countries; but it also attracted criticism (Borchorst and Siim 2002).

Women have long been part of the state's workforce, initially in routine and low-paid jobs. Rising levels of women's education worldwide have made possible a growing role in administration and policy-making. In Australia the officials responsible for gender equality, at national and state level, were jokingly called 'femocrats'. Their story is vividly told by Hester Eisenstein – who spent some time as a femocrat herself – in her book *Inside Agitators* (1996). Special units responsible for gender equity were created within government departments, and these units set to work with great energy. They were particularly effective in public education, but also supported women's health centres, refuges, anti-violence campaigns, and anti-discrimination measures in workplaces.

By the 1990s another strategy had become influential, especially in Europe: gender mainstreaming. Rather than set up separate units, all parts of government were tasked to implement gender-equity policies in the course of their regular work. This was taken up by the UN and by many national governments, for instance in the form of gender budgets and data-collecting requirements.

A report from the Philippines suggests the difficulties this strategy met, including small budgets and lack of interest by senior bureaucrats. 'Men still dominated decision making in the political spheres, rural development agencies, rural organizations and even the homes' (Illo 2010: 149). A more recent study from Finland, a country noted for gender equality, gives an equally sharp picture of failure. Hanna Ylöstalo (2016) conducted research in that country's Ministry of Defence. There was a national policy for mainstreaming gender equity, and a high-level committee to oversee it. The high-level committee understood what it was about, but officials down the line often did not. Mainstreaming is an unfamiliar word in Finnish, there was much confusion about what practical measures were required, and there was little back-up. The legislation was soft: reform was supposed to happen harmoniously, and there were no penalties attached to non-compliance. So out in the organization there was passive resistance, with other issues given priority; or the gender policy was simply interpreted as promoting existing organizational goals of efficiency, competitiveness, etc. Very little changed.

From a broader perspective, the state is only one of society's centres of power. A familiar definition of the state is the institution that holds a monopoly of the legitimate use of force in a given territory. That definition supposes that there is agreement across the society on what is legitimate, which is not always true, and it ignores other kinds of force such as domestic violence. Husbands beating their wives to enforce obedience is a widespread practice, that used to be legal and in many communities still is acceptable. Can we regard husbands as a 'power'? Conventional political analysis does not; but husbands' right to their wives' sexual and domestic services has often been recognized in law, religion and custom.

The biggest weakness of the old model of the gendered state, however, was that it emerged from the nation-states of the global North and did not think beyond them. That model did not consider the imperial state, the post-colonial state, or the transnational state. But these forms of the state have been coming more into focus in gender research.

The gender dynamics of the imperial state have been explored for many colonies of the old empires. We have, for instance, studies of colonial-era gender legislation in Bengal (Sinha 1995), military power in Natal (Morrell 2001), and convicts, work and sexuality in Van Diemen's Land (Reid 2007).

Post-colonial states have also come in for close attention. Achille Mbembe's celebrated book *On the Postcolony* (2001) makes a withering critique of corrupt and violent patriarchal rule in one country of Central Africa. In the more recently decolonized parts of the world, including Central and Western Africa, the Middle East and North Africa, South and South-East Asia, the state structures left by colonialism lacked legitimacy and often cut arbitrarily across geographical and cultural landscapes. Many of these countries have been racked with conflict that turned into military coups or internal war. The masculinized military forces of the colonial era provided the core of many post-colonial state elites, including some of the largest, in Pakistan, Nigeria, Indonesia and Egypt.

In other countries where the leadership of guerrilla forces gained control of the post-colonial state, including Vietnam, Algeria, Zimbabwe and Cuba, the result was a one-party authoritarian regime. Even where a civilian leadership remained in control, as in India, the attempt to hold together a new republic and the drive for economic development valorized a hegemonic masculinity focused on authority and rational calculation. This regime too, in its drive for economic development, was willing to override local communities and traditions (Nandy 1987).

Particularly interesting and well-documented is the story of the Turkish state. This was the first modern republic in the Islamic world and became an important model for post-colonial regimes in the twentieth century. General Mustafa Kemal, a hero of the First World War, came to power at a time of desperate crisis, and drove out occupying forces in what amounted to a war of independence. He then led a modernizing elite in setting up a secular state. Emancipation of women was famously on Kemal's agenda from the 1920s on. Women still have a presence in Turkish public life, though there has been a strong patriarchal backlash recently (Engin and Pals 2018).

Until the current Islamist regime of Recep Tayyip Erdoğan's Justice and Development Party (AKP), the army that Kemal had created remained the dominant force in the Turkish republic. As Emma Sinclair-Webb (2000) shows in a very interesting ethnographic study, compulsory military service in Turkey has been a rite of passage into manhood, connected with national identity. But it is also a site of tension: professional soldiers, especially the officers, regard the conscripts as poor material. The army does not rely on an already-established masculinity, but tries to shape young men in a specific mould.

The army's capacity to impose its agenda, however, has run into difficulty. It could not defeat the long-running Kurdish rebellion, and it has been marginalized by the rise of political Islam, especially since the failed coup attempt in 2016. The Erdoğan regime has its own tool for shaping masculinity in the segregated religious schools it has sponsored. A recent study by Cenk Ozbay and Ozan Soybakis (2020) argues that this history has produced divided versions of hegemonic masculinity. Most are shaped by the contending political forces. But there is now another, less politicized version, a more cosmopolitan definition of Turkish masculinity that places high value on gender equality and nonviolence.

Kemal's republican regime, together with the Soviet Union in its early days, were the first notable examples of state feminism – the deliberate attempt to improve women's rights and conditions by official action from above. By the mid-1970s, versions of state feminism driven by women had emerged in a number of countries, including India (Rai and Mazumdar 2007).

This responded to a vibrant history of women's political engagement in post-colonial countries. Independence movements often attempted to mobilize women's support. It is notable that there has been extensive, and varied, activism by women in the world's biggest Muslim-majority country, Indonesia (Robinson 2009). Readers will recall the story of Kartini (chapter 4), whose memory is preserved by these movements.

From Chile and Brazil to Pakistan and Indonesia, women have become prominent political leaders and heads of government. The post-colonial state in India provided an environment in which a strong feminist movement could develop, and non-feminist women who had elite connections could rise to power. It is striking that of the five successor states to the British Indian Empire, four have had women Prime Ministers and the fifth nearly did (Burma with Aung San Suu Kyi). Sirimavo Bandaranaike, who became Prime Minister of Sri Lanka in 1960, was the first elected woman head of government in the world.

A comparative study of Chile and Nigeria by Philomina Okeke-Ihejirika and Susan Franceschet (2002) points to specific conditions for the success of state feminism. In Chile, women were prominent in the struggle against the Pinochet dictatorship. Feminists gained access to the top levels of state power during the transition to democracy. In 2006 Michelle Bachelet, a social democrat who had been part of the resistance, was elected President of Chile. But in Nigeria, though women were involved in the struggle for independence, and though feminist groups have persisted, the post-independence military regimes had no place for feminist ideas. Instead, they promoted tame women's organizations led by the wives of the real rulers – borrowing the US idea of the 'first lady'. These organizations pursued a mild welfare agenda and a conservative view of women's place.

The Chinese revolution tells another story of containment. The Maoist slogan 'women hold up half the sky' was an attack on feudal attitudes and laws which had previously enforced the subordination of women (Stacey 1983). Working-class and peasant women have always been part of the workforce, and women recruited into factory work drove the 'south China economic miracle' of the 1980s and 1990s. But apart from one case of nepotism, women have not been admitted to the political leadership. In the hybrid-capitalist China ruled by Mao's successors, the top levels of national power are entirely held by men.

Plainly all states are gendered, but their gendering varies a great deal. This is the underlying idea of a recent global study by Mala Htun and Laurel Weldon, *The Logics of Gender Justice: State Action on Women's Rights Around the World* (2018). Htun and Weldon compiled a huge bank of information about policies and their implementation in 70 countries over 30 years, 1975–2005. They found the issues could be sorted into three dimensions, which they called status politics (e.g. voting rights, anti-violence measures), doctrinal politics (e.g. abortion rights, which contest religious doctrines), and class politics (e.g. women's economic rights). Advances and retreats on one of these dimensions could occur independently of others: for instance, government action on status issues like violence was easier to get than on doctrinal issues. The global picture, it seems, is very diverse – but not completely random.

Htun and Weldon's research involved a huge effort, but was not designed to provide information for campaigns for gender justice. There are other approaches designed for that. A notable example is the 'social watch' methodology developed in Chile by the Grupo Iniciativa Mujeres, later broadened across Latin America. It was described by the project coordinator Teresa Valdés as 'a strategy for citizen monitoring of gender equity'. The ICC (*Indice de compromiso cumplido*, index of achieved commitments) is not based on an abstract definition of gender justice. It is based on the specific policy commitments locally embedded in national legislation, administrative rules or adoption of international agreements, which can be leveraged by social movements. The ICC has three kinds of indicators: measures of 'political will', such as enactment of gender quota laws; measures of 'process', such as municipal programmes for domestic violence victims; and measures of 'result', such as the ratio between men's and women's incomes (Valdés 2001; Valdés et al. 2003).

State policy about gender relations constantly involves men. This is shown clearly in Turkey, where different parts of the state have pursued conflicting agendas for the shaping of hegemonic masculinities. Other states have encouraged men to work towards gender equality. Scandinavian countries have most experience with this, described in Øystein Holter's *Can Men Do It? Men and Gender Equality – the Nordic Experience* (2003). Only a few generations ago, the Nordic countries were socially conservative places with sharp gender divisions of labour. They now lead the world in women's representation in the public realm, men's involvement in childcare, and other measures. The state's role in that change has been crucial, for instance in providing financial support for fathers' involvement in the care of young children. Men do change, Holter argues, and public policy can make the difference.

But many states have been changing in the last generation in ways that make power *less* accountable to women. Women's increased presence in the public realm is counterbalanced by a decline of the public realm itself. The economic policies sometimes called 'neoliberalism' – deregulating markets, reducing taxes and public services, and privatizing public assets – have the effect of transferring wealth and power into institutions dominated by men.

These trends have hollowed out welfare sectors on which large numbers of women depend, for resources and for jobs. They also affect the gendered relations between society and nature. The case of water privatization in post-colonial states has been well documented by feminists (Larner and Laurie 2010), arguing that pro-market policies commodify water ecosystems. Care for people and for environment is marginalized by the pursuit of profit. Not surprisingly, these policies are implemented through the narrowly-focused managerial masculinity described in chapter 7. Privatizing water was supposed to be inclusive for women, but actually reaffirms neoliberal individualism (Roberts 2008).

Partly because of the greater insecurity created by deregulated economies, there has recently been a striking surge of neo-conservative and nationalist political movements. Some have successfully used populist methods to gain power; and once in office, they promote an authoritarian model of masculinity. The Orbán regime in Hungary, the Modi government in India and the Trump administration in the United States are examples. The most striking case, however, is the Putin regime in Russia. Elizabeth Wood's (2016) examination of Putin's strategy shows how a display of hypermasculinity has been an integral part of his politics. The image involves not just the famous photos of the man bare-chested on his horse, but also his media displays of dominance through rough language and aggressive treatment of interviewers and opponents.

We have come a long way from the idea of the state as simply patriarchal, and also from the idea of the women-friendly state. Both models represent real possibilities, but trends towards them are open to contestation and are sometimes reversed. We can say something more. The state not only reflects, it also *forms* gender patterns and gender relations. State agencies, whether they intend it or not, are active players in the gender order.

Gender politics on a world scale

The old colonial empires were in themselves a kind of transnational state. Some turned into large nation-states, notably Russia and the United States. The others broke up, through independence struggles, into separate nation-states – often still connected by language, trade and investment links, and military alliances.

As the old empires declined, there has been a striking growth of institutions that link territorial states without themselves having a territorial base. They include the International Labour Organization, the League of Nations, the United Nations, UN agencies such as the World Bank, International Monetary Fund and World Health Organization, and the rich countries' Organisation for Economic Co-operation and Development. There are also regional unions of states such as the European Union, the African Union and Mercosur.

Mostly the gender regimes of these agencies copy those of the conventional states that gave rise to them. They are mainly staffed and controlled by men, as Cynthia Enloe's (1990) pioneering study of gender in the diplomatic world showed. Negotiations between states, over economic relations or military and security issues, are still mainly conducted by men. UN Women (2019) summarizes the position:

> Women continue to be largely excluded from negotiating peace. ... Between 1992 and 2018, women constituted 13 per cent of negotiators, 3 per cent of mediators and only 4 per cent of signatories in major peace processes tracked by the Council on Foreign Relations.

Yet women have gained some ground in the arena of international relations. The United Nations set up a Commission on the Status of Women as early as 1946, and later established several global agencies to pursue gender equality. In 2010 these were merged into the single body called UN Women. International aid agencies now generally have women's or gender programmes, and many NGOs do the same.

There are widely known policy documents supporting gender equality. The most famous is the 1948 *Universal Declaration of Human Rights*, which forbids discrimination on the basis of sex (as well as other grounds, notably race) in its Article 2. Also well-known are the 1979 UN *Convention on the Elimination of All Forms of Discrimination against Women*, known as CEDAW, and the wide-ranging *Beijing Declaration* from the Fourth UN World Conference on Women in 1995. When the United Nations adopted its Millennium Development Goals in 2000, one of the eight major goals was to 'promote gender equality and empower women'. This was repeated and expanded in the Sustainable Development Goals adopted in 2015.

Democratizing gender relations in global institutions is straightforward in concept but endlessly difficult in practice. It means getting wage equality in transnational corporations, ending misogyny and homophobia in international media, gaining equal representation of women and men in international forums, ending gender discrimination in international labour markets, and creating anti-discrimination norms in the public culture.

A worldwide agency of change exists in the international state agencies just described. Support from influential men, such as the UN Secretary-General, has been important in opening spaces for women's groups. Feminist movements have a presence, even if a limited one, in international meetings (Stienstra 2000). There is a less visible presence of gay and lesbian movements, particularly in human rights agencies and UNAIDS, the joint United Nations programme on HIV/AIDS. The growth of a broad 'human rights' agenda in international forums has been important in winning support for gender equality principles. Conventions such as CEDAW are widely known, though how far principles have been turned into practice varies greatly from one country to another (Zwingel 2016).

It is not only through state institutions that gender equity is pursued internationally. Millie Thayer (2010) speaks of a 'feminist counterpublic', vast and heterogeneous, that exists on an international scale. Regional and global networks have developed. Valentine Moghadam in *Globalizing Women* (2005) describes transnational feminist networks that work on issues ranging from the gender dimensions of structural adjustment and trade to the position of women in Muslim-majority countries. Other international networks deal with gay and lesbian rights, and the role of men in gender equality.

The most important effects of this pressure have been on development agendas. From the 1940s to the 1960s a global apparatus of development aid was created. Improving the literacy, skills and knowledge of girls and women was seen as a key move in economic and social development. Consequently, in most parts of the world a large social investment was made in elementary education for girls and in literacy programmes for rural and working-class women. Equality has not yet been reached, but compared with some other areas of life documented in UN reports (see *https://undocs.org/E/2019/68*), education remains one of the gender-equality success stories.

Beyond the education agenda, aid agencies funded dams, machinery, fertilizers, roads and other tools of economic growth. Before long it became obvious that not only were men in charge of the aid programmes, but most of the benefits also went to men. Often women's lives were most disrupted, particularly in rural areas where development projects mean environmental damage. The response was the 'Women in Development' agenda, which feminists urged on aid agencies from the 1970s, to expand the funds directed towards women in poor countries. In the 1990s a major debate occurred around this agenda. Some argued that a focus on women alone was ineffective, that men too had to become change agents if gender equality was to be achieved. A 'Gender and Development' strategy was proposed, including men and masculinities. Others argued that bringing men into the only part of the global development agenda where women had actually gained control would reinforce patriarchy. Since then the debates have expanded to include intersectionality, sexual politics, and decolonial perspectives (Harcourt 2016).

Similar issues arose in the 'gender mainstreaming' debates. It became important, therefore, to look at the specific role of men in gender politics. This issue was discussed in UN forums in the late 1990s and early 2000s, using the new research on masculinities that had emerged since the 1980s. This culminated in a policy document, *The Role of Men and Boys in Achieving Gender Equality*, adopted by the 2004 meeting of the UN Commission on the Status of Women (Lang et al. 2008). It is the first broad international agreement on this issue.

The forces pushing for gender democracy in global arenas are still weak in relation to the size of the problem. They have little influence on transnational corporations and global markets. Obedience to anti-discrimination laws in head office does not prevent transnational corporations behaving badly in the 'global factory', as shown by the scandals about Nike's use of heavily-exploited labour in making its sports gear. Transnational corporations' search for cheap labour around the world often leads them, and their local suppliers, to exploit the weak industrial position of women. This is especially the case where unions are hammered down, as in free-trade zones that governments have set up to attract international capital (Marchand and Runyan 2011).

Even in the United Nations system there is no unified force for change. The World Conferences on Women were important, but among the delegations attending were some from conservative governments opposed to gender equality, both Catholic and Muslim. So these conferences saw sharp conflict over issues of abortion, contraception and lesbianism. Even the concept of 'gender' was under attack at Beijing, because it was supposed by right-wing forces to be a code word for feminism (Benden and Goetz 1998). Largely because of these conflicts, the conferences have now ended – a significant win for conservatives. In the early twenty-first century, the rise of neo-conservative and nationalist governments in many countries has impacted international forums even more strongly, putting advocates of gender equality on the defensive.

During the 1980s, differences between gender orders around the world were widely discussed. The idea of third world feminism emerged, as shown in chapter 4. While equality between women and men could be seen as a mark of modernity, it could also be portrayed as Western cultural imperialism. Even within the metropole, versions of feminism which emphasized women's individual autonomy aroused opposition from women of ethnic minorities who valued solidarity with the men of their communities in struggles against racism and neo-colonial domination.

The issues here are difficult. The modern international order grew out of the violent history of imperialism. A democratic agenda must contest the legacies of empire and colonization: the many forms of racism, and the inequalities between global North and global South. The colonial system of the past, like the globalized world economy of the present, was based on the institutionalized power of men. But anti-colonial struggles, too, were almost everywhere led by men and often valorized violent masculinities. The iconic image of Che Guevara in his beret should be a reminder of this. Guevara, though a doctor, was a particularly violent figure in the Cuban revolutionary movement.

In post-colonial regimes, the men of local elites have often been complicit with businessmen from the metropole in the exploitation of women's labour, as noted in chapter 7. Arms trafficking similarly involves alliances between the men who control local military forces and the men who run arms manufacturing corporations in the global North. In the Philippines, Thailand, Mexico and some other places, men of local elites have created international sex trade destinations. Rejecting gender equality in the name of 'religion' or 'the family' or 'Asian values' or 'African culture' is a familiar ploy of privileged men clinging to power.

A successful response to these problems can only come from activists and theorists in the majority world, from the social movements they speak to, and from the networks and counter-publics that link them. General statements such as CEDAW get read in different ways, but with enough overlap to allow many practical measures to be taken, such as the expansion of education.

Efforts at globalization from below involve the same logic of overlap. Without exact agreement on concepts or even goals, enough common ground can be found to make practical action possible. In a valuable essay called 'Transnational solidarity' (2002), Manisha Desai finds several common themes in women's resistance to neoliberal restructuring: asserting a right to work, struggling for a better quality of life, and sustainability. These issues can be the basis of South/South connections, which are always difficult to organize but are immensely important for gender justice on a world scale.

The stakes in gender politics

What is at stake in these struggles? Generally speaking, the people who benefit from social and economic inequalities have an interest in defending them, while those who bear the costs have an interest in ending them. This difference begins with inequalities between men and women, but soon becomes more complicated as we probe into the details.

Chapter 7 introduced the concept of the patriarchal dividend, the benefits to men as a group from maintaining an unequal gender order. Money income was the focus there, but money is not the only kind of benefit. Others are authority and respect, personal services, control of housing, access to institutional power, emotional support, sexual pleasure and control over one's own body.

The patriarchal dividend is the main stake in contemporary gender politics. Its scale makes patriarchy worth defending. The small band of sex role reformers in the 1970s who attempted to persuade men that Women's Liberation was good for them were undoubtedly right in saying that hegemonic masculinity had its costs. But the same reformers hopelessly underestimated the patriarchal dividend. They missed what very large numbers of men gain from current arrangements in terms of power, income, authority, peer respect or sexual access.

The stakes in gender politics also include the harm done by a given gender order. That includes rape, sexual harassment, sexualized imagery in the media, and sexual abuse of children and youth – all underpinned by inequalities of power and respect. Gender harm is also found in the effects of specific gender formations in personal life. Femininities that make adolescent girls anxious and self-conscious about their bodies are harmful in a very material way. Contemporary hegemonic masculinities are dangerous when they promote occupational stress, arms races, strip mining and deforestation, hostile labour relations, or the abuse of technologies. In the long run, such masculinities are harmful to men as well as to women.

But if gender in these respects is harmful, it is in other respects a source of pleasure, creativity and other greatly valued things. Gender organizes adult sexual relationships, and caring relations with children, which are sources of personal delight and growth. Gender is integral to the cultural wealth of most regions in the world, from *Noh* plays to hiphop and video games. It is difficult to imagine Shakespeare's plays, Homer's *Iliad*, Joyce's *Ulysses*, Rumi's poetry, the *Ramayana* or Bergman's films without gender. The joys, tensions and disasters of gender relations are among the most potent sources of creativity.

It is an attractive feature of recent queer politics that it has rediscovered the energy of gender practices by shifting them off their conventional axes. Starting with the US direct action group Queer Nation in 1990, a great deal of creativity has been unleashed. Pleasure in gender display, in erotic inventiveness, in alternative embodiments and games with gendered language, are very evident. Studies of elementary schools show how children take pleasure in learning to do gender (Thorne 1993). The lifelong gender projects discussed in chapter 6 are not tales of woe; for great numbers of people they are complex and satisfying accomplishments.

The stakes in gender politics, then, include the value of gender as well as its harm. Given these possibilities, gender politics has to be understood as more than an interest-group struggle over inequalities. In the most general sense, gender politics is about the *steering* of the gender order in history. It is not something new; it is contestation over the endless process of making and re-making gender relations.

It is usually clear what gender reform movements are fighting against – discriminatory laws, gender-based violence, social oppression. But what are they fighting for? Where do they want to steer society, in the long run? Chapter 7 mentioned the work of J. K. Gibson-Graham on economic arrangements that could come after capitalism. There is a tradition of utopian fiction about gender-equal futures, and it would be good to have more thinking in this spirit.

Many feminists think that gender is inherently about inequality, and that harm is unavoidable in any gender system. Logically, then, they aim at the abolition of gender. A clear statement is made by the US sociologist

Judith Lorber in *Breaking the Bowls: Degendering and Feminist Change* (2005). Recognizing that gender, however interwoven with other social structures, 'still exerts an enormous organizing, socializing and discriminatory power', Lorber sees two possible responses: acts of individual rebellion, or a strategy of de-gendering. She argues for de-gendering families, workplaces and politics, seeking the abolition of gender wherever it is found, and defining 'a world without gender' as the goal.

But there is another possibility: a strategy of gender democracy. This seeks to equalize gender orders, rather than shrink them to nothing. On the argument of this book, gender does not, in itself, imply inequality. The fact that there are gender orders with seriously different levels of inequality is some evidence in support. The social struggles that have actually moved gender relations some distance towards equality suggest this is a practicable goal. The gender-equality policy regime of the Nordic countries is an example on the large scale. The intimate politics that produced the fairer families described in the United States (Risman 1998) and South Africa (Sideris 2005) are examples on the small scale.

A strategy of gender democratization, rather than gender abolition, has some points to recommend it. It allows us to preserve many gendered pleasures, cultural riches and traditions that people value, as well as contesting the injustices of gender orders. Democratizing gender does not require isolating the reproductive arena from social structures and institutions. Rather, it means organizing on equal and inclusive lines the social processes involved in conception, birth, baby care and child rearing, as well as paid labour and political representation.

This strategy connects gender reform with other fronts of democratic struggle. Environmental issues are now perhaps the most demanding of all, and democratized gender relations will contribute to sustainable forms of economic and political life. No strategy of gender reform will be easy – on that, everyone agrees. But these look like significant advantages.

Afterword

As I said at the beginning, noticing gender is easy, understanding it is a great challenge. This book has traced many ways that gender relations shape our fates. The environment, the economy, government, communications, sexuality, childhood, community and religion are all involved with gender.

Galvanized by injustice and violence, social movements have made powerful criticisms of the gender order. These movements have changed the situations of women in many parts of the world, have changed the situations of gay, lesbian, bisexual and transgender groups, and have changed our thinking about men and masculinities. Yet they have encountered powerful resistance from media, church and state, and have faced troubling questions about sexuality, race, class and indigeneity.

The field of gender studies has developed in close relationship with these movements. Practical politics often makes use of research findings of the kind presented in this book. Gender theorists have struggled to articulate ideas that will support or guide action to transform the gender order. 'What is to be done?' remains the central question, and debates within gender theory matter because the stakes are so high. That is the reason the book argues against a 'de-gendering' strategy for feminism. To assume that gender inevitably means inequality is to undervalue direct struggles to democratize gender relations, whether in families, economies or states, as well as undervaluing cultural and social diversity.

The criterion of democratic action in gender relations is the same as in all forms of democratic action: moving towards equality of participation, power and respect. This principle applies to relations within *any* gender order, and it applies to relations between gender orders globally. It is impossible to avoid conflicts, as shown by the debates in forums such as the Latin American *encuentros* and the UN World Conferences on Women. Yet progressive movements cannot evacuate global arenas just because democratic practice is difficult. Anti-democratic forces are certainly not evacuating them.

Gender research and its applications in practice are now under attack in a more systematic way than ever before. The homophobic, anti-trans and anti-feminist campaigns mentioned in chapter 8, sometimes called the 'anti-gender' crusade, have been linking up around the world. Their effects have already been seen in UN forums and in Hungary, Bolivia, Brazil and Australia. The Hungarian government has moved to close down gender studies in universities, and that move could soon be copied by other authoritarian governments.

It is therefore important to think carefully about how gender analysis is to be done in future. Gender analysis needs many workers – but they live in different circumstances. Given the history of colonization and the huge inequalities of the contemporary world, solidarity can be very difficult. Aileen Moreton-Robinson (2000) shows in her critique of White feminism in Australia that goodwill is not enough. Myths about women's solidarity are common (Cornwall et al. 2008). Good theory has to think beyond immediate appearances and grapple with the structures of inequality. Movements need to build practices of solidarity, however imperfect they may be.

Knowledge about gender has to be reconsidered again and again, in the light of changing gender dynamics. To develop the field requires an energetic commitment to listen, learn and cooperate. Given this, I am convinced that gender research, theory and organizing can play a growing role in making a more democratic and survivable world.

References

Aboim, Sofia. 2010. *Plural Masculinities: The Remaking of the Self in Private Life*. Farnham: Ashgate.

Acker, Joan. 1990. 'Hierarchies, jobs, bodies: A theory of gendered organizations', *Gender and Society*, 4 (2): 139–58.

Adler, Alfred. 1992 [1927]. *Understanding Human Nature*, translated by C. Brett. Oxford: Oneworld.

Agarwal, Bina. 1988. *Structures of Patriarchy: State, Community, and Household in Modernising Asia*. New Delhi: Kali for Women.

Agarwal, Bina. 1994. *A Field of One's Own: Gender and Land Rights in South Asia*. Cambridge: Cambridge University Press.

Agarwal, Bina. 1997. '"Bargaining" and gender relations: Within and beyond the household', *Feminist Economics* 3 (1): 1–51.

Agarwal, Bina. 2010. *Gender and Green Governance: The Political Economy of Women's Presence Within and Beyond Community Forestry*. Oxford: Oxford University Press.

Ahmed, Sarah. 2008. 'Open forum: Some preliminary remarks on the founding gestures of the "New Materialism"', *European Journal of Women's Studies* 15 (1): 23–39.

Alexievich, Svetlana. 2017 [1985]. *The Unwomanly Face of War*. London: Penguin Classics.

Altman, Dennis. 1972. *Homosexual: Oppression and Liberation*. Sydney: Angus & Robertson.

Ampofo, Akosua Adomako, Josephine Beoku-Betts, Wairimu Ngaruiya Njambi and Mary Osirim. 2004. 'Women's and gender studies in English-speaking sub-Saharan Africa: A review of research in the social sciences', *Gender & Society* 18 (6): 685–714.

Armstrong, Pat and Hugh Armstrong. 1990. *Theorizing Women's Work*. Toronto: Garamond.

Arnfred, Signe. 2003. 'African gender research: A view from the North', *CODESRIA Bulletin* 2003 no. 1: 6–9.

Arnot, Madeleine, Miriam David and Gaby Weiner. 1999. *Closing the Gender Gap: Postwar Education and Social Change*. Cambridge: Polity.

Ault, Elizabeth. 2013. '"You can help yourself/but don't take too much": African American motherhood on *The Wire*', *Television & New Media* 14 (5): 367–85.

Australian Bureau of Statistics. 2017. *4906.0 – Personal Safety, Australia, 2016.* Online at https://www.abs.gov.au/ausstats/abs@.nsf/mf/4906.0, accessed 20.5.2020.

Badran, Margot. 1988. 'The feminist vision in the writings of three turn-of-the-century Egyptian women', *British Journal of Middle Eastern Studies* 15 (1–2): 11–20.

Baigent, Dave. 2016. 'Resisting and accommodating the masculinist gender regime in firefighting'. Pp. 175–85 in Elaine Enarson and Bob Pease, eds., *Men, Masculinities and Disaster.* Abingdon and New York: Routledge.

Bakare-Yusuf, Bibi. 2003. '"Yorubas don't do gender": A critical review of Oyeronke Oyewumi's *The Invention of Women: Making an African Sense of Western Gender Discourses', African Identities* 1 (1): 121–43.

Barbieri, Teresita de. 1992. 'Sobre la categoria genero. Una introduccion teorico-metodologica', *Revista Interamericana de Sociologia* 6: 147–78.

Barrett, Frank J. 1996. 'Gender strategies of women naval officers', in *Women's Research and Education Institute: Conference on Women in Uniformed Services.* Washington, DC.

Bauer, Robin, Josch Hoenes and Volker Woltersdorff, eds. 2007. *Unbeschreiblich Männlich: Heteronormativitätskritische Perspektiven.* Hamburg: Männerschwarm.

Beauvoir, Simone de. 1972 [1949]. *The Second Sex.* Harmondsworth: Penguin.

Bebel, August. 1971 [1879]. *Women under Socialism [Die Frau und der Sozialismus].* New York: Schocken Books.

Bem, Sandra L. 1974. 'The measurement of psychological androgyny', *Journal of Consulting and Clinical Psychology* 42: 155–62.

Benden, Sally and Anne-Marie Goetz. 1998. 'Who needs [sex] when you can have [gender]? Conflicting discourses on gender at Beijing'. Pp. 19–38 in Cecile Jackson and Ruth Pearson, eds., *Feminist Visions of Development: Gender, Analysis and Policy.* London: Routledge.

Bennett, Jane. 2010. *Vibrant Matter: A Political Ecology of Things.* Durham, NC: Duke University Press.

Bettencourt, B. Ann and Norman Miller. 1996. 'Gender differences in aggression as a function of provocation: A meta-analysis', *Psychological Bulletin* 119 (3): 422–7.

Bettie, Julie. 2003. *Women Without Class: Girls, Race, and Identity.* Berkeley: University of California Press.

Bhaskaran, Suparna. 2004. *Made in India: Decolonizations, Queer Sexualities, Trans/national Projects.* New York: Palgrave Macmillan.

Blamires, Alcuid, ed. 1992. *Woman Defamed and Woman Defended: An Anthology of Medieval Texts.* Oxford: Clarendon Press.

Borah, R. and S. Nandi. 2012. 'Reclaiming the feminist politics of "SlutWalk"', *International Feminist Journal of Politics* 14 (3): 415–21.

Borchorst, Anette and Birte Siim. 2002. 'The women-friendly welfare states revisited', *NORA* 10 (2): 90–8.

Bracke, Sarah and David Paternotte. 2016. 'Unpacking the sin of gender', *Religion & Gender* 6 (2): 143–54.

Bulbeck, Chilla. 1988. *One World Women's Movement*. London: Pluto Press.

Bulbeck, Chilla. 1997. *Living Feminism: The Impact of the Women's Movement on Three Generations of Australian Women*. Cambridge: Cambridge University Press.

Bulbeck, Chilla. 1998. *Re-orienting Western Feminisms: Women's Diversity in a Postcolonial World*. Cambridge: Cambridge University Press.

Burton, Clare. 1987. 'Merit and gender: Organisations and the mobilisation of masculine bias', *Australian Journal of Social Issues* 22 (2): 424–35.

Butler, Judith. 1990. *Gender Trouble: Feminism and the Subversion of Identity*. New York: Routledge.

Caplan, Pat, ed. 1987. *The Cultural Construction of Sexuality*. London: Tavistock.

Carrigan, Tim, Raewyn Connell and John Lee. 1985. 'Toward a new sociology of masculinity', *Theory and Society* 14 (5): 551–604.

Carrington, Kerry. 2015. *Feminism and Global Justice*. Abingdon: Routledge.

Cassano, Graham, Jessica Payette and Rima Lunin Schultz. 2019. *Eleanor Smith's* Hull House Songs: *The Music of Protest and Hope in Jane Addams's* Chicago. Leiden: Brill.

Chang, Kimberly A. and L. H. M. Ling. 2000. 'Globalization and its intimate other: Filipina domestic workers in Hong Kong'. Pp. 27–43 in Marianne H. Marchand and Anne Sisson Runyan, eds., *Gender and Global Restructuring*. London: Routledge.

Chapkis, Wendy. 1997. *Live Sex Acts: Women Performing Erotic Labor*. New York: Routledge.

Chodorow, Nancy. 1978. *The Reproduction of Mothering: Psychoanalysis and the Sociology of Gender*. Berkeley: University of California Press.

Clarke, Averil. 2011. *Inequalities of Love: College-Educated Black Women and the Barriers to Romance and Family*. Durham, NC: Duke University Press.

Cockburn, Cynthia. 1983. *Brothers: Male Dominance and Technological Change*. London: Pluto Press.

Collins, Patricia Hill. 1991. *Black Feminist Thought: Knowledge, Consciousness, and the Politics of Empowerment*. New York: Routledge.

Collyer, Fran, Raewyn Connell, João Maia and Robert Morrell. 2019. *Knowledge and Global Power: Making New Sciences in the South*. Melbourne: Monash University Publishing.

Committee on the Status of Women in India. 1975. *Towards Equality: Report of the Committee on the Status of Women in India*. New Delhi: Government of India.

Comte, Auguste. 1875–7 [1851–4]. *System of Positive Polity, or, Treatise on Sociology*. 4 vols. London: Longmans Green.

Connell, Catherine. 2010. 'Doing, undoing, or redoing gender? Learning from the workplace experiences of transpeople', *Gender & Society* 24 (1): 31–55.

Connell, Raewyn. 1987. *Gender and Power: Society, the Person and Sexual Politics*. Cambridge: Polity.

Connell, Raewyn. 1990. 'The state, gender, and sexual politics', *Theory and Society* 19 (5): 507–44.

Connell, Raewyn. 1995. *Masculinities*. Cambridge: Polity.

Connell, Raewyn. 2000. *The Men and the Boys*. Cambridge: Polity.

Connell, Raewyn. 2006a. 'Glass ceilings or gendered institutions? Mapping the gender regimes of public sector worksites', *Public Administration Review* 66 (6): 837–49.

Connell, Raewyn. 2006b. 'The experience of gender change in public sector organizations', *Gender, Work and Organization* 13 (5): 435–52.

Connell, Raewyn. 2012a. 'Gender, health and theory: Conceptualizing the issue, in local and world perspective', *Social Science & Medicine* 74 (11): 1675–83.

Connell, Raewyn. 2012b. 'Inside the glass tower: The construction of masculinities in finance capital'. Pp. 65–79 in P. McDonald and E. Jeanes, eds., *Men, Wage Work and Family*. Abingdon: Routledge.

Corman, June, Meg Luxton, David Livingstone and Wally Seccombe. 1993. *Recasting Steel Labour: The Stelco Story*. Halifax, NS: Fernwood.

Cornwall, Andrea, Elizabeth Harrison and Ann Whitehead. 2008. *Gender Myths and Feminist Fables: The Struggle for Interpretive Power in Gender and Development*. Oxford: Blackwell Publishing.

Crenshaw, Kimberlé. 1989. 'Demarginalizing the intersection of race and sex: A black feminist critique of antidiscrimination doctrine, feminist theory and antiracist politics', *University of Chicago Legal Forum* 1989: 139–68.

Cupples, Julie. 2005. 'Love and money in an age of neoliberalism: Gender, work, and single motherhood in postrevolutionary Nicaragua', *Environment and Planning A* 37 (2): 305–22.

Daly, Mary. 1978. *Gyn/Ecology: The Metaethics of Radical Feminism*. Boston: Beacon Press.

Darwin, Charles. 1928 [1859]. *The Origin of Species*. London: Dent.

Davies, Bronwyn. 1993. *Shards of Glass: Children Reading and Writing beyond Gendered Identities*. Sydney: Allen & Unwin.

DeKeseredy, Walter S. and Amanda Hall-Sanchez. 2018. 'Male violence against women in the global South: What we know and what we don't know'. Pp. 883–900 in Kerry Carrington, Russell Hogg, John Scott and Máximo Sozzo, eds., *The Palgrave Handbook of Criminology and the Global South*. Basingstoke: Palgrave Macmillan.

Delphy, Christine. 1984 [1970]. 'The main enemy'. Translated in *Close to Home: A Materialist Analysis of Women's Oppression*. London: Hutchinson.

Dennis, Alex. 2018. 'The strange survival and apparent resurgence of socio-biology', *History of the Human Sciences* 31 (1): 19–35.

Desai, Manisha. 2002. 'Transnational solidarity: Women's agency, structural adjustment, and globalization'. Pp. 15–33 in N. Naples and M. Desai, eds., *Women's Activism and Globalization: Linking Local Struggles and Transnational Politics*. New York: Routledge.

Donaldson, Mike. 1991. *Time of our Lives: Labour and Love in the Working Class*. Sydney: Allen & Unwin.

Donnelly, Kristin and Jean M. Twenge. 2017. 'Masculine and feminine traits on the Bem Sex-Role Inventory, 1993–2012: A cross-temporal meta-analysis', *Sex Roles* 76: 556–65.

Dowsett, Gary W. 1996. *Practicing Desire: Homosexual Sex in the Era of AIDS*. Stanford, CA: Stanford University Press.

Dowsett, Gary W. 2003. 'Some considerations on sexuality and gender in the context of AIDS', *Reproductive Health Matters* 11: 21–9.

Dull, Diana and Candace West. 1991. 'Accounting for cosmetic surgery: The accomplishment of gender', *Social Problems* 38 (1): 54–70.

Eagly, Alice H. 1987. *Sex Differences in Social Behavior: A Social-Role Interpretation*. Hillside, NJ: Lawrence Erlbaum.

Eagly, Alice H., David I. Miller, Christa Nater, Michèle Kaufmann and Sabine Sczesny. 2020. 'Gender stereotypes have changed: A cross-temporal meta-analysis of U.S. public opinion polls from 1946 to 2018', *American Psychologist* 75 (3): 301–15.

d'Eaubonne, Françoise. 1974. *Le Féminisme ou la mort*. Paris: Pierre Horay. Extract translated as 'Feminism or death', pp. 64–7 in E. Marks and I. de Courtivron, eds., *New French Feminisms: An Anthology*. Amherst: University of Massachusetts Press, 1980.

Eisenstein, Hester. 1996. *Inside Agitators: Australian Femocrats and the State*. Sydney: Allen & Unwin.

Eisenstein, Hester. 2009. *Feminism Seduced: How Global Elites Use Women's Labor and Ideas to Exploit the World*. Boulder, CO: Paradigm Publishers.

Elias, Juanita. 2008. 'Hegemonic masculinities, the multinational corporation, and the developmental state: Constructing gender in "progressive" firms', *Men and Masculinities* 10 (4): 405–21.

Elliott, Karla. 2020. *Young Men Navigating Contemporary Masculinities*. Cham: Palgrave Macmillan.

Ellis, Havelock. 1928. *Eonism and other Supplementry Studies. Studies in the Psychology of Sex*, vol. VII. Philadelphia: F. A. Davis.

Enarson, Elaine and Bob Pease, eds. 2016. *Men, Masculinities and Disaster*. Abingdon and New York: Routledge.

Engels, Friedrich. 1970 [1884]. *The Origin of the Family, Private Property and the State*, in Marx/Engels Selected Works. Moscow: Progress Publishers.

Engin, Ceylan and Heili Pals. 2018. 'Patriarchal attitudes in Turkey 1990–2011: The influence of religion and political conservatism', *Social Politics* 25 (3): 383–409.

Enloe, Cynthia. 1990. *Bananas, Beaches and Bases: Making Feminist Sense of International Politics*. Berkeley: University of California Press.

Epstein, Cynthia Fuchs. 1988. *Deceptive Distinctions: Sex, Gender and the Social Order*. New Haven, CT: Yale University Press.

Epstein, Cynthia Fuchs. 2007. 'Great divides: The cultural, cognitive, and social bases of the global subordination of women', *American Sociological Review* 72 (1): 1–22.

Ericson, Mathias and Ulf Mellström. 2016. 'Firefighters, technology and masculinity in the micro-management of disasters'. Pp. 165–74 in Elaine

Enarson and Bob Pease, eds., *Men, Masculinities and Disaster*. Abingdon and New York: Routledge.

Erikson, Erik H. 1950. *Childhood and Society*. London: Imago.

Ernst, Michelle, Lih-Mei Liao, Arlene B. Baratz and David E. Sandberg. 2018. 'Disorders of sex development/intersex: Gaps in psychosocial care for children', *Pediatrics* 142 (2): e20174045.

Espinosa, Cecilia. 2013. 'Malentendidos productivos: "Clivaje de género" y feminismo en un organisación de trabajadores desocupados de Argentina', *La Ventana* 37: 289–323.

Firestone, Shulamith. 1970. *The Dialectic of Sex: The Case for Feminist Revolution*. New York: Morrow.

Franzway, Suzanne. 2001. *Sexual Politics and Greedy Institutions*. Sydney: Pluto Press.

Franzway, Suzanne and Mary. M. Fonow. 2011. *Making Feminist Politics: Transnational Alliances Between Women and Labor*. Champaign: University of Illinois Press.

Fregoso, Rosa Linda. 1993. *The Bronze Screen: Chicana and Chicano Film Culture*. Minneapolis: University of Minnesota Press.

Freud, Sigmund. 1953 [1900]. *The Interpretation of Dreams*, in Complete Psychological Works, vols. 4–5. London: Hogarth.

Freud, Sigmund. 1953 [1905]. 'Fragment of an analysis of a case of hysteria', in Complete Psychological Works, vol. 7. London: Hogarth.

Freud, Sigmund. 1953 [1905]. *Three Essays on the Theory of Sexuality*, in Complete Psychological Works, vol. 7. London: Hogarth.

Freud, Sigmund. 1958 [1911] 'Psycho-analytic notes on an autobiographical account of a case of paranoia (dementia paranoides)', in Complete Psychological Works, vol. 12. London: Hogarth.

Freud, Sigmund. 1955 [1918]. 'From the history of an infantile neurosis', in Complete Psychological Works, vol. 17. London: Hogarth.

Freud, Sigmund. 1961 [1930]. *Civilization and its Discontents*, in Complete Psychological Works, vol. 21. London: Hogarth.

Frosh, Stephen, Ann Phoenix and Rob Pattman. 2002. *Young Masculinities: Understanding Boys in Contemporary Society*. Basingstoke: Palgrave.

Gallo, Ester and Francesca Scrinzi. 2016. *Migration, Masculinities and Reproductive Labour: Men of the Home*. London: Palgrave Macmillan.

Garbagnoli, Sara and Massimo Prearo. 2017. *La Croisade 'anti-genre': Du Vatican aux manifs pour tous*. Paris: Éditions Textuel.

Gauthier, Xavière. 1981. 'Is there such a thing as women's writing?' Pp. 161–4 in Elaine Marks and Isabelle de Courtivron, eds., *New French Feminisms: An Anthology*. London: Harvester.

Geary, David C. 1998. *Male, Female: The Evolution of Human Sex Differences*. Washington, DC: American Psychological Association.

Gekoski, Anna, Jacqueline M. Gray, Joanna R. Adler and Miranda A. H. Horvath. 2017. 'The prevalence and nature of sexual harassment and assault against women and girls on public transport: An international review', *Journal of Criminological Research, Policy & Practice* 3 (1): 3–16.

Gherardi, Silva and Barbara Poggio. 2001. 'Creating and recreating gender order in organizations', *Journal of World Business* 36 (3): 245–59.

Ghoussoub, Mai. 2000. 'Chewing gum, insatiable women and foreign enemies: Male fears and the Arab media'. Pp. 227–35 in Mai Ghoussoub and Emma Sinclair-Webb, eds., *Imagined Masculinities: Male Identity and Culture in the Modern Middle East*. London: Saqi Books.

Gibson-Graham, J. K. 1996. *The End of Capitalism (As We Knew It): A Feminist Critique of Political Economy*. Oxford: Blackwell.

Gibson-Graham, J. K. 2011. 'A feminist project of belonging for the Anthropocene', *Gender, Place & Culture* 18 (1): 1–21.

Glass Ceiling Commission. 1995. *A Solid Investment: Making Full Use of the Nation's Human Capital. Recommendations*. Washington, DC: Federal Glass Ceiling Commission.

Global Health 50/50. 2020. *COVID-19 Sex-disaggregated data tracker*, updated to 22.4.2020. Online at globalhealth5050.org/covid19/, accessed 29.4.2020.

Glucksmann, Miriam [writing as Ruth Cavendish]. 1982. *Women on the Line*. London: Routledge & Kegan Paul.

Glucksmann, Miriam. 2000. *Cottons and Casuals: The Gendered Organisation of Labour in Time and Space*. Durham: Sociologypress.

Goldberg, Steven. 1993. *Why Men Rule: A Theory of Male Dominance*. Chicago: Open Court.

Gottfried, Heidi. 2013. *Gender, Work, and Economy: Unpacking the Global Economy*. Cambridge: Polity.

Gottfried, Heidi. 2015. *The Reproductive Bargain: Deciphering the Enigma of Japanese Capitalism*. Leiden: Brill.

Griggs, Claudine. 1996. *Passage Through Trinidad: Journal of a Surgical Sex Change*. Jefferson, NC: McFarland & Company.

Grosz, Elizabeth. 1994. *Volatile Bodies: Towards a Corporeal Feminism*. Sydney: Allen & Unwin.

Gutmann, Matthew and Catherine Lutz. 2010. *Breaking Ranks: Iraq Veterans Speak Out Against the War*. Berkeley: University of California Press.

Habermas, Jürgen. 1976. *Legitimation Crisis*. London: Heinemann.

Hacker, Helen Mayer. 1957. 'The new burdens of masculinity', *Marriage and Family Living* 19: 227–33.

Halpern, Diane F. and Mary L. LaMay. 2000. 'The smarter sex: A critical review of sex differences in intelligence', *Educational Psychology Review* 12 (2): 229–46.

Harcourt, Wendy. 2009. *Body Politics in Development: Critical Debates in Gender and Development*. London: Zed Books.

Harcourt, Wendy, ed. 2016. *The Palgrave Handbook of Gender and Development*. Basingstoke: Palgrave Macmillan.

Harding, Sandra. 1986. *The Science Question in Feminism*. Ithaca, NY: Cornell University Press.

Harper, Catherine. 2007. *Intersex*. Oxford: Berg.

He-Yin Zhen. 2013 [1907]. 'On the question of women's liberation'. Pp.

53–71 in Lydia H. Liu, Rebecca E. Karl and Dorothy Ko, eds., *The Birth of Chinese Feminism: Essential Texts in Transnational Theory*. New York: Columbia University Press.

Herdt, Gilbert H. 1981. *Guardians of the Flutes: Idioms of Masculinity*. New York: McGraw-Hill.

Hernes, Helga. 1987. *Welfare State and Women Power: Essays in State Feminism*. Oslo: Norwegian University Press.

Hird, Myra. 2009. 'Feminist engagements with matter', *Feminist Studies* 35 (2): 329–56.

Hochschild, Arlie Russell. 1983. *The Managed Heart: Commercialization of Human Feeling*. Berkeley: University of California Press.

Hocquenghem, Guy. 1978 [1972]. *Homosexual Desire*, translated by D. Dangoor. London: Allison & Busby.

Holland, Dorothy C. and Margaret A. Eisenhart. 1990. *Educated in Romance: Woman, Achievement, and College Culture*. Chicago: University of Chicago Press.

Holmes, Morgan, ed. 2009. *Critical Intersex*. Farnham: Ashgate.

Holter, Øystein Gullvåg. 2003. *Can Men Do It? Men and Gender Equality – the Nordic Experience*. Copenhagen: Nordic Council of Ministers.

Holter, Øystein Gullvåg. 2005. 'Social theories for researching men and masculinities: Direct gender hierarchy and structural inequality'. Pp. 15–34 in Michael S. Kimmel, Jeff Hearn and Raewyn Connell, eds., *Handbook of Studies on Men and Masculinities*. Thousand Oaks, CA: Sage.

hooks, bell. 1984. *Feminist Theory: From Margin to Center*. Boston: South End Press.

Hountondji, Paulin J. 1997. 'Introduction: Recentring Africa'. Pp. 1–39 in Paulin J. Hountondji, ed., *Endogenous Knowledge: Research Trails*. Dakar: CODESRIA.

Htun, Mala. 2003. *Sex and the State: Abortion, Divorce, and the Family under Latin American Dictatorships and Democracies*. Cambridge: Cambridge University Press.

Htun, Mala, Francesca R. Jensenius and Jami Nelson-Nuñez. 2019. 'Gender-discriminatory laws and women's economic agency', *Social Politics* 26 (2): 193–222.

Htun, Mala and Laurel Weldon. 2018. *The Logics of Gender Justice: State Action on Women's Rights Around the World*. Cambridge: Cambridge University Press.

Hultman, Martin and Paul M. Pulé. 2018. *Ecological Masculinities: Theoretical Foundations and Practical Guidance*. Abingdon and New York: Routledge.

Hyde, Janet S. 1984. 'How large are gender-differences in aggression? A developmental meta-analysis', *Developmental Psychology* 20 (4): 722–36.

Hyde, Janet S. 2005. 'The gender similarities hypothesis', *American Psychologist* 60 (6): 581–92.

Hyde, Janet S. and Nita M. McKinley. 1997. 'Gender differences in cognition: Results from meta-analyses'. Pp. 30–51 in P. J. Caplan,

M. Crawford, J. S. Hyde and J. T. E. Richardson, eds., *Gender Differences in Human Cognition*. New York: Oxford University Press.

Illo, Jeanne Frances I. 2010. *Accounting for Gender Results: A Review of the Philippine GAD Budget Policy*. Manila: Women and Gender Institute, Miriam College.

ILO (International Labour Organization). 2018. *World Employment Social Outlook: Trends for Women 2018*. Online at https://www.ilo.org/wcmsp5/groups/public/---dgreports/---dcomm/---publ/documents/publication/wcms_619577.pdf, accessed 9.4.2020.

ILO (International Labour Organization). 2018/19. *Global Wage Report 2018/19: What Lies Behind Gender Pay Gaps*. Online at https://www.ilo.org/global/publications/books/WCMS_650553/lang--en/index.htm, accessed 10.6.2020.

Inter-Parliamentary Union. 2019. 'Women in national parliaments: Situation as of 1st October 2019'. Online at http://www.ipu.org/wmn-e/world.htm.

Irigaray, Luce. 1985 [1977]. *This Sex Which is Not One*, translated by C. Porter and C. Burke. Ithaca, NY: Cornell University Press.

Jackson, Peter A. 1997. '*Kathoey*><Gay><Man: The historical emergence of gay male identity in Thailand'. Pp. 166–90 in L. Manderson and M. Jolly, eds., *Sites of Desire, Economies of Pleasure*. Chicago: University of Chicago Press.

Jaffee, Sara and Janet S. Hyde. 2000. 'Gender differences in moral orientation: A meta-analysis', *Psychological Bulletin* 126 (5): 703–26.

Jewkes, Rachel and Robert Morrell. 2010. 'Gender and sexuality: Emerging perspectives from the heterosexual epidemic in South Africa and implications for HIV risk and prevention', *Journal of the International AIDS Society* 13 (1): http://www.jiasociety.org/content/13/1/6.

Juana Inés de la Cruz, Sor. 2009 [1691]. *The Answer: La Respuesta*, ed. Electa Arenal and Amanda Powell. New York: The Feminist Press.

Kanter, Rosabeth. 1977. *Men and Women of the Corporation*. New York: Basic Books.

Kartini. 2014. *The Complete Writings 1898–1904*. Clayton: Monash University Publishing.

Kemper, Theodore D. 1990. *Social Structure and Testosterone: Explorations of the Socio-bio-social Chain*. New Brunswick, NJ: Rutgers University Press.

Keough, Leyla J. 2006. 'Globalizing "postsocialism": Mobile mothers and neoliberalism on the margins of Europe', *Anthropological Quarterly* 79 (3): 431–61.

Kippax, Susan, Raewyn Connell, Gary W. Dowsett and June Crawford. 1993. *Sustaining Safe Sex: Gay Communities Respond to AIDS*. London: Falmer Press.

Kirkwood, Julieta. 1986. *Ser Política en Chile: Las Feministas y los Partidos*. Santiago: FLACSO.

Klein, Alan M. 1993. *Little Big Men: Bodybuilding Subculture and Gender Construction*. Albany, NY: State University of New York Press.

Kling, Kristen, Janet Shibley Hyde, Caroline J. Showers and Brenda

N. Buswell. 1999. 'Gender differences in self-esteem: A meta-analysis', *Psychological Bulletin* 125 (4): 470–500.

Kollontai, Alexandra. 1977. *Selected Writings*, translated by A. Holt. London: Allison & Busby.

Komarovsky, Mirra. 1946. 'Cultural contradictions and sex roles', *American Journal of Sociology* 52: 184–9.

Krafft-Ebing, Richard von. 1965 [1886]. *Psychopathia Sexualis*, 12th edn. New York: Paperback Library.

Kristeva, Julia. 1984 [1974]. *Revolution in Poetic Language*. New York: Columbia University Press.

Kulkarni, Mangesh, ed. 2019. *Global Masculinities: Interrogations and Reconstructions*. Abingdon and New York: Routledge.

Lancet, The. 2020. 'Editorial: The gendered dimensions of COVID-19', *The Lancet* 395 (10231): 1168.

Lang, James, Alan Greig and Raewyn Connell, in collaboration with the Division for the Advancement of Women. 2008. *The Role of Men and Boys in Achieving Gender Equality*. 'Women 2000 and Beyond' series. New York: United Nations Division for the Advancement of Women/ Department of Economic and Social Affairs. Electronic version at: http. www.un.org/womenwatch/daw/w2000.html.

Laplanche, J. and J.-B. Pontalis. 1973. *The Language of Psycho-Analysis*. New York: Norton.

Larner, Wendy and Nina Laurie. 2010. 'Travelling technocrats, embodied knowledges: Globalising privatisation in telecoms and water', *Geoforum* 41 (2): 218–26.

Laurie, Nina. 2011. 'Gender water networks: Femininity and masculinity in water politics in Bolivia', *International Journal of Urban and Regional Research* 35 (1): 172–88.

Lei, Xiaojing, Kay Bussey, Phillipa Hay, Jonathan Mond, Nora Trompeter, Alexandra Lonergan and Deborah Mitchison. 2019. 'Prevalence and correlates of sexual harassment in Australian adolescents', *Journal of School Violence*. Online at https://doi.org/10.1080/15388220.2019.1699800.

Lenz, Ilse. 2017. 'Genderflexer? Zum gegenwärtigen Wandel der Geschlechterordnung'. Pp. 181–214 in Ilse Lenz, Sabine Evertz and Saida Ressel, eds., *Geschlecht im flexibilisierten Kapitalismus? Neue UnGleichheiten*. Wiesbaden: Springer VS.

Lindberg, Sara M., Janet S. Hyde, Jennifer L. Petersen and Marcia Linn. 2010. 'New trends in gender and mathematics performance: A meta-analysis', *Psychological Bulletin* 136 (6): 1123–35.

Litfin, Karen. 1997. 'The gendered eye in the sky: A feminist perspective on earth observation satellites', *Frontiers* 18 (2): 26–47.

Lopata, Helena Z. and Barrie Thorne. 1978. 'On the term "sex roles"', *Signs* 3 (3): 718–21.

Lorber, Judith. 2005. *Breaking the Bowls: Degendering and Feminist Change*. New York: Norton.

Luttrell, Wendy. 1997. *Schoolsmart and Motherwise: Working-Class Women's Identity and Schooling*. New York: Routledge.

Luxton, Meg. 2006. 'Feminist political economy in Canada and the politics of social reproduction'. Pp. 11–44 in Kate Bezanson and Meg Luxton, eds., *Social Reproduction: Feminist Political Economy Challenges Neo-Liberalism*. Montreal: McGill-Queen's University Press.

Mac an Ghaill, Máirtín. 1994. *The Making of Men: Masculinities, Sexualities and Schooling*. Buckingham: Open University Press.

Maccoby, Eleanor E. and Carol Nagy Jacklin. 1975. *The Psychology of Sex Differences*. Stanford, CA: Stanford University Press.

MacGregor, Sherilyn. 2009. 'A stranger silence still: The need for feminist social research on climate change', *The Sociological Review* 57 (2): 124–40.

MacKinnon, Catharine A. 1983. 'Feminism, Marxism, method and the state: Towards feminist jurisprudence', *Signs* 8 (4): 635–58.

Madrid, Sebastián. 2016. 'La formación de masculinidades hegemónicas en la clase dominante: el caso de la sexualidad en los colegios privados de elite en Chile', *Sexualidad, Salud y Sociedad: Revista Latinoamericana* 22: 369–98.

Madrid, Sebastián, Teresa Valdés and Roberto Celedón, eds. 2020. *Masculinidades en América Latina: Veinte Años de Estudios y Políticas para la Igualdad de Género*. Santiago: Universidad Academia de Humanismo Cristiano.

Malinowski, Bronisław. 1927. *Sex and Repression in Savage Society*. London: Routledge & Kegan Paul.

Malos, Ellen, ed. 1980. *The Politics of Housework*. London: Allison & Busby.

Mama, Amina. 1997. 'Heroes and villains: Conceptualizing colonial and contemporary violence against women in Africa'. Pp. 46–62 in M. J. Alexander and C. T. Mohanty, eds., *Feminist Genealogies, Colonial Legacies, Democratic Futures*. New York: Routledge.

Mane, Purnima and Peter Aggleton. 2001. 'Gender and HIV/AIDS: What do men have to do with it?', *Current Sociology* 49 (1): 23–37.

Manivannan, Sharanya. 2016. *The High Priestess Never Marries*. Noida, Uttar Pradesh: HarperCollins Publishers India.

Mannon, Susan E. 2006. 'Love in the time of neo-liberalism: Gender, work, and power in a Costa Rican marriage', *Gender & Society* 20 (4): 511–30.

Marchand, Marianne H. and Anne Sisson Runyan, eds. 2011. *Gender and Global Restructuring: Sightings, Sites and Resistances*, 2nd edn. Abingdon: Routledge.

Martin, Patricia Yancey. 2003. '"Said and done" versus "Saying and doing": Gendering practices, practicing gender at work', *Gender & Society* 17 (3): 342–66.

Mbembe, Achille. 2001. *On the Postcolony*. Berkeley: University of California Press.

Mead, Margaret. 1963 [1935]. *Sex and Temperament in Three Primitive Societies*. New York: William Morrow.

Melville, Herman. 1969 [1853]. 'Bartleby the Scrivener'. Pp. 159–90 in D. J.

Burrows and F. R. Lapides, eds., *Alienation: A Casebook*. New York: Crowell.

Mernissi, Fatima. 1985 [1975]. *Beyond the Veil: Male–Female Dynamics in Modern Muslim Society*. London: Saqi Books.

Merrick, Teri. 2019. 'From "Intersex" to "DSD": A case of epistemic injustice', *Synthese* 196: 4429–4447.

Messerschmidt, James W. 2004. *Flesh and Blood: Adolescent Diversity and Violence*. Lanham, MD: Rowman & Littlefield.

Messner, Michael. 2007. *Out of Play: Critical Essays on Gender and Sport*. Albany, NY: State University of New York Press.

Metz-Göckel, Sigrid and Ursula Müller. 1985. *Der Mann: Die Brigitte-Studie*. Hamburg: Beltz.

Mies, Maria. 1986. *Patriarchy and Accumulation on a World Scale: Women in the International Division of Labour*. London: Zed Books.

Mill, John Stuart. 1912 [1869]. 'The subjection of women'. In *J. S. Mill: Three Essays*. London: Oxford University Press.

Mills, Albert J. and Peta Tancred, eds. 1992. *Gendering Organizational Analysis*. Newbury Park, CA: Sage.

Misra, Joya. 2018. 'Categories, structures, and intersectional theory'. Pp. 111–30 in James W. Messerschmidt et al., eds., *Gender Reckonings: New Social Theory and Research*. New York: New York University Press.

Mitchell, Juliet. 1966. 'Women: The longest revolution', *New Left Review* 40: 11–37.

Mitchell, Juliet. 1974. *Psychoanalysis and Feminism*. New York: Pantheon Books.

Moghadam, Valentine M. 2005. *Globalizing Women: Transnational Feminist Networks*. Baltimore: Johns Hopkins University Press.

Moghadam, Valentine M. 2013. 'What is democracy? Promises and perils of the Arab Spring', *Current Sociology* 61 (4): 393–408.

Mohanty, Chandra Talpade. 1991. 'Under Western eyes: Feminist scholarship and colonial discourses'. Pp. 51–80 in C. T. Mohanty, A. Russo and L. Torres, eds., *Third World Women and the Politics of Feminism*. Bloomington: Indiana University Press.

Mohanty, Chandra Talpade. 2003. *Feminism Without Borders: Decolonizing Theory, Practicing Solidarity*. Durham, NC: Duke University Press.

Mohwald, Ulrich. 2002. *Changing Attitudes towards Gender Equality in Japan and Germany*. Munich: Iudicium.

Moodie, T. Dunbar, with Vivienne Ndatshe. 1994. *Going for Gold: Men, Mines and Migration*. Johannesburg: Witwatersrand University Press.

Moreton-Robinson, Aileen. 2000. *Talkin' Up to the White Woman: Indigenous Women and Feminism*. St. Lucia: University of Queensland Press.

Morgan, Robin, ed. 1970. *Sisterhood is Powerful: An Anthology of Writings from the Women's Liberation Movement*. New York: Vintage.

Morgan, Ruth, Charl Marais and Joy Rosemary Wellbeloved, eds. 2009. *Trans: Transgender Life Stories from South Africa*. Auckland Park: Fanele.

Morrell, Robert. 2001. *From Boys to Gentlemen: Settler Masculinity in Colonial Natal 1880–1920*. Pretoria: University of South Africa.

Mudimbe, Valentine. 1994. *The Idea of Africa*. Bloomington: Indiana University Press.

Najmabadi, Afsaneh. 2014. *Professing Selves: Transsexuality and Same-Sex Desire in Contemporary Iran*. Durham, NC: Duke University Press.

Namaste, Viviane K. 2000. *Invisible Lives: The Erasure of Transsexual and Transgendered People*. Chicago: University of Chicago Press.

Namaste, Viviane K. 2011. *Sex Change, Social Change: Reflections on Identity, Institutions, and Imperialism*. Toronto: Canadian Scholars' Press.

Nandy, Ashis. 1987. *Traditions, Tyranny and Utopias: Essays in the Politics of Awareness*. New Delhi: Oxford University Press.

Nery, João W. 2011. *Viagem Solitária: Memórias de um Transexual Trinta Anos depois*. São Paulo: Leya.

Ng, Janet and Janice Wickeri, eds. 1996. *May Fourth Women Writers*. Hong Kong: Chinese University of Hong Kong.

Nilsson, Arne. 1998. 'Creating their own private and public: The male homosexual life space in a Nordic city during high modernity', *Journal of Homosexuality* 35 (3–4): 81–116.

Odih, Pamela. 2007. *Gender and Work in Capitalist Economies*. Maidenhead: Open University Press.

OECD (Organisation for Economic Co-operation and Development). 2019. *Pension Markets in Focus*. Online at www.oecd.org/daf/fin/private-pensions/pensionmarketsinfocus.htm, accessed 13.4.2020.

OECD. 2020. *Distribution of teachers by age and gender*. Table in *OECD. Stat*. Online at https://stats.oecd.org/Index.aspx?DataSetCode=EAG_PERS_SHARE_AGE, accessed 14.5.2020.

Ogasawara, Yuko. 1998. *Office Ladies and Salaried Men: Power, Gender, and Work in Japanese Companies*. Berkeley: University of California Press.

Okeke-Ihejirika, Philomina E. and Susan Franceschet. 2002. 'Democratisation and state feminism: Gender politics in Africa and Latin America', *Development and Change* 33 (3): 439–66.

Oyéwùmí, Oyèrónké. 1997. *The Invention of Women: Making an African Sense of Western Gender Discourses*. Minneapolis: University of Minnesota Press.

Ozbay, Cenk and Ozan Soybakis. 2020. 'Political masculinities: Gender, power and change in Turkey', *Social Politics* 27 (1): 27–50.

Paap, Kris. 2006. *Working Construction: Why White Working Class Men put Themselves – and the Labor Movement – in Harm's Way*. Ithaca, NY: Cornell University Press.

Pahl, Jan M. and Raymond E. Pahl. 1971. *Managers and their Wives: A Study of Career and Family Relationships in the Middle Class*. London: Allen Lane.

Parsons, Talcott and Robert F. Bales. 1956. *Family Socialization and Interaction Process*. London: Routledge & Kegan Paul.

Pascoe, C. J. 2012. *Dude, You're a Fag: Masculinity and Sexuality in High School*, New edn. Berkeley: University of California Press.

Pearce, Ruth, Igi Moon, Kat Gupta and Deborah Lynn Steinberg, eds. 2019. *The Emergence of Trans: Cultures, Politics and Everyday Lives*. Abingdon: Routledge.

Perkins, Roberta. 1983. *The 'Drag Queen' Scene: Transsexuals in Kings Cross*. Sydney: Allen & Unwin.

Perkins, Roberta and Frances Lovejoy. 2007. *Call Girls: Private Sex Workers in Australia*. Crawley: University of Western Australia Press.

Peteet, Julie. 1994. 'Male gender and rituals of resistance in the Palestinian Intifada: A cultural politics of violence', *American Ethnologist* 21 (1): 31–49.

Petersen, Jennifer and Janet Hyde. 2011. 'Gender differences in sexual attitudes and behaviors: A review of meta-analytic results and large datasets', *Journal of Sex Research* 48 (2–3): 149–65.

Pfau-Effinger, Birgit. 1998. 'Gender cultures and the gender arrangement – a theoretical framework for cross-national research', *Innovation* 11: 147–66.

Pizan, Christine de. 1983 [1405]. *The Book of the City of Ladies*. London: Pan Books.

Pleck, J. H. and J. Sawyer, eds. 1974. *Men and Masculinity*. Englewood Cliffs, NJ: Prentice-Hall.

Plumwood, Val. 1994. *Feminism and the Mastery of Nature*. London: Routledge.

Pringle, Rosemary. 1989. *Secretaries Talk: Sexuality, Power and Work*. Sydney: Allen & Unwin.

Promundo and International Center for Research on Women. 2015. *International Men & Gender Equality Survey (IMAGES) Background and Key Findings*. Online at www.promundoglobal.org/resources/international-men-and-gender-equality-survey-images-background-and-key-findings, accessed 17.3.2019.

Prudham, Scott. 2009. 'Pimping climate change: Richard Branson, global warming, and the performance of green capitalism', *Environment and Planning A* 41 (7): 1594–613.

Radcliffe, Sarah A., Nina Laurie and Robert Andolina. 2004. 'The transnationalization of gender and reimagining Andean indigenous development', *Signs* 29 (2): 387–416.

Rai, Shirin and Vina Mazumdar. 2007. 'Emerging state feminism in India: A conversation with Vina Mazumdar, Member Secretary to the First Committee on the Status of Women in India', *International Feminist Journal of Politics* 9 (1): 104–11.

Ratele, Kopano. 2014. 'Currents against gender transformation of South African men: Relocating marginality to the centre of research and theory of masculinities', *NORMA: International Journal for Masculinity Studies* 9 (1): 30–44.

Ray, Raka. 1999. *Fields of Protest: Women's Movements in India*. Minneapolis: University of Minnesota Press.

Reddy, Gayatri. 2006. *With Respect to Sex: Negotiating Hijra Identity in South India*. New Delhi: Yoda Press.

Reid, Kirsty. 2007. *Gender, Crime and Empire: Convicts, Settlers and the State in Early Colonial Australia*. Manchester: Manchester University Press.

Reynolds, Robert. 2002. *From Camp to Queer: Re-making the Australian Homosexual*. Melbourne: Melbourne University Press.

Rippon, Gina. 2019. *The Gendered Brain: The New Neuroscience that Shatters the Myth of the Female Brain*. London: The Bodley Head.

Risman, Barbara J. 1986. 'Can men "mother"? Life as a single father', *Family Relations* 35: 95–102.

Risman, Barbara J. 1998. *Gender Vertigo: American Families in Transition*. New Haven, CT: Yale University Press.

Risse, Leonora. 2019. '50 years after Australia's historic "equal pay" decision, the legacy of "women's work" remains', *The Conversation*. Online at https://theconversation.com/50-years-after-australias-historic-equal-pay-decision-the-legacy-of-womens-work-remains-118761, accessed 4.4.2020.

Roberson, James E. and Nobue Suzuki, eds. 2003. *Men and Masculinities in Contemporary Japan: Dislocating the Salaryman Doxa*. London: Routledge.

Roberts, Adrienne. 2008. 'Privatizing social reproduction: The primitive accumulation of water in an era of neoliberalism', *Antipode* 40 (4): 535–60.

Roberts, Celia. 2000. 'Biological behaviour? Hormones, psychology and sex', *NWSA Journal* 12: 1–20.

Robinson, Kathryn. 2009. *Gender, Islam, and Democracy in Indonesia*. Abingdon: Routledge.

Rogers, Lesley. 2000. *Sexing the Brain*. London: Phoenix.

Roper, Michael. 1994. *Masculinity and the British Organization Man since 1945*. Oxford: Oxford University Press.

Rosenberg, Rosalind. 1982. *Beyond Separate Spheres: Intellectual Roots of Modern Feminism*. New Haven, CT: Yale University Press.

Rowbotham, Sheila. 1969. *Women's Liberation and the New Politics*. Nottingham: Spokesman.

Rubin, Gayle. 1975. 'The traffic in women: Notes on the "political economy" of sex'. Pp. 157–210 in R. R. Reiter, ed., *Toward an Anthropology of Woman*. New York: Monthly Review.

Rubin, Henry. 2003. *Self Made Man: Identity and Embodiment Among Transsexual Men*. Nashville, TN: Vanderbilt University Press.

Saffioti, Heleieth. 1969. *A Mulher na Sociedade de Classes: Mito e Realidad*. Petrópolis: Vozes.

Sahlins, Marshall. 1977. *The Use and Abuse of Biology: An Anthropological Critique of Sociobiology*. London: Tavistock.

Sartre, Jean-Paul. 1968. *Search for a Method*, translated by H. Barnes. New York: Vintage.

Sawyer, Jack. 1974 [1970]. 'On male liberation'. Pp. 170–3 in J. H. Peck and J. Sawyer, eds., *Men and Masculinity*. Englewood Cliffs, NJ: Prentice-Hall.

Schilt, Kristen and Matthew Wiswall. 2008. 'Before and after: Gender transitions, human capital, and workplace experiences', *The B. E. Journal of Economic Analysis & Policy* 8 (1): article 39.

Schofield, Toni, Raewyn Connell, Linley Walker, Julian Wood and Dianne L. Butland. 2000. 'Understanding men's health and illness: A gender-relations approach to policy, research, and practice', *Journal of American College Health* 48 (6): 247–56.

Schools Commission (Australia). 1975. *Girls, School and Society*. Canberra: Schools Commission.

Schreiner, Olive. 1978 [1911]. *Woman and Labour*. London: Virago.

Scott, Joan W. 1986. 'Gender: A useful category of historical analysis', *American Historical Review* 91 (5): 1053–75.

Scott, Joan W. 2016. 'Gender and the Vatican', *Religion & Gender* 6 (2): 300–1.

Segal, Lynne. 1994. *Straight Sex: Rethinking the Politics of Pleasure*. London: Virago.

Seifert, Ruth. 1993. *Individualisierungsprozesse, Geschlechterverhältnisse und die soziale Konstruktion des Soldaten*. Munich: Sozialwissenschaftliches Institut der Bundeswehr.

Serrano-Amaya, José Fernando. 2018. *Homophobic Violence in Armed Conflict and Political Transition*. Palgrave Macmillan.

Shen, Zhi. 1987. 'Development of women's studies – the Chinese Way. Sidelights of the National Symposium on Theoretical Studies on Women', *Chinese Sociology and Anthropology* 20: 18–25.

Shiva, Vandana. 1989. *Staying Alive: Women, Ecology and Development*. London: Zed Books.

Sideris, Tina. 2005. '"You have to change and you don't know how!": Contesting what it means to be a man in a rural area of South Africa'. Pp. 111–37 in Graeme Reid and Liz Walker, eds., *Men Behaving Differently*. Cape Town: Double Storey Books.

Sinclair-Webb, Emma. 2000. 'Our Bülent is now a commando: Military service and manhood in Turkey'. Pp. 65–92 in Mai Ghoussoub and Emma Sinclair-Webb, eds., *Imagined Masculinities: Male Identity and Culture in the Modern Middle East*. London: Saqi Books.

Sinha, Mrinalini. 1995. *Colonial Masculinity: The 'Manly Englishman' and the 'Effeminate Bengali' in the Late Nineteenth Century*. Manchester: Manchester University Press.

Spivak, Gayatri Chakravorty. 1988. *In Other Worlds: Essays in Cultural Politics*. New York: Routledge.

Stacey, Judith. 1983. *Patriarchy and Socialist Revolution in China*. Berkeley: University of California Press.

Stauffer, Robert H. 2004. *Kahana: How the Land was Lost*. Honolulu: University of Hawai'i Press.

Stienstra, Deborah. 2000. 'Dancing resistance from Rio to Beijing: Transnational women's organizing and United Nations conferences, 1992–6'. Pp. 209–24 in M. H. Marchand and A. S. Runyan, eds., *Gender and Global Restructuring*. London: Routledge.

Stockholm International Peace Research Institute. 2020. *Financial Value of the Global Arms Trade*. Online at https://www.sipri.org/databases/financial-value-global-arms-trade, accessed 26.3.2020.

Stoller, Robert J. 1968. *Sex and Gender, vol. 1: On the Development of Masculinity and Femininity*. London: Hogarth Press.

Strathern, Marilyn. 1978. 'The achievement of sex: Paradoxes in Hagen gender-thinking'. Pp. 171–202 in E. Schwimmer, ed., *The Yearbook of Symbolic Anthropology*. London: Hurst.

Stryker, Susan. 2008. *Transgender History*. Berkeley, CA: Seal Press.

Stryker, Susan and Stephen Whittle, eds. 2006. *The Transgender Studies Reader*. New York: Routledge.

Taga Futoshi. 2007. 'The trends of discourse on fatherhood and father's conflict in Japan'. Paper to the fifteenth biennial conference of the Japanese Studies Association of Australia, Canberra, July 2007.

Tanaka Kazuko. 1977. *A Short History of the Women's Movement in Modern Japan*, 3rd edn. Japan: Femintern Press.

Taymour, Aisha. 2001 [1892]. *Mir'at Al-Ta'mmul fi Al-Umur* [The Mirror of Contemplating Affairs]. Mohandessin: Women and Memory Forum.

Temkina, Anna. 2008. *Sexual Life of Women: Between Subordination and Freedom*. St Petersburg: European University at St Petersburg.

Thayer, Millie. 2010. *Making Transnational Feminism: Rural Women, NGO Activists, and Northern Donors in Brazil*. Abingdon: Routledge.

Thorne, Barrie. 1993. *Gender Play: Girls and Boys in School*. New Brunswick, NJ: Rutgers University Press.

Tienari, Janne, Anne-Marie Søderberg, Charlotte Holgersson and Eero Vaara. 2005. 'Gender and national identity constructions in the cross-border merger context', *Gender, Work & Organization* 12 (3): 217–41.

Tinsman, Heidi. 2000. 'Reviving feminist materialism: Gender and neoliberalism in Pinochet's Chile', *Signs* 26 (1): 145–88.

Tomsen, Stephen. 2013. *Violence, Prejudice and Sexuality*. New York: Routledge.

Tsing, Anna L. 1993. *In the Realm of the Diamond Queen: Marginality in an Out-of-the-Way Place*. Princeton, NJ: Princeton University Press.

Tsing, Anna L. 2004. *Friction: An Ethnography of Global Connection*. Princeton, NJ: Princeton University Press.

Turley, Emma L. 2016. '"Like nothing I've ever felt before": Understanding consensual BDSM as embodied experience', *Psychology & Sexuality* 7 (2): 149–62.

UNESCO (United Nations Educational, Scientific and Cultural Organization). 2003. *Gender and Education for All: The Leap to Equality*. Paris: UNESCO Publishing.

United Nations Secretary-General. 2020. *Policy Brief: The Impact of COVID-19 on Women*. Online at https://www.unwomen.org/-/media/headquarters/attachments/sections/library/publications/2020/policy-brief-the-impact-of-covid-19-on-women-en.pdf?la=en&vs=1406, accessed 29.4.2020.

UN Women. 2019. *Facts and Figures: Peace and Security*. Online at https://www.unwomen.org/en/what-we-do/peace-and-security/facts-and-figures#_Notes, accessed 13.4.2020.

Vaerting, Mathilde [writing as Mathilde and Mathias Vaerting]. 1981 [1921]. *The Dominant Sex: A Study in the Sociology of Sex Differentiation*. Westport, CT: Hyperion.

Valdés, Teresa. 2001. *El Índice de Compromiso Cumplido – ICC: Una Estrategia Para el Control Ciudadano de la Equidad de Género*. Santiago de Chile: FLACSO.

Valdés, T., Ana María Muñoz and Alina Donoso. 2003. *Han Avanzado Las Mujeres? Indice de Compromiso Cumplido Latino Americano*. Santiago de Chile: FLACSO.

Vickers, Jill. 1994. 'Notes toward a political theory of sex and power'. Pp. 174–93 in H. L. Radtke and J. S. Henderikus, eds., *Power/Gender*. London: Sage.

Viloria, Hida. 2017. *Born Both: An Intersex Life*. New York: Hachette Books.

Viveros Vigoya, Mara. 2002. *De Quebradores y Cumplidores: Sobre Hombres, Masculinidades y Relaciones de Género en Colombia*. Bogotá: Universidad Nacional de Colombia.

Viveros Vigoya, Mara. 2018a. *Les Couleurs de la masculinité: Expériences intersectionelles et pratiques de pouvoir en Amérique latine*. Paris: La Découverte.

Viveros Vigoya, Mara. 2018b. 'Race, indigeneity, and gender: Lessons for global feminism'. Pp. 90–110 in James W. Messerschmidt et al., eds., *Gender Reckonings: New Social Theory and Research*. New York: New York University Press.

Waetjen, Thembisa. 2004. *Workers and Warriors: Masculinity and the Struggle for Nation in South Africa*. Urbana: University of Illinois Press.

Waetjen, Thembisa and Gerhard Maré. 2001. '"Men amongst men": Masculinity and Zulu nationalism in the 1980s'. Pp. 195–206 in R. Morrell, ed., *Changing Men in Southern Africa*. London: Zed Books.

Wajcman, Judy. 1998. *Managing like a Man: Women and Men in Corporate Management*. Cambridge: Polity and Sydney: Allen & Unwin.

Walby, Sylvia. 1990. *Theorizing Patriarchy*. Oxford: Basil Blackwell.

Walby, Sylvia. 1997. *Gender Transformations*. London: Routledge.

Ward, Lester. 1883. *Dynamic Sociology or Applied Social Science*. New York: D. Appleton and Company.

Warren, Karen, ed. 1997. *Ecofeminism: Women, Culture, Nature*. Bloomington: Indiana University Press.

West, Candace and Don H. Zimmerman. 1987. 'Doing gender', *Gender & Society* 1 (2): 125–51.

WHO (World Health Organization). 2013. *Global and Regional Estimates of Violence against Women: Prevalence and Health Effects of Intimate Partner Violence and Non-Partner Sexual Violence*. Online at https://www.who.int/reproductivehealth/publications/violence/9789241564625/en/, accessed 12.4.2020.

Williams, Christine L. 1989. *Gender Differences at Work: Women and Men in Nontraditional Occupations*. Berkeley: University of California Press.

Williams, Walter L. 1986. *The Spirit and the Flesh: Sexual Diversity in American Indian Culture*. Boston: Beacon Press.

Wollstonecraft, Mary. 1975 [1792]. *Vindication of the Rights of Woman*. Harmondsworth: Penguin.

Wood, Elizabeth A. 2016. 'Hypermasculinity as a scenario of power', *International Feminist Journal of Politics* 18 (3): 329–50.

Wood, Leila, Sharon Hoefer, Matt Kammer-Kerwick, José Rubén Parra-Cardona and Noël Busch-Armendariz. 2018. 'Sexual harassment at institutions of higher education: Prevalence, risk, and extent', *Journal of Interpersonal Violence*. Online at https://journals.sagepub.com/doi/full/10.1177/0886260518791228.

World Bank. 2020. *Life expectancy at birth, total (years)*. Data table. Online at https://data.worldbank.org/indicator/sp.dyn.le00.in, accessed 6.5.2020.

World Wide Web Foundation. 2015. *Women's Rights Online: Translating Access into Empowerment*. Online at http://webfoundation.org/docs/2015/10/womens-rights-online21102015.pdf, accessed 15.5.2020.

Xaba, Thokozani. 2001. 'Masculinity and its malcontents: The confrontation between "struggle masculinity" and "post-struggle masculinity" (1990-1997)'. Pp. 105–24 in Robert Morrell, ed., *Changing Men in Southern Africa*. Pietermaritzburg: University of Natal Press.

Yan Hairong. 2008. *New Masters, New Servants: Migration, Development and Women Workers in China*. Durham, NC: Duke University Press.

Ylöstalo, Hanna. 2016. 'Organizational perspective to gender mainstreaming in the Finnish state administration', *International Feminist Journal of Politics* 18 (4): 544–58.

Zaloom, Caitlin. 2006. *Out of the Pits: Traders and Technology from Chicago to London*. Chicago: University of Chicago Press.

Zell, Ethan, Zlatan Krizan and Sabrina R. Teeter. 2015. 'Evaluating gender similarities and differences using metasynthesis', *American Psychologist* 70 (1): 10–20.

Zulehner, Paul M. and Rainer Volz. 1998. *Männer im Aufbruch: Wie Deutschlands Männer sich selbst und wie Frauen sie sehen*. Ostfildern: Schwabenverlag.

Zwingel, Susanne. 2016. *Translating International Women's Rights: The CEDAW Convention in Context*. London: Palgrave Macmillan.

Author index

Subject index